TRIBUNALS AND GOVERNMENT

LAW IN CONTEXT
Editors: Robert Stevens (Professor in Law in Yale University)
and William Twining (Professor of Law in the University of
Warwick)

Already published:

Tribunals and Government

J. A. FARMER

Barrister and Solicitor of the Supreme Court of New Zealand;
formerly Fellow of Gonville and Caius College, Cambridge

WEIDENFELD AND NICOLSON

London

Weidenfeld and Nicolson
11 St John's Hill
London SW11

ISBN 0 297 76837 9 cased
ISBN 0 297 76861 1 paperback

Printed in Great Britain by
Willmer Brothers Limited
Birkenhead

CONTENTS

Foreword

Administrative tribunals have evolved and proliferated in this country over a long period of time. They now represent one of the most important institutions of government, dealing with such varied spheres as social services, licensing, housing, industrial relations and immigration. What are their manifest and latent functions in society? How do they operate in practise? Should they be viewed as substitutes for courts, as quasi-courts, as a branch of the administration or as convenient devices for enabling ministers and officials to exercise influence without public accountability? To what extent is it valid to make any generalization about tribunals?

These and other questions are examined in this book both at a general level and through a detailed examination of the workings of selected tribunals. The author is well-qualified to undertake this task. As a scholar specializing in Public Law he is familiar not only with the relevant legal literature but also with the writings of political scientists and others concerned with decision-making in government. He has had first-hand experience of tribunals in action both as a legal practitioner and as a scholar. As a New Zealander, resident in England for several years, he is able to observe tribunals in England from the perspective of one who has had experience of other jurisdictions.

R.B.S.
W.L.T.

Preface

In an earlier work in the 'Law in Context' series, Michael Zander commented on the paucity of writing on the subject of tribunals.* To some extent, therefore, this book may help to provide information and material on what is without doubt a much-neglected area of the legal system and public administration. But my object in undertaking a work of this kind was more than just to fill a gap in the literature. Rather it was to attempt a different approach to the study of legal institutions in a relatively specialized but important area. In particular, it had seemed to me that the existing assumptions about the function of tribunals, their structure and procedures and the processes by which decisions were taken, warranted closer examination. Tribunals tend to be viewed as little more than cheaper, quicker, more informal courts. I had long felt that there was much more to the subject than this. The very distinction between a court and a tribunal seemed for a start to bristle with problems which had received little attention. No doubt the fictions and assumptions which continue to persist about the role of the courts, despite the attention of the many jurists who have endeavoured to expose the political and social realities of the judicial system, do not help to clarify the tribunal picture. But traditional views of the function and operation of tribunals have, it seemed to me, ignored the importance and the potential which they have as instruments by which the affairs of the country are managed. To this extent, the decision-making processes of tribunals may often be better compared – at least in functional terms – with those operating in government departments and other more obviously administrative institutions.

* *Cases and Materials on the English Legal System* (1973), p. 45.

Some years ago, the Editor of *Public Law* made an analogous point when he lamented that 'there are no books on administrative law which approach the subject through the administrative process, by showing the way in which decisions are taken and the political and legal forces which shape those decisions.'* His words were taken up by the American lawyer, Professor K. C. Davis, who, in a scathing attack on the jurisprudence of English administrative law, said: 'Scholars, commentators and educators – in both law and political science – ought to be digging into the details and realities of the administrative process in operation in the ministries and in the tribunals, the major problems ought to be identified, solutions ought to be proposed, the pros and cons ought to be debated and developed both orally and in writing, and administrators and judges ought to be drawing from the enlightenment that would thus be made available.'† The best way to write a book on administrative law, he thought, 'would be by going into the ministries and the tribunals, finding out what the legal problems are concerning the administrative process, and then discussing them in the light of the statutes and the case law.'‡

It is of course one thing to see the problem and to state in general terms the method by which it should be attacked. It is another to succeed. I am painfully aware of how far short this work falls of the objectives which have inspired me to write it. Nevertheless, it is hoped that as a modest attempt to provide a different perspective of an important part of the legal and administrative machinery, some new insights may be found to emerge which will assist those working and studying in the field of public law and administration. In this respect, I have been especially mindful of the value of a more contextual approach to the study of tribunals in English Legal System and Administrative Law courses. My own experience of teaching these subjects has left me convinced that the subject of tribunals in fact provides a most suitable vehicle by which the law student can be helped to see the political and social context in which legal institutions (and the law itself) operate. I would hope too that students of public administration might find an equal benefit in this study.

Inevitably during the writing of this book many have given

* [1961] P.L. 339.
† *English Administrative Law – An American View* [1962] P.L. 139.
‡ *Ibid.*, 141.

generously of their time, assistance and encouragement. I have first and foremost been fortunate in the fact that chairmen and members of many different kinds of tribunals, Government officials in various ministries and departments, and the secretaries and clerks to a number of tribunals have related their experiences to me without reservation. The willingness of tribunal members to discuss informally with me hearings which I have previously attended has been particularly enlightening. In this respect it must be said that it is not intended in this book to reveal any confidences, but the value of such discussions in general terms has nevertheless been immeasurable.

Within academic circles, I also owe a debt to many. Professors R. M. Jackson, C. J. Hamson and S. A. de Smith at different times and in different ways advised and encouraged me. Dr P. J. Evans, who was engaged on research and writing himself at Cambridge, never hesitated to give up his valuable time to discuss with me the ill-formed ideas and concepts with which I struggled during the writing of the book. Dr Keith Hawkins also acted as a valued sounding-board and other colleagues at Gonville and Caius College, by establishing a happy and relaxed working environment, contributed much to the completion of this work.

To Robert Stevens and William Twining has fallen the unenviable task of reading the manuscript and of providing suggestions and criticisms. They have done this with both patience and friendship and I sincerely hope that they are aware of my immense gratitude to them.

It has perhaps become customary to thank one's wife for showing stoic fortitude during the writing of a book. I have been especially fortunate in being able as well to discuss much of the book with my wife but neither to her nor to any of the others listed above should the shortcomings of this work be attributed.

Auckland, New Zealand
November 1973   James Farmer

I

Introduction

If asked what a court is and what it looks like, most people refer to an elderly judge, robed in red, wigged and gowned counsel, a panel of twelve jurors and a defendant in the dock. The courtroom is thought of as a place of high drama, a place where witnesses are broken down under fierce cross-examination, a place where (as Lord Goodman recently said) lawyers are wont to break into dog latin. The function of the court is seen as determining questions of innocence and guilt or, at a more sophisticated level, disputes of fact or law.

That picture is not of course entirely accurate. The range of courts is much wider than is generally thought. There is the world of difference between the High Court Judge and jury and the bench of lay magistrates; or between the Court of Appeal and a County Court Judge. More than that, there is a wide variety of specialized Courts – courts-martial, ecclesiastical courts, the Court of Protection, Restrictive Practices Court, Commercial Court, National Industrial Relations Court – which can be subdivided further and which depart from the layman's picture of 'the courts of law'.

In another sphere, which is seldom regarded as related to the work of the courts, most people also have a general idea of how the business of government is carried on. The image of Whitehall is that of Cabinet ministers in chauffeur-driven black cars hurrying to Downing Street for top-level policy conferences; a hierarchy of civil servants nearby, working behind closed doors promulgating in the form of specific directives and regulations the policies and orders of their ministerial masters; the despatch of these instructions to government offices in the regions, where ultimately a junior or subordinate behind a counter administers them to the uncomprehending citizen.

The administration of government does not in reality conform to this simplistic picture either. There is, firstly, a complex structure of local government which in part complements and in part overlaps with the work of central government. Then there are government agencies such as the BBC, the National Coal Board and the public utilities which co-exist with both central and local government and which operate with a greater or lesser degree of autonomy from both.

When we turn to what are generally referred to as tribunals (most commonly called administrative tribunals and special tribunals) the layman's picture is rather more hazy. If pressed, he would probably describe three wise men behind a long desk listening to evidence or argument, not necessarily addressed by a lawyer, frequently asking searching questions and at the end giving a brief but incisive report or decision. But he would have great difficulty in describing the context of the tribunal's inquiry. That it is not determining issues of innocence or guilt would be acknowledged readily enough. Sometimes it might appear to be questions of causation – as in the case of an ad hoc tribunal of inquiry investigating an aircraft disaster – that arise for determination. Or it might be an issue of fact, as with a national insurance tribunal deciding whether a worker had been dismissed for misconduct, or an issue of law. In other instances, however, a particular tribunal might not even be seen as making a decision, but, at best, compiling a report with recommendations (for example, as to a wage settlement which might be acceptable).

The distinction between different kinds of tribunals is indeed more difficult to draw than that between different kinds of courts. Even the fact that some are ad hoc (established for a particular inquiry and then disbanded) and that some are permanent and continuing is not always appreciated. Professor R. M. Jackson has said, truly enough, that the 'most marked characteristic of special tribunals is that they are a very mixed lot'.[1]

And a mixed lot they certainly are. No one is quite sure how many there are, although in 1963 Professor H. W. R. Wade calculated that there were over two thousand in England and Wales, if all the tribunals of different kinds in each locality were counted separately. As he also pointed out, this list was in no way finite because new tribunals are constantly being established.[2]

Since that time, there is no doubt but that the list has grown considerably, with, for example, the addition of rent assessment committees, industrial tribunals and immigration tribunals and the continued expansion of previously existing tribunals.

There is in fact scarcely an area of human activity where tribunals do not exist. They flourish in particular in the social services (national insurance, supplementary benefits, war pensions and national health), in licensing jurisdictions (transport, liquor retailing, cinema, theatres), in housing (rent), and in industry. Indeed wherever there is government regulation, tribunals tend to proliferate.

The very diversity and number of tribunals has tended to obscure the functions which they exercise and the purposes for which they are created. Traditionally, in fact, tribunals have been seen as a part of, or at most complementary to, the judicial system. To that extent and in nearly every respect, they are viewed simply as alternatives within that system to courts of law. Hence in most discussions of their operation, emphasis is usually placed on those procedural and institutional features where they are thought to fall short of, or sometimes exceed, the comparable characteristics of regular courts. Thus, two such examples which have excited much comment (both favourable and unfavourable) are the comparative lack of legal representation in tribunals and their general willingness to relax or dispense with the legal rules of evidence.

The assumption that tribunals in their entirety constitute a part of the judicial system does, however, obscure a number of important facts which it is hoped here to highlight.

First, there are those tribunals which operate in a context where the use of a court would not be considered at all appropriate. That is, some tribunals really constitute alternatives to departmental or ministerial decision-making rather than court-substitutes. Thus, on a traditional analysis these tribunals may be thought to exist outside the judicial system altogether, either because their decisions partake of a greater content of policy-making than is generally regarded as proper in ordinary courts, or because their decisions are not directly enforceable at law and therefore constitute recommendations only. Many of the tribunals discussed in the next chapter (Tribunals and Economic Policy) are of this type.

Secondly, the judicial system itself cannot necessarily be

regarded as falling outside the business of the State and therefore (together with its institutions) should perhaps be considered as a part of the general administration of government, along with the civil service, public corporations and local authorities. Pertinent to this point are complex questions of accountability and sovereignty but if the rather crude political analysis is adopted that Government Ministers and their closest advisers are responsible for the formulation of matters of general policy and that the rest of the administration is concerned only to implement the detail of that policy, the general proposition should not offend constitutional lawyers overmuch.

The principle behind this point was made in another context and in another way in 1900 by F. J. Goodnow:

The fact is, then, that there is a large part of administration which is unconnected with politics, which should therefore be relieved very largely, if not altogether, from the control of political bodies. It is unconnected with politics because it embraces fields of semi-scientific, quasi-judicial and quasi-business or commercial activity – work which has little if any influence on the expression of the true State will.[3]

The thesis that is put forward in this book that tribunals properly form a part of the administration may be surprising to many. But it is the very failure to recognize this fact which has served to inhibit the effectiveness and growth of tribunals in many areas of governmental regulation where their use would otherwise provide a major contribution.

The third point is that, historically, jurisdiction entrusted to tribunals has not always been allocated as a rational exercise in decision-making. Nor for that matter have many of the newer statutory jurisdictions which have been added to those administered at common law by the courts. Often the allocation of a jurisdiction to either a tribunal or to a court, in preference to its retention within the department, is purely a matter of historical accident or political whim or convenience. There are fads and fashions which come and go in this area as elsewhere and there are also developments which defy any rational analysis.

Perhaps because of their haphazard and piecemeal historical development, there is much scepticism about tribunals and their position within the overall structure of the State. Many see them, or some of them, as being under the thumb of the government of the day or being directly controlled by ministers and their departments under the *guise* of independent agencies. Considerable controversy thus surrounds the use of tribunals in certain areas because, it is said, the adoption of the tribunal form of administration leads to a remoteness from political and parliamentary accountability without necessarily always achieving a real independence in decision-making from government interference.

A good example of this kind of objection is to be seen in the immigration tribunals which were established in 1969 to determine appeals against decisions by immigration officers or by the Home Secretary refusing entry into Britain or ordering deportation from Britain. The tribunals, and the appeal rights themselves, were introduced against a common law background which had not provided for any substantive or procedural rights to the individual alien.[4] The question of immigration had been essentially a matter of executive discretion with the Home Secretary as final arbiter. The Immigration Appeals Act 1969 transferred this final discretion to the immigration appeal tribunal, although the Act also made provision for the definition of rules and principles by which the tribunal, and the immigration adjudicators who were to operate under the tribunal as the first level of appeal, were to exercise that discretion. The announcement of the new scheme and the corresponding shift of decisional power in immigration cases attracted the comment of Quintin Hogg (now Lord Hailsham, L.C.) in the Commons debates on the Bill that a tribunal was not, in his view, 'the proper authority to decide questions of policy which are embodied in the rather obscure phrase "discretion" which the tribunal can impose upon the Secretary of State, and therefore upon Parliament, without Parliament retaining control over it.'[5] The same point was also made more fully by a Conservative backbencher:

The Home Secretary made no bones about this when he said, quite frankly, that whereas in the past he had been on the receiving end of representations from hon. Members on both sides about this or that case, whether the discretion had been rightly exercised and someone perhaps excluded who should have been let in, or the other way round, in future he would be relieved of this difficult function because the final responsibility would rest with the adjudicator or the tribunal. The Home Office would retain the initiative, that is, the initial decision would be made by the Home Office, but the final decision would be made by a judicial body.

This is about immigration, but does it not raise quite general considerations with which this House ought by now to concern itself? With others, I have watched a growing tendency for the powers of Parliament – the discretion of the Executive, which is much the same thing, since we control the Executive – to be farmed out to bodies which are remote from political control. Where the decision is one of fact, or concerned with the innocence or guilt of a specified offence, it is right that judicial procedures should be used and political pressures minimised, but where the decision is a political one, it is surely very dangerous for this House to see the ultimate power pass away beyond its reach and scope. That is a growing tendency.[6]

We shall see that this is a debate which has recurred, in different guises, over and over again in the area of governmental decision-making. Should the authority or official taking a decision be subject to political control or not? Should policy-making bodies or those entrusted with wide discretion be required always to account to Parliament? What is the proper function of an independent agency or tribunal?

It is a debate which surrounded the establishment of the Restrictive Practices Court[7] and, more recently, the rent scrutiny boards under the Housing Finance Act 1972.[8] It is a debate which has also been aired from time to time in relation to the important field of land use planning. Here appeal decisions lie to the Secretary of State who, oddly enough, adopts a judicial or tribunal form of proceeding, by appointing an inspector to hold a full public hearing at which interested or affected parties may appear (with counsel or solicitor), present evidence and submissions and cross-examine opposing witnesses. The ultimate decision, however, remains that of the Secretary of State who is free to accept or reject his inspector's report at will. It is worth looking at the reasons for establishing this machinery in a little more detail.

The basic explanation for leaving the final decision in the hands of the minister in planning cases was given by Professor de Smith not long after town planning machinery in its modern form was first established. 'The Minister is responsible for the co-ordination of national planning policy', he said, an aim which 'cannot be achieved without the closest liaison with the many other Departments which may be affected by development schemes.'

Furthermore, he continued, planning appeals cannot be

regarded as mere *lites inter partes*; the 'respective merits of the disputants may have to be viewed in the light of overriding considerations of national policy, the best judge of which is likely to be the Minister.'[9]

These points are undoubtedly compelling but there are other, unanswered, questions about the nature of town planning which will have a bearing on the preference for ministerial decision-making. Is town planning to be viewed *primarily* as a national activity or is it of greater importance locally? Should planners be motivated principally by the economics of different kinds of land use, having regard to national patterns and needs of supply, production and employment? Or are the physical and environmental aspects of land use of overriding concern?

A view of planning which stresses the needs of the locality and the importance of the immediate physical environment perhaps encompasses more naturally an appellate tribunal operating regionally and paying closer regard to evidence on local conditions. Both Australia and New Zealand use town planning tribunals in this way and the results are evident in a more fragmented and individualized (but less coherent) type of planning than exists in Britain.

The use of a tribunal in the planning field arguably shows a greater regard for the individual's position as against the all-embracing power of government bureaucracy. Certainly, it has been concern for the increasingly weak position of the individual citizen which has led to the establishment in many areas of independent tribunals exercising a protective or safeguarding role.

This in fact was one of the principal reasons behind the introduction of immigration appeal rights administered through a system of independent adjudication as described briefly above. The Wilson Committee, whose report and recommendations had preceded the decision to adopt the tribunal system,[10] had empasized the vulnerability of prospective immigrants who had neither procedural nor substantive rights in relation to entry. The Committee also felt that, while a decision to refuse entry might well be proper and in accordance with law in a particular case, this would not always be apparent to the would-be immigrant and his relatives. For that reason alone, it was said, an open, independent decision-making process would be preferable to an entirely administrative process in which the person most affected took no substantial part.

Similar questions have also arisen in other sensitive areas involving the freedom of the individual. In many cases the lack of any substantive legal rights or the susceptibility to legal restrictions or liabilities impels the establishment of procedural safeguards. The more vulnerable the individual's position, the greater the demand for such protection. Hence the conferment of powers of internment of citizens in Northern Ireland suspected of terrorist activities, because of the seriousness to the citizen affected by the exercise of such powers and their potential abuse, led eventually, as a result of public outcry, to the provision of a system of independent review.

It is this area of individual liberty which reveals most acutely the strain between the political and parliamentary mechanism by which the exercise of governmental or State power is controlled and the alternative machinery signified by independent tribunals. In the famous House of Lords internment case during the Second World War – *Liversidge* v. *Anderson*[11] – Lord Macmillan excused the refusal of the majority of the Lords to review the grounds on which the Home Secretary had exercised his powers to intern persons believed to be of enemy origin or association, by pointing to the fact that the Home Secretary was a responsible officer of State who was accountable to Parliament for his actions and decisions.[12]

Yet the doctrine of ministerial responsibility, while of course of fundamental constitutional importance, has been too uncertain and inconsistent in its scope and application to provide an entirely satisfactory reassurance, and, probably for this very reason, the demand for independent review has increased in recent times. The establishment of the office of Parliamentary Commissioner of Administration, or Ombudsman, is an important manifestation of this development. It is interesting too that the form of that office reflects the basic tension between the system of parliamentary control and the alternative one of tribunal control. The defects of the tribunal form of investigation and decision-making have not escaped notice and there are therefore attractions in adopting the kind of in-between mechanism that the Ombudsman represents.

In this respect, the advantages of the Ombudsman's office are both procedural and institutional. Investigation of a dispute or case will not be hampered by the limitations of the hearing-type of proceeding. Information can be gained by telephone or through correspondence, evidential rules or requirements hardly have application and the whole process of inquiry is comparatively effective and quick. The conduct of the investigation is an independent one but ultimately, because the Ombudsman's decisions take the form of recommendations and reports to Parliament, there is no loss of Parliamentary control.[13]

While the English Ombudsman has not generally been accorded the same success as his counterparts in other countries[14] the combination of independent inquiry and retention of parliamentary control have led to a preference for similar machinery to deal with complaints against the police. Thus, shortly before the time of writing, it had just been announced by the Home Secretary in the Commons that a type of *ex post facto* review along Ombudsman lines would be introduced to deal with such complaints.[15]

These have previously been dealt with under the Police Act of 1964 by internal investigation, often conducted by an officer from another force. Occasionally, *ad hoc* independent commissions or tribunals of inquiry have been established, either administratively by the Home Secretary or by parliamentary resolution under the more formal provisions of the Tribunals of Inquiry (Evidence) Act 1921. Early in 1970, *Justice* put forward proposals for all complaints to be sent to an independent full-time investigator who would report initially to the chief constable; if the report were adverse to a police officer, then the matter would go to an independent tribunal for investigation and determination.

The police have, not unnaturally, resisted the concept of independent tribunal investigation and to that extent the new system of informal review represents something of a compromise. It is interesting to note that, while lawyers have been in the forefront of the reformers who sought change in police procedures, complaints by the public against lawyers continue to be investigated internally by the respective professional bodies.

By contrast with the new provisions relating to the police, complaints against doctors and dentists who come under the National Health Service have ultimately been determined by a National Health Service Tribunal which has the power to remove the practitioner from the national health list. But the independence and impartiality of these tribunals has been called into question and the fact that they sit in private and that legal representation is barred has been severely criticized. Professor Street has attributed their unsatisfactory operation to the Ministry of Health giving 'the practitioners what the BMA and other pressure groups insisted on as the price of accepting the National Health Service.'[16]

There are clearly dangers in establishing a tribunal which purports to provide an independent, impartial safeguard if it cannot in fact genuinely fulfil that role *and* give the appearance of doing so. Thus, when the immigration appeal tribunals were first established, concern that there might be cases where considerations of national security were at stake led to an exception being made to the normal arrangements which eventually had most unfortunate consequences. In that instance, the legislation provided that where, on any immigration appeal, it appeared to the Secretary of State that the original decision had been taken in the interests of national security, that appeal could be referred directly to the Immigration Appeals Tribunal specially constituted on an *ad hoc* basis by the Secretary of State and the Lord Chancellor acting jointly.[17] The decision of that Tribunal was not to bind the Home Secretary, however, so that in this type of case its decision was in effect advisory only. Moreover, the special tribunal was empowered to hear evidence in the absence of the appellant and his legal representatives where the Secretary of State certified that considerations of national security were relevant to that evidence.

It is now history that these provisions were used but once, in order to confirm the expulsion from Britain of the German student radical Rudi Dutschke in 1970. Dutschke had originally been permitted to enter England temporarily to recuperate from operations caused by his being shot in Germany by a right-wing opponent. Subsequently, he applied to and was accepted by the University of Cambridge for post-graduate research. The Home Secretary, however, determined that Dutschke's continued presence would be undesirable, Dutschke appealed and, on a national security certification being given, the case came before a special tribunal.

Certain parts of the evidence were heard *in camera* in the absence of Dutschke and his lawyers, by authority of the provisions referred to above. This evidence was crucial, for, although Dutschke had denied taking part in any political activities since his arrival in England or of having any such future intention, Security Service evidence given in his absence was accepted by the tribunal as successfully contradicting these assertions. Given the importance of this evidence, the tribunal's subsequent comment that during the *ex parte* proceedings the members of the tribunal had 'kept the principles of natural justice in the forefront of their minds', attained little credibility.[18]

Following the Dutschke case, the special procedure provided was abolished by the Immigration Act of 1971. In its place, it was simply provided that, where the Home Secretary certified that it would be contrary to the public good on the grounds (*inter alia*) that considerations of national security were affected, no appeal would lie to an immigration tribunal. The decision was thus entirely that of the Home Secretary, reached by him without the assistance of a tribunal investigation. We are thus back into the uncomplicated position of ministerial decision-making and traditional accountability. Given the peculiar features of national security requirements, it is doubtful whether any other course is practical.[19]

Just as the 'national security' immigration tribunal provisions represented a (rather unsatisfactory) compromise between independent inquiry and ministerial decision-making, so too the prisoner parole procedures introduced by the Criminal Justice Act of 1967 reflected similar tensions and concern that ultimate control of a politically sensitive area should not be handed over completely to a body which was not accountable to Parliament.

When the Bill, containing the new provisions for release on licence, was introduced, it provided no machinery at all for independent review. The Home Secretary was to make the decision whether or not to release in each case after having regard to recommendations made by an informal local prison review committee consisting of the governor of the prison, a senior district probation officer and a member of the board of visitors. On the second reading for the Bill, the then Home Secretary, Mr Roy Jenkins, acknowledged that the choice between this system and an independent parole board was not an easy one and invited the views of both sides of the House.[20]

Criticisms were not slow in forthcoming. Mr Quintin Hogg, while agreeing that the decision to release on parole is 'not necessarily a judicial or quasi-judicial function', thought that 'there is a quasi-judicial element in it, especially as involving the right of the individual ... to make his own representations.' He thought also that it was a decision which should not only be detached from politics but should also 'be seen to be detached from politics.' Decisions of this kind did not in any event, he said, lend themselves very easily to the day-to-day business of parliamentary questions.[21]

Other Opposition speakers expressed similar doubts. Mr Mark Carlisle said that there was a grave danger that practical expediency, based on the state of crowding in prisons and the state of preparedness of the probation service, would be determinative and that there would not be a 'fair, judicial consideration of the individual man's case.'[22] The matter was further debated in committee and, following continuing criticism, the Bill when reported back to the House contained substantial amendments to the administrative machinery.

It was provided in particular that there would be a parole board but that the board would, after due inquiry, report its investigations to the Home Secretary who would remain responsible for the final decision. The board's decisional powers were also dependent on the Secretary of State in another respect, insofar as it was only empowered to investigate those individual cases which the Secretary referred to it. This initial screening process places tribunals in a potentially vulnerable position. As we shall see in a later chapter, the effectiveness of the National Board for Prices and Incomes under the Wilson Government dwindled dramatically when wage references from the department dried up as the Government decided that it was politically expedient to relax its incomes policy.

In the debate on the Amendment, Mr Jenkins confirmed that the local prison review committees would remain as 'part of the Home Office machinery, rather than part of the Board machinery.' A member of the committee would see the prisoner informally before the committee's report was sent to the Home Secretary for his decision as to whether the case should be forwarded on to the parole board for investigation. In justifying the new arrangements, Mr Jenkins stated that it was important that there should not be created 'a complete divorce' between the prison department and the parole board. Such a development would be bad for the morale of the prison department, he said, because it would 'turn its officers into gaolers and nothing else.' Furthermore, it would be harmful to the development of the prisoner if the process of selection for parole were to operate independently of the various other decisions relating to his detention and rehabilitation which had also to be taken at different times.[23]

Although he welcomed the new changes, Mr Hogg put a rather different interpretation on the reasons for adopting a system of co-determination. The adoption of the pre-filtering process would, he said, 'go some way to alleviate what I know was the Department's internal opposition to the creation of a board.'[24]

It would seem, therefore, that political pressures (within departments and outside) contribute substantially to the kind of half-way measure adopted here. The new machinery adopted for dealing with complaints against the police and the peculiar procedural features of national health service tribunals would also seem to fall into this category. So too do many of the tribunals and agencies concerned with matters of economic policy – for example, the Monopolies Commission – which will be discussed in this book.

The parole board has now been operating fairly successfully for some five years but critics of the basic structure and procedures remain unquieted. Chief among these is Dr Keith Hawkins, who, following a comparative study of parole systems in the United States of America, remains convinced that an independent parole board is the best solution. 'Most of the procedural weaknesses in the present parole system can be attributed to a considerable extent to the requirement that the Secretary of State makes the final decision as to parole in all cases', he says. He points in particular to the delays and to the appearance of remoteness and impersonality which the Home Secretary's role engenders.[25]

It is understood that removal of formal decision-making power from the Secretary of State to the board is opposed by some officials in the Home Office on the grounds that parole remains a politically sensitive area because of the danger of a prisoner committing a crime while on licensed release. The fact is that analogous considerations apply to the release of patients from mental hospitals. Here a patient has a statutory right to apply at any time to a mental health review tribunal for a determination as to whether or not he should continue to be detained in hospital. That determination is final and binding and is made by a tribunal which is in no way subject to ministerial fiat.

The areas of political sensitivity are hardly constant but their selection must often appear a matter of expediency. If it is true that tribunals cannot or should not be entrusted with sensitive decisions or should only be allowed to take such decisions where the Government retains suitable controls or a final power of veto, then the establishment of the various incomes-control agencies, the National Industrial Relations Court and the Restrictive Practices Court, would seem difficult to justify. And what is one to make of the claim by the minister in *Padfield* v. *Minister of Agriculture, Fisheries and Food*[26] that he would not exercise his statutory power to refer a complaint about price distribution to an independent tribunal for investigation because it would be difficult politically for him to refuse to adopt and implement the tribunal's report? If that was so, how did the statutory machinery ever get established in the first place?

It would be a mistake, however, to view tribunal decision-making solely in terms of political accountability (important though that aspect of their functioning is). In a recent work, John Garrett points out that 'government has acquired an array of policy-making, legislative, judicial, service, supervisory, inspectorial, representational, transaction-processing and production functions which together present a managerial task of a range and complexity rarely encountered in any other form of organization.'[27] It is a thesis of this book that tribunals (of considerably differing kinds) provide an increasingly important instrument of management by which *all* those functions can be exercised.

2

Tribunals and economic policy

There is no government in Britain in modern times which has not placed the promotion of economic growth at the forefront of its objectives. Even Labour Governments, committed to socialist principles and to a more equal distribution of wealth, have accepted the philosophy of the larger cake as the best means by which the living standards of the poorer classes can be raised.[1] Successive governments of different colours have therefore directed their various economic policies to the fulfilment of the basic objective of growth. On the other hand they have recognized that unbridled economic activity can, and does, have serious harmful social effects. Economic policies have thus been matched with social policies which help to ameliorate the adverse consequences of the drive for growth. In both these areas of policy, tribunals of different kinds play an important part in assisting to formulate policy and in applying it. This chapter, therefore, will attempt to provide an examination of those activities of the State where tribunals operate and, in some cases, where they do not operate but where they might have been expected. Special emphasis will be put on the reasons and advantages which have been thought relevant to the choice of a tribunal as the instrument by which the relevant economic or social policy is to be fulfilled.

1. ECONOMIC POLICIES AND ECONOMIC GROWTH

The whole range of economic policies supporting the objective of economic growth is vast and covers everything from foreign exchange control to marketing regulations. Four basic policies only are selected for discussion here and while it is confidently stated that each of them is of major importance, it must also be said that their choice is occasioned as much from the point of view of their relevance to institutional decision-making as from a base of economic priority. The policies are:

(a) the provision of tax incentives and investment grants, discriminatory in nature, in favour of particular industrial activities or particular regions;
(b) the control of inflation, principally by prices and incomes policies;
(c) the regulation of industrial relations and the control of strikes;
(d) the maintenance of free competition as the greatest stimulus to growth.

(a) *Discriminatory tax incentives and investment grants*

From the point of view of growth potential some industrial and economic activities are seen to be more advantageous than others. Similarly it is often thought necessary to encourage economic activity (generally or of a particular kind) in certain regions or areas. The reasons in this latter instance are partly social (for example, to solve an unemployment problem in a depressed area or to relieve congested cities in the south east); but they are also based on a supposition that there will be economic advantages in such a policy (for example, cheaper land, readily available manpower, potential for the growth of allied and supporting industries). In respect of both particular activities and the locations in which they ought to be encouraged to take place, the Selective Employment Payments Act 1966 (and its later amendments) embodied major economic policy of the last Labour Government as to the direction in which it thought economic growth ought to lie.[2] Industrial tribunals, which had been established under the Industrial Training Act 1964[3] were given the task of determining disputes as to when an employer was engaged on an activity which would be deemed to be economically beneficial so as to receive a financial incentive or at least not to be fiscally penalized. The whole subject of selective employment tax and the industrial tribunals will be dealt with in detail in a later chapter but at this juncture it should be recorded that there was relatively little discussion on the allocation of decision-making powers under the statute to a tribunal which was in essence of the independent court-substitute kind. Mr Heath, then Leader of the Opposition, did express some concern at the choice of a tribunal over a court but the major attack of the Opposition was directed to the inadequacy of the statutory criteria which the tribunals were to apply. From an examination of the operation of the Act and its administration by the tribunals, it will be concluded that this was a problem with which the tribunals coped remarkably well but that an overemphasis on the case-by-case approach may have placed an excessive strain on the expertise and knowledge of industry upon which they heavily relied.

Perhaps of even greater importance – and certainly so to the encouragement of regional economic activity – have been the various statutes passed since 1960 which have been designed to enable financial grants to be made to industrialists willing to invest in certain depressed localities. The principal legislation is now provided by the Local Employment Act and the Industry Act, both passed in 1972, but they were preceded by a whole plethora of statutes, most of which still survive in part : these include the Control of Offices and Industrial Development Act 1965, the Industrial Development Act 1966, the Industrial Reorganization Corporation Act 1966, the Local Employment Act of 1960 (and amendments) and the Town and Country Planning Act 1971. The basic powers given to the Secretary of State are very broad[4] and he may, for example, make grants towards approved capital expenditure for providing buildings, machinery or plant, or mining works.[5] He may also make loans or subscribe for shares.[6] In addition he may make payments towards the removal and settlement of workers[7] and he or any other appropriate minister, may, with the consent of the Treasury, make grants or loans towards the better provision of basic services in development areas.[8] The discretion in each case is very large and it is not surprising therefore that, as the legislation developed through the 1960s and early 70s extending the Secretary of State's powers, increased concern should have been expressed at the danger of wrongful or improper or arbitrary discrimination. Parliamentary accountability existed of course to protect such abuses but this remedy is not always seen to be an effective one. The first of the local assistance statutes to be passed was the Local

Employment Act 1960 and it set the form which has since been followed by not providing either a right of appeal or a right to a hearing or the right to be given reasons for the minister's decision. As one writer has pointed out, however, the spirit of the Franks Report[9] is very well observed in the practical working of the machinery; applications are processed as follows:

The applicant for a loan or a grant is asked by the Advisory Committee (of the Board of Trade) to fill in a detailed questionnaire and submit accounts and other material. The secretary of the committee travels round the country to meet applicants and tries to put them on the right lines. Many applicants only begin to formulate their claims precisely as the process of investigation gets under way. Though no reasons are given formally it would be made clear to the applicant if a new application, e.g., for a lesser amount would be more likely to succeed. Such a new application is in effect tantamount to an appeal.[10]

The workings of the Local Employment Act have been examined by the Select Committee on Estimates, which expressed concern at the lack of any formal reasons for the rejection of an application. The Board of Trade was insistent, however, that such a requirement would have destroyed the easy contact which existed between applicant and investigating officer. A similar view was also put forward in the Commons debate on the Industrial Development Bill of 1966. The Government's attitude here was that an informal process of this nature was ultimately based on goodwill rather than on a strict application of rules.[11] It was conceded that it would certainly have been possible to give reasons but, in the Government's view, an industrialist who had been negotiating under the informal procedure would in fact know far more of the reasons behind the decision than could emerge from formal reasons.[12] The Board of Trade also operated an 'internal hierarchy of appeals'[13] or informal review machinery as it is perhaps better described. It should be emphasized here that the administrative process under these statutes was entirely departmental. There was no question, for example, of an appeal going to an independent tribunal and indeed an Opposition amendment proposing an appeal tribunal under the Control of Offices Bill 1965 was firmly rejected. The Board of Trade's decision to grant or refuse an office development permit, it was said, was 'essentially a policy decision which involves weighing the case of the applicant, not against some fixed or measurable criteria but against a judgment on the national distribution of employment policy.'[14] The provision of an appeal tribunal would mean that an 'independent tribunal would ... be dictating economic decisions to the Government'.[15] This last point is a crucial one; as we shall see, it is made over and over again, not only in relation to matters of economic policy but also on any matter of major political importance (for example, immigration) where ministerial accountability is thought to be necessary.

The Heath Conservative Government, which succeeded the Labour Government that had refused to establish an independent appeal tribunal 'dictating economic decisions', was not surprisingly even less enamoured with the concept of autonomous agencies exercising decision-making powers in this field. The Labour Government had in fact established one autonomous agency – the Industrial Reorganization Corporation, which was set up under the Industrial Reorganization Corporation Act of 1966. The Corporation's general functions were to promote or assist the reorganization or development of any industry or, at the request of the Secretary of State, to establish, develop, promote or assist the establishment or development of any industrial enterprise. For this purpose the Corporation was given specific power to acquire or hold and dispose of securities, form companies, provide and guarantee loans and acquire and provide premises, plant, machinery and other equipment.[16] The Corporation was made subject to ministerial direction on matters 'of a general character' but the Secretary of State was required to consult with the Corporation first before issuing such directions.[17] The new Conservative Government, in enacting the Industry Act 1972, made its dislike of the Industrial Reorganization Corporation plain, notwithstanding the Secretary of State's powers of direction. The Secretary of State for Trade and Industry, Mr John Davies, said on the second reading of the Bill:

... the nature of mechanism to undertake the selective assistance envisaged has been the subject of much consultation. There are those who propound the virtues of an external agency or agencies, modelled on the pattern of the Labour Administration's IRC: they extol its independence and adaptability. But we have serious objections to such a mechanism. It handles public money without a proper degree of accountability to Parliament and its institutions. It intervenes in the market at its own whim. It becomes a force of manipulation and coercion. This is precisely what we do not want to see the kind of selective support that we favour become.

We have therefore decided that the mechanism should be part of Government itself, though staffed and counselled to a substantial extent by those experienced in the promotion of industrial projects and recruited from industry and commerce.[18]

It is not irrelevant in this context to mention that the Industry Act 1972 was seen and acknowledged as representing a fairly dramatic turnaround of Conservative policy on the issue of regional economic development and government support and assistance to industry generally; it is not surprising therefore that, in feeling its way in a new and unwelcome direction, the Government should wish to retain as much control as possible.

The Industry Act 1972 also replaced the advisory committee which had been established under the Local Employment Act 1972 by a body known as the Industrial Development Board. In other words tribunal assistance, in the form of an advisory body, was retained.[19] It is interesting to compare the Secretary of State's relationship with the Local Employment Act advisory committee on the one hand, and with the Industry Act Advisory Board on the other. The Secretary of State, in considering applications for building grants, was empowered to consult the advisory committee if he saw fit;[20] consultation was thus discretionary.[21] In relation to his more general powers of making grants, loans and subscribing for shares, however, it was mandatory for the Secretary of State in every instance to act in accordance with recommendations made by the committee.[22] On the other hand the committee, in making such recommendations, was required to 'act in accordance with general directions given to them by the Secretary of State with the consent of the Treasury'.[23] The Treasury's role is obviously a crucial one for, in so far as the Secretary of State exercised control over the advisory committee, so too the Treasury exercised control over the Secretary of State. Treasury consent has also been required in respect of grants given under the Industry Act but the new Advisory Board is now no longer subject to ministerial (or treasury) direction. Whether this should be a matter for rejoicing is, however, doubtful as the Board's recommendations are not now binding on the Secretary of State in any event, though the latter must, if required by the Board, lay a statement before

Parliament in any case where he has acted contrary to the Board's recommendations.[24]

There is thus a plain reluctance to allow tribunals to provide more than advisory assistance in this area. The concept of an independent tribunal having powers of final determination free of ministerial or treasury direction has been consistently rejected. It was rejected also in relation to the granting of office development permits under the Control of Offices and Industrial Development Act 1965.[25] The decision to grant such a permit, the minister said, was 'essentially a policy decision which involves weighing the case for the applicant, not against some fixed or measurable criteria, but against a judgement on the national distribution of employment policy'. This was 'a matter for ministerial judgment, with the emphasis changing from time to time as between one place and another'.[26] Similarly, in relation to the issue of industrial development certificates (for buildings of more than a specified area), the suggestion of an independent appeals tribunal was rejected by the Hunt Committee which reported on *The Intermediate Areas* because of the flexibility and sensitivity of the whole policy and the consequential 'lack of permanent and readily applicable criteria'.[27] The comment may be added that the crucial factor was not flexibility, for policy-oriented tribunals have often been praised for their flexibility and adaptability, but rather sensitivity.

(b) and (c) *The control of inflation and the regulation of industrial relations*

The forces which produce inflation are many and varied but the battle against it has centred very much on the restraint of price and, more particularly, wage increases. There are many economists who argue that price and wage restraint as such is impractical and that a greater use of subsidies, discriminatory taxation and welfare benefits provides the better hope of success. Nevertheless, prices and incomes policies designed to curb increases which are not matched by productivity gains have been the central feature of governmental anti-inflation policy in recent years. Independent agencies have played a key role in the administration of these policies, as they have also in relation to the conduct of industrial relations. This latter topic will be examined in detail in a later chapter; it is associated here with the control of inflation because in both matters, and for the same reasons, successive governments have found the concept of independent decision-making an attractive one. There is, in short, a moral appeal that can be made to respect and observe the edicts of 'impartial', 'independent' bodies which have no axe to grind and which, it is said, base their decisions on a detached examination of the merits of individual cases. Or, in the case of the National Industrial Relations Court in the summer of 1972, base their decisions on a detached application of the law of the land.[28]

This type of reasoning was evident with the establishment in 1957 of the first of the various prices and incomes agencies: the Council on Prices, Productivity and Incomes, a three-member body chaired by Lord Cohen, which inevitably came to be called the 'Three Wise Men'. The Council had general review powers only and was charged with examining and reporting from time to time on changes in prices, productivity and incomes. It had no power to rule on specific cases but it was independent of the Government. Andrew Shonfield has commented on the effect of this fact:

... the Government was no doubt moved by the hope that these people would achieve a quasi-judicial standing and that their recommendations on economic policy, even if unpopular, would have a compelling moral force, like those of judges handing down the law. This idea of bringing in a species of economic judiciary, to supplement the efforts of an executive in need of wider support for its policies ... lay behind the establishment of the 'Council on Prices Productivity and Incomes' ... which was supposed to provide the country with *ex cathedra* judgments on the permissible increase in wages ... and so on.[29]

The Three Wise Men issued three reports and, following a change in personnel in 1960, a final report in 1961. Many thought that this institutional experiment had not been a success: 'People kept noticing the unstated political assumptions staring through the cracks in the facade of expert economic argument', said Shonfield and others expressed critical views also.[30]

In November 1962 a new independent body, the National Incomes Commission, was established. Its function was to review income matters where the cost was borne by the Exchequer (apart from pay in the nationalized industries, the higher civil service and doctors and dentists) and also to examine retrospectively any specific pay settlement, whether in the public or private sector (other than an arbitration award). In each case, it was dependent on a government reference; it could not, in other words, initiate an investigation itself.[81] This was also to be a feature (and a weakness) of the Labour Government's successor to the Commission – the National Board for Prices and Incomes. The National Incomes Commission was handicapped considerably also by its inability to gain trade union approval, a matter not irrelevant to the operation of the various institutions and agencies established by the Industrial Relations Act 1971. On the other hand the Commission's procedures and investigatory methods were wide-ranging and to some extent showed a healthy willingness to eschew purely judicial techniques of fact-finding and decision-making. Its basic method of investigation was as follows.[82] It relied upon a wide variety of sources of information : its own knowledge, published information, written submissions, oral evidence and enquiries initiated for the reference. It began its proceedings by seeking written submissions from all interested parties and also placed a notice in the press inviting information and submissions from any other persons. Background information about the industry and available data concerning wage rates, earnings, profits and productivity were supplied by government departments; in some cases academic researchers made contributions. All submissions were circulated amongst the contributors and given to the press. Public oral hearings were then held at which written submissions could be expanded and other contributions commented on. The Commission retained the right to question witnesses but no cross-examination or legal representation was allowed. No special enquiries of its own were undertaken by the Commission and Alan Fels has observed that it was therefore very much in the hands of the co-operating parties for its information; often this information was of limited use.[83] In the end the lack of a strong research branch of its own and an over-reliance on existing information, mainly supplied by interested parties, proved to be its Achilles' heel. According to Fels :

Nearly all reports were weakened in one crucial respect or another by NIC's inability to reach a definite finding, either on a vital issue of fact, or even on the central question of whether or not an agreement was against the national interest. This was largely because it followed the approach of a Court of Inquiry or legal tribunal or Royal Commission of relying for evidence mainly on what co-operating parties submitted and what was already available in a published form or happened to have been the subject of recent academic research. On some questions, such as managerial efficiency in the engineering and shipbuilding industries, independent enquiries would have been necessary for a sound judgment to have been made. The weakness of its investigations lessened the force of its findings, and at times led it to some rather simplistic findings.[34]

If the National Incomes Commission was not as adventurous or as effective in investigating references as it might have been, its successor, the National Board for Prices and Incomes, established by the Labour Government in 1965, opened up new vistas for inquiry and decision-making by independent agencies. In five years it published 170 reports; seventy-nine on pay, sixty-seven on prices, ten related to both pay and prices, nine general study references and five general reports. The Board was assisted by having extremely well-qualified staff with both specialist and inter-disciplinary skills; in its *Final General Report* it said that among the members and staff there were 'experts in such fields as economics, industrial relations, accounting, statistics and management operations, their effectiveness being the greater because they acted as a single instrument of investigation'. But its procedures were revolutionary in that it conducted its own inquiries and did not rely on others to supply basic factual information. The Board also commissioned outside experts – particularly management consultants but also academics on occasion – to aid them on specific matters, though it claimed in its *Second General Report* in answer to criticism of this practice that these did not intrude into the area of policy determination.[35] All this is not to say that the Board did not seek and obtain information from interested parties and otherwise listen to their views; they did, but unlike most judicial and quasi-judicial bodies they were not in the position of having little option but to base their determinations on the material supplied by the parties. The whole process is perhaps aptly summed up as one of informal consultative investigation[36] under which interested parties were consulted informally at different stages during the investigation on different matters and for different purposes. Thus, the parties were contacted immediately after a reference had been received from the department and preliminary meetings arranged at which the purpose of the inquiry was outlined, submissions invited and necessary arrangements made for future contact. Great emphasis was placed on obtaining the willing co-operation of the parties; the Board did have legal powers for questioning witnesses or obtaining information but never once used them. During the conduct of the investigation, members of the investigating team went 'into the field' and interviewed many persons at all levels of management and work force. Although the primary purpose of the interviews was to obtain factual and technical information, the opportunity was also taken to obtain opinions about an industry and its operations. Subsequently the investigating team and the designated board member would meet with the parties, separately and privately, in order to argue out different points and even basic matters of policy. In particular, alternative conclusions were put to the parties in order to gauge their reaction and to obtain rebuttals; there was a reluctance, however, to use draft reports as the basis of such discussions, though the Board was aware of the importance of keeping in touch with the parties right up to the time of publication and submission of its report to the minister. For this reason the Board came in for some criticism, especially from trade unions, on the grounds that it was being rather secretive and underhand; its practice of putting to a party at a consultation the views of another, opposing, party so that a reaction might be obtained did not assist in this respect. It is to be noted that the Commission on Industrial Relations, which has to a considerable extent modelled its methods of investigation on those used by the Board, has not adopted this particular feature of the Board's proceedings; instead, it openly reveals its tentative conclusions at a certain point for the express purpose of trying to seek some form of agreement from the parties, or at least a modification of initial standpoints.

It must be said that the Prices and Incomes Board did not escape strong criticism on many grounds of substance. Perhaps the most serious was the charge that it effectively destroyed the Labour Government's incomes policy by approving under the 'productivity' exception many wage settlements which were truly inflationary but, dressed up in appropriate language, were passed off as productivity agreements. Some estimates of these phoney agreements have been put as high as fifty per cent of all approvals given by the Board, though Professor Clegg, who was a member of the Board, while accepting that there were phoney deals puts the figure very much lower.[37] Fels is more cautious than most. The necessary evidence, he feels, is not at hand to make a firm assessment; he concedes, however, that the productivity criterion, in bringing about some changes in the wage structure and the bargaining process, may have been inflationary.[38] There may have been some confusion of goals here. Certainly the Labour Government wished to encourage greater productivity and to reform wage bargaining procedures to enable this to occur more easily; but to seek reforms of such substance by providing a loophole in its incomes policy was an open invitation to escape by simply changing the form. Government responsibility was not only pinned to the soundness of the actual policy, however. It was also related in large part to the administration of the scheme; for the Board was dependent on the Department (initially on the Department of Economic Affairs, later on the Department of Employment and Productivity) for its references. It could not initiate an investigation itself and, although at times it put some pressure on the Department to refer particular wage settlements or price increases to it, it was in this respect at the Department's mercy. Eventually, the number of references did dry up to a trickle; Fels concludes that 'there were serious omissions in the reference of above-norm nationally negotiated wage rate agreements even before the total breakdown of the policy in July 1969' and practically no local settlements notified to the Department were referred to the Board.[39] The Board itself commented in its *Third General Report* that it was not satisfied that the Government had been pursuing a 'sufficiently purposeful stategy for price references to the Board'.[40] The rest is history.

Following the election of the Conservative Government in 1970 the fate of the Prices and Incomes Board was never in doubt. The Conservatives had been consistent critics of the Labour prices and incomes policy and made plain their view that legal restrictions were not the answer. The Board was therefore wound up completely within a few months, although it had in fact already ceased to investigate wage settlements. In its place was instituted the 'unofficial norm' policy, exercised through persuasion and appeals to the national interest, by which it was sought to induce the parties to wage negotiations to agree on increases below a stated figure (around eight per cent). Price stability would follow automatically, it was said, assisted by tougher legislation to be introduced on the control of monopolies and price-fixing agreements. This policy was in fact more complex than is generally thought. At its crudest level it meant that wage claims in the public sector were resisted fiercely; a fact attested to by the lengthy and bitter strikes in the Post Office and the coal mines. But the policy also worked through government pressure on Wages Councils, wage arbitrators,[41] and the Department of Employment's Conciliation Service.[42] There were clearly dangers in this course and the wisdom of the Government at that time must be questioned. It would seem likely that the high-water mark of its folly was the ill-fated applications made by the Secretary of State for Employment to the National Industrial Relations Court for cooling-off and compulsory ballot orders in the case of the railways workers' pay claim in early 1972.[43] It is now generally acknowledged that these orders simply served to harden union resolve and thus were a major factor in the substantial increase which was eventually agreed. After the Wilberforce Court of Inquiry[44] had recognized that the miners constituted a 'special case', deserving of an increase well above the unofficial norm, it became only a matter of time before there was a reversion to legal controls exercised through a standing independent agency. A wages and prices freeze[45] late in 1972 was followed by the Counter-Inflation Act 1973 which established two agencies called respectively the Price Commission and the Pay Board.

The Prices and Incomes Board, in its *Final Report*, had expressed the view very forcefully that wages and prices should be dealt with together under the auspices of a single agency; to the extent that these two matters are inter-related and do overlap, the creation of two agencies is likely to cause problems and to inhibit the efficacy of the overall policy.[46] It is probably this fear which has, however, led to the inclusion in the 1973 Act of a provision enabling the two agencies to be amalgamated at any time by Order in Council.[47] The general functions and position of the agencies are not dissimilar to those of the Prices and Incomes Board, though there are some interesting differences.[48] The principal one is that under the new legislation the Treasury is given the task of preparing a code for the guidance of the agencies and including 'practical guidance for those concerned in decisions on levels of prices and pay'. The code is to be promulgated by statutory instrument and may be changed from time to time by similar process. Before doing so, however, the Treasury must consult with the agencies and with 'such representatives of consumers, persons experienced in the supply of goods or services, employers and employees and other persons as they think appropriate'.[49] The concept of a code containing guidelines is a useful one and bears direct comparison with that provided under the Industrial Relations Act; it is noteworthy in the case of the Counter-Inflation Act that the Treasury has assumed open responsibility for the formulation of the code. The relationship between autonomous agencies, individual ministers and the Treasury has often been obscured except where, as in the case of investment grants discussed above, expenditure of public moneys has been involved.

The Price Commission and Pay Board are not so obviously dependent on ministerial decision as to the cases which they may investigate and give rulings on; in addition, their determinations are not simply recommendatory but have direct legal effect and are legally enforceable. The Act provides that in each instance the appropriate agency may restrict the prices or charges for the sale of goods or the performance of services in the course of business, or, as the case may be, the remuneration (of whatever kind) which is paid.[50] But it is also provided that:

The Minister[51] may, in such cases as appear to him appropriate, by order make provision to ensure that the Agencies receive notice of increases in any prices, charges or remuneration in time to consider whether the increases conform with the relevant provisions of the code, and whether the Agencies should exercise the powers conferred by the following provisions of this Act in order to prevent those increases.[52]

Again, therefore, ultimate control is retained by the minister as to the scope of the agencies' jurisdiction and as to the occasions on which they may exercise their powers.[53] This is not necessarily a bad thing in principle: indeed, it is argued in Chapter 8 that it is precisely this arrangement that potentially is the most effective and flexible form of administration. But, in an area where a Government wishes to stress the independence and impartiality of a decision-making agency, control of this kind may ultimately serve to bring the agency into disrepute.

(d) *The maintenance of free competition*

The idea that free competition among traders ensures price stability, adequate consumer protection, greater productivity and generally an efficient free enterprise or capitalist system dies hard.

Many of our modern laws and institutions are dedicated to achieving that basic objective. Chief among the agencies are the Restrictive Practices Court and the Monopolies Commission, as different in form and composition as chalk from cheese, yet both performing tasks with the same goal in mind. Indeed, the Restrictive Practices Court, when it was established in 1956, took over from the Monopolies Commission one of the jobs which it had been performing since its inception in 1948: that of deciding whether or not certain trade and price-fixing agreements were contrary to the public interest. The establishment of the Court gave rise to misgivings for, although it was clear that restrictive practice laws needed to be enforced more rigorously, many felt that the Government itself should have assumed responsibility for doing so. The debates on the Restrictive Trade Practices Bill raised this issue directly and attention was focused also on the ability of a judicial proceeding to determine matters of economic policy. It was true that the new court was to have economic experts who would sit with the high court judge who presided over it and the Bill did provide certain criteria to which the Court was to have regard in measuring agreements against the public interest. But ultimately it was clear that the Court would be developing policy in a largely uncharted area. The chief (Labour) Opposition spokesman, Sir Lynn Ungoed-Thomas (later a High Court judge himself), objected that the function of a court was to interpret and administer law, not to make it. 'This Bill', he said, 'hands over to this court governmental and parliamentary power'. Judgements of courts are founded upon law or upon facts, he said, but in this instance the decision would be a political and economic one.[54] To the Government's reply that the courts were well used to dealing with economic and social matters, at least on an individual level, and that they often had to determine questions of reasonableness (something which is difficult to classify as either law or fact), Sir Lynn rejoined:

It has been said that the courts are accustomed to decided whether a thing is reasonable or not; of course they are. Whenever they assess damages they assess what is a reasonable amount. That argument begs the question, which is the ambit within which reasonableness has to be exercised. If it is within a justiciable issue, then the courts of law exercise reasonableness, but no one will suggest that because there is an exercise of reasonableness in Budget decisions therefore Budget decisions are things which ought to be submitted to a court of law.[55] Justiciability [he concluded] depends not upon reasonableness or unreasonableness, or upon whether or not it is an individual case, but essentially upon the nature of the issue that has to be considered by the body that we set up. We know that the function of the court of law is to apply the general rules of law to the facts of a particular case. The rules and the definition are there and the Court interprets the definition as part of its function in applying it to the facts of the case.[56]

The economic decisions which the Restrictive Practices Court would make were not, he thought, of this kind. They were essentially, governmental decisions.

Notwithstanding these doubts the Court's initial performances received warm praise. In the leading study made of its operations, Stevens and Yamey reported in 1956 that: 'So far the Court has received an almost exclusively eulogistic reception; and the praise has come from all directions.'[57] Judges, newspapers, economic journals, left-wing writers, right-wing writers, political parties, all to varying degrees of enthusiasm approved of the work the Court had done in the years following its establishment.[58] Stevens and Yamey themselves were noticeably less enthusiastic. A full analysis of the decisions of the Court up to that time led them to conclude that in some judgements there were 'unresolved internal inconsistencies' and that in others 'necessary steps in the analysis appear to be missing, or the full implications of particular findings or facts are not drawn out'. Sometimes, they said, 'the theoretical bases of the analysis appear to be unconvincing'.[59] They were hesitant too about the procedure which the Court followed. The Court does in fact have its own procedural rules and these do provide for some important differences from those operating in the Queen's Bench Division of the High Court. Thus, it is expressly provided that:

Where it appears to the Court . . . that the Court would be assisted in determining any issue in the proceedings by the admission of evidence (whether oral or documentary) which would not otherwise be admissible under the law relating to evidence, the Court may make an order allowing the admission of such evidence.[60]

Interlocutory applications too are determined by the judge of the Court except where he otherwise directs and this, in theory at least, gives him a greater degree of control over the conduct of the case and over the settlement of the relevant issues than would be

possible where a master heard such applications.[61] More than
that, it is expressly provided in the rules that the Registrar of
Restrictive Trading Agreements *must* apply to the Court for
directions as soon as practicable after replies have been delivered
by the respondents (or the time for their doing so has expired) to
the answer delivered by the Registrar to the statement of case.
The purpose of this provision, the rule states, is to provide 'an
occasion for the consideration of the preparations for the final
hearing so that:

(1) all matters which can be dealt with (including, in Scotland,
    any preliminary question of relevance or sufficiency of speci-
    fication arising on the pleadings) on interlocutory applications
    and have not already been dealt with may, so far as possible,
    be dealt with; and
(2) such directions may be given as to the future course of the
    proceedings as appear best adapted to secure the just, expedi-
    tious and economical disposal thereof.'[62]

Stevens and Yamey are not convinced, however, that the
procedure of the Restrictive Practices Court is significantly different in practice from that of the Queen's Bench Division: 'The
case begins with the exchange of pleading, and then follows the
customary pre-trial procedures.' In the Court itself, 'the same
effort is made to keep the proceedings within the normal bounds
of the ordinary courts. The strict distinction between barrister
and solicitor is retained. Counsel preserve the English tradition of
orality, and the Court has shown a reluctance to sit *in camera*. . . .
In general . . . there has been an increasing assimilation of the
operation of the Court to that of an ordinary court.'[63]

The Confederation of British Industry has also been very
critical of the Court and pressed the Government to repeal the
Restrictive Trade Practices Acts and to abolish the Court totally.
The CBIs objection to the Court was that it has interpreted the
relevant provisions of the Act too rigidly with the result that
conditions imposed on agreements are exceedingly difficult to
satisfy. The CBI was especially critical as to the procedure
followed by the Court:

The defence of an agreement before the court is lengthy (one case
has exceeded nine years), costly and the absence of any system of
speedy clearance has operated seriously to the detriment of the business community. The result in practice has been to prevent the

formation or cause the revocation of a number of rationalization, specialization and other agreements which would have improved industrial efficiency and would have been beneficial to the public interest.... We also consider that the procedure of a trial before a court has led to the taking of a number of technical points in inter-locutory proceedings and is generally inappropriate for the handling of what are often economic problems of great complexity.[64]

The proposals which the CBI made for the replacement of the Restrictive Practices Court are interesting for they raise issues which are fundamental to the role of the judicial process. The CBI recommended the appointment of an official to be known as the Registrar of Restrictive Trade Practices who would have wide powers of initial investigation of restrictive trading agreements and who would also have a discretion to discuss these agreements with the firms concerned. If he were unable to negotiate a satis-factory informal settlement he would refer the matter to the Secretary of State with a view to a formal reference then being made to the Monopolies Commission (reconstituted as a more expert body than at present).[65] The Commission would then investigate the matter 'on an inquisitorial basis' and certain classes of restrictive agreements would be regarded as being *prima facie* contrary to the public interest. On the other hand 'certain procedural safeguards' (unspecified) would be provided to 'ensure that respondents have an opportunity of both knowing and of adequately testing the evidence against them'.

Ultimately the Fair Trading Act did extend the provisions of the 1956 Act to include agreements and arrangements between suppliers of services which involve restrictions upon the supply or acquisition of services other than services of a professional nature. It also transferred to a new officer known as the director general of fair trading the functions formerly exercised by the Registrar of Restrictive Trading Agreements.[66] But it left the Court unchanged.

The establishment of the office of director general of fair trad-ing, together with other changes made by the 1973 Fair Trading Act, went some way towards meeting serious criticisms of substance which had been made continuously about the Mono-polies Commission from the time of its inception. The Commis-sion had been created by the Monopolies and Restrictive Practices (Inquiry and Control) Act of 1948 as an investigative body which would undertake inquiries into monopoly matters referred to it by the President of the Board of Trade under powers given to him by the Act. References could be made in respect of any class of goods where it was thought that a third of the goods specified had been supplied or acquired in the United Kingdom either by a single firm or by a number of firms who effectively operated a closed shop among themselves.[67] The establishment of the Restrictive Practices Court in 1956 took away from the Commission's jurisdiction restrictive trading agreements[68] but the Monopolies and Mergers Act 1965 gave the Commission important new functions, notably the power to inquire into restrictive practices and monopoly situations in the supply of services (as referred by the Board of Trade) and to investigate mergers referred to it by the Board of Trade. Special provisions were also included enabling the Commission to inquire into newspaper mergers, a matter thought to be not so much one of economic concern as of 'freedom of speech, free expression of opinion, and the public interest'.[69] The tendency, therefore, seems to be to entrust the investigation of new and extended monopoly matters to the Commission, rather than the Court,[70] perhaps indicating that dissatisfaction with the judicial solution provided in 1956 now exceeds the concern previously felt about the Monopolies Commission which led to the adoption of that solution.

Membership of the Commission has been characterized by part-timers who are drawn from a wide range of professional life and who are of the highest distinction in their various fields. Originally the Board of Trade had power to appoint between four and ten members but in 1953 the maximum number was increased to twenty-five to enable the Commission to sit in groups and so conduct a number of inquiries at the one time; the 1956 Act took away this power and also reduced the number of members. However, the enlargement of the Commission's jurisdiction in 1965 saw an increase also in the number of members and on this occasion power was given to add further members by statutory instrument. As at 31 December 1972 there was a full-time chairman, a part-time deputy chairman and seventeen part-time members. In addition, a special panel of seven was maintained from which the Secretary of State was empowered under the 1965 legislation to appoint extra members to take part in any investigation into a newspaper merger. As of the same date, the Commission employed a staff of sixty-four (including four who were part-time).[71]

By virtue of the quality of its membership the Monopolies Commission has enjoyed a high reputation but, like the National Board for Prices and Incomes, its effectiveness has been severely limited by its inability to undertake inquiries of its own initiative. Under both the 1948 and the 1965 Acts it was empowered only to investigate such monopoly matters as were referred to it by the President of the Board of Trade (now the Secretary of State for Trade and Industry). Further, the Commission's conclusions were in no way directly enforceable but were at best in the nature of recommendations for the Secretary of State. The latter was given power by the legislation to make orders to prevent or remedy any conditions or arrangements operating against the public interest, as found by the Commission.[72] From the point of view of the Secretary of State the Monopolies Commission thus provides a highly expert, reputable agency which assumes full responsibility for the conduct of inquiries into monopoly matters and whose findings are likely to be treated with the highest respect as those of an expert, independent body. But it is an agency which will only act when the Secretary of State commands and whose conclusions are also subject to his determination as to the action which should be taken. This is not said cynically but simply to show that ultimately the Secretary of State has retained full control over the extent to which action will be taken in monopoly situations while relinquishing it completely in the actual investigation of specific cases.

The relationship between the Commission and the Secretary of State is undoubtedly a delicate one. Three specific examples will illustrate the point. The first concerned the investigation by the Commission into the supply of household detergents.[73] The Commission, in its report of 3 August 1966, found that Unilever and Procter and Gamble held forty-four and forty-six per cent by value respectively of the total market; that the vast amounts of money spent by these companies on advertising and promotion effectively prevented the entry of new suppliers into the market and also resulted in wasteful expenditure. The net result, the Commission said, had been excessively high profits for both companies and high prices for the consumer. The Commission made various recommendations as to the action that should be taken to remedy the situation. These remedies were not, however, adopted by the Board of Trade. Instead, negotiations were entered into between the Board of Trade and the companies concerned and on 26 April 1967 the President (Mr Douglas Jay) announced in the Commons that the companies had agreed voluntarily to make fully available an alternative range of top-quality soap powders and synthetic detergent powders at a price twenty per cent below that of existing products; the companies also undertook to keep prices pegged for two years in respect of those detergents covered by the Commission's report.[74] This announcement immediately brought an angry retort from an Opposition member:

Is the President of the Board of Trade aware that there is nothing in the Monopolies and Mergers Act which gives him power to carry out these negotiations, and that he has acted with grave constitutional impropriety? Will he now say whether he intends to continue his policy of government by Ministerial decree, or will pass laws to justify what he has been trying to do?[75]

Constitutionally proper or not, it is clear that the report of an independent agency coupled with the minister's legal powers of enforcement, had certainly provided a very effective bargaining weapon for the minister, highlighting a function of agency utility which has not been previously emphasized.

The second case concerned the proposed merger between the Slater Walker and Hill Samuel Groups. On 22 May 1973 it was announced that there would be no reference to the Monopolies Commission. Subsequently, the Minister for Trade and Consumer Affairs, Sir Geoffrey Howe, explained in the Commons that, while the merger satisfied the so-called size of assets test, it did not pass the market share test so that the total situation would remain fully competitive.[76] Opposition speakers, in criticizing the decision to allow the merger to proceed without an inquiry by the Commission, thought that 'matters of this kind [should] be considered by an independent body, not behind closed doors, so that the public can understand what is happening and what are its ramifications'.[77] Concern was also expressed as to certain (unpublished) assurances which had been given by the companies to the minister.[78] In defending this position, the minister stated that the undertakings which had been given would be published in due course and said:

In deciding whether or not to subject any particular change in industrial organisation for inquiry by the Monopolies Comission one seeks to satisfy oneself about a number of existing facts and possible future decisions in relation to the merged organisation.

In doing that, one acquires, inevitably and rightly, indications and assurances as to the way in which the proposed organisation is likely to see its commercial future. These assurances are useful indications in reaching a decision about the instant matter.

They are also part of the background that can be taken into account in any future decisions to be taken. It would be foolish to disregard the opportunity of getting some indication as to the future probable development of the merged organisation.[79]

In winding up the discussion the minister also emphasized what he described as the two-stage nature of monopoly proceedings – the minister's decision to refer a case to the Commission for consideration, the inquiry and report by the Commission and (he might have added) the minister's further decision as to what action should be taken. At the initial stage it would be plainly easier, he said, as a matter of political convenience to say 'Let it be referred' and the responsibility would then be lifted from the Government's shoulders.[80] One wonders, however, whether a decision not to implement Monopolies Commission recommendations is in fact much more politically inconvenient than a decision not to refer a case to the Commission for investigation.[81]

The third case was that – also in May 1973 – of a government decision to refer to the Monopolies Commission for investigation the supply of certain kinds of photocopiers. It was stated that the reference was to be restricted to what are known as plain paper copiers and would not extend to other kinds of copiers, including high volume rotary duplicators. The objection taken to this course of action was that the terms of reference were too narrow. According to the director general of the Business Equipment Trade Association, the reference was a misuse of legislative powers in that 'If you define your field narrowly enough, everything is a monopoly'.[82] Certainly there is a point of substance here. In determining the breadth and scope of any inquiry or investigation, the person or agency responsible for defining the terms of reference possesses a discretionary power which may well be decisive of the ultimate outcome of the inquiry. Nor has the Monopolies Commission itself been willing, generally speaking, to broaden its inquiries by taking account of 'public interest' factors other than those of market share, asset size and other pure monopoly criteria. Thus, unlike the National Board for Prices and Incomes, it has not investigated or taken account of managerial efficiency or industrial relations.[83] And, according to Professor Peston, the Commission has relied on simple textbook assumptions of profit maximization in static conditions in determining the likely behaviour of companies; it has commissioned very little work from universities or from management consultants so that 'although in principle all or nearly all the problems that have confronted it are cost-benefit problems, the Commission appears to have been happy merely to survey whatever evidence is easily available and then apply their judgment to it'.[84]

The net result has been that the Commission's effectiveness has been severely limited both by the comparative superficiality of its inquiries and by its dependence on ministerial reference and implementation. Alister Sutherland, an economist, has commented that radical structural remedies, including the dissolution of monopolies, have not been considered adequately because the Commission has not even attempted to assess the costs and benefits of such alternative strategies. Thus, he says, the Commission 'has inevitably fallen back *either* on remedies of an essentially temporary nature (cut prices; reform specified exclusionary tactics); *or* on a more rapid introduction of a more permanent remedy, reduction in tariff, which is likely to be forced upon the UK anyway as part of the general slow chipping away of protective barriers in GATT'.[85] Sutherland also saw the dependence of the Commission on ministerial reference as preventing it assuming a role as permanent auditor of behaviour and performance in markets where structure ought to remain non-competitive (at least for the time being) because of the demonstrated weight of scale economies.[86]

The Fair Trading Act 1973 has not gone so far as to permit the Commission to initiate investigations of its own accord but it has by the creation of the new office of director general of fair trading, reduced the Commission's dependence on ministerial reference and thus removed in some part the degree of political arbitrariness which was previously so apparent in the taking of the decision to refer. Under the Act the director is required to give information and assistance to the Secretary of State about monopoly situations and uncompetitive practices (*inter alia*) and to make recommendations to him for action. He also has the power to make monopoly references himself, except in relation to goods or services which are the subject of a statutory monopoly or which are regulated by a statutory body (for example, electricity, letter post, port and air navigation facilities). The director must, however, communicate any reference made by him to the Secretary of State, who may within fourteen days direct the Commission not to proceed with the reference. In addition the Secretary of State retains the power to make references to the Commission himself or in conjunction with any other minister; references as to newspaper mergers remain the sole prerogative of the Secretary of State. That the latter ultimately retains control is also seen in a provision in the Act which empowers the Secretary of State to issue general directions about the considerations to which the director is to have regard in the discharge of his functions.

Nor has the Act altered the responsibility of the Secretary of State for the implementation (by statutory order) of Monopoly Commission recommendations, or the taking of other action in accordance with commission findings. But it has introduced an interesting new provision under which the director may be required by the appropriate minister to negotiate, on the basis of a report of the Commission on either a monopoly or merger reference, the securing of undertakings to remedy or prevent any adverse consequences referred to in the report. The director may further be required to keep under review the carrying out of any such undertaking or any action taken in compliance with any order made upon the basis of the report. There is a comparable provision under the restrictive trade practices part of the Act which enables the director, in his capacity as registrar of the Restrictive Practices Court, to seek a written assurance from any person carrying on business who has persistently maintained a course of conduct which is detrimental and unfair to consumers in the United Kingdom. If negotiations for the obtaining of a satisfactory undertaking break down, or if any undertaking given is not observed, the director is empowered to institute proceedings before the Restrictive Practices Court.

The development of negotiatory procedures leading to enforcement through 'voluntary' undertakings is not new to England. The Alkali and Factories Inspectorates, as well as River Boards and Authorities, have traditionally relied on systems of voluntary enforcement through negotiation and persuasion, though the threat of prosecution has undoubtedly acted as a powerful incentive to companies to be reasonable. On a broader scale the Press Council, and now the City Panel on Take-overs and Mergers, have acted as voluntary regulatory agencies, in the one case maintaining standards of journalism according to a largely unwritten code of professional ethics and developing principles through case-law, and in the other ensuring that shareholders and investors are given adequate information in relation to take-overs and mergers. Neither system can operate without the consent of the regulated; agreement has, however, been readily forthcoming because, as stated in the introduction to the 1969 version of the City Code, the choice is between 'a system of voluntary self-discipline' and 'regulation by law enforced by officials appointed by Government'.[87] The introduction of a director general of fair trading with the power to negotiate for voluntary undertakings in relation to monopolies and mergers is therefore likely to be welcomed by industry. In so far as there had been previous occasions when the Secretary of State had sought and obtained similar assurances, the practice may prove not to be qualitatively different. But the interposition of a statutory officer, unpressured by daily political expediencies, is a step in the right direction.

2. THE MITIGATION OF THE CONSEQUENCES OF GROWTH

While the main thrust of government has been the promotion of economic growth, an important and necessary corollary has been provided by the policies which have been designed to mitigate the more undesirable effects of that growth. Policies which restrain and control economic activity in 'the public interest' most obviously perform this function; but much social policy also is directed to that end. Our social security laws, for example, may express humanitarian ideals; they also, however, help to maintain capitalist goals by mollifying and disguising their worst effects. The same is true of legislation providing for rent control and regulation. To this extent and from one point of view, the tribunals operating in these fields[88] can be seen as performing a necessary supportive role to our present economic system. The fact that some of these tribunals are appellate bodies and therefore exist as safeguards against the exercise of arbitrary governmental power does not destroy this thesis but rather lends greater credibility to it. A sop to our consciences, the cynic might say.

Similar points might be made about those laws and policies (and tribunals) which operate to protect the consumer against exploitation; those which constitute licensing systems; and those which provide planning and environmental control of the abuses of an industrial economy. Lest the general point be overemphasized, however, it must also be said that some social policies do serve to protect the citizen in his dealings with the organs of state and to maintain his liberties and rights as an individual. This basic objective can be seen behind our laws of immigration, mental health, internment (and release) and in the processing of complaints, the assessment of taxation and the provision of compensation for personal injury. The rest of this chapter (and the three following chapters) will therefore endeavour to examine the role which tribunals play in carrying out policies in many of these areas.

(a) *Consumer protection*

For over three-quarters of a century, the Sale of Goods Act has provided the most obvious source of statutory protection to consumers and purchasers of goods. A weakness of the Act, as far as the consumer is concerned, has of course been the fact that it has allowed 'contracting out' by vendors of their implied obligations under the Act.[89] Much more serious, however, have been the problems faced by consumer plaintiffs in enforcing valid claims against recalcitrant traders and manufacturers. The deficiencies and expense of court proceedings in this area have excited much comment and examination in recent years. Chief among them was the Consumer Council's Report, *Justice Out of Reach – A Case for a Small Claims Court*. The Consumer Council itself, funded by government money, acted as an informal complaint-receiving body; opinion was, however, sharply divided as to its efficacy and its abolition was one of the first moves of the incoming Conservative Government in 1970.

The Council's report focused attention on the fact that the County Courts, which were themselves originally established as small claims courts, had come to be used mainly for debt collecting by firms who sell on credit. The Council said that, unless backed by a trade union or an insurance company, 'the individual simply does not take his dispute to a court for a decision'. And, for reasons of expense, solicitors normally advised against court proceedings.

The Consumer Council, in making proposals for institutional

change which would improve the position of an individual consumer, was much attracted by the North American concept of small claims courts – operating mostly in the evenings and from which legal representation was normally barred. The Council ultimately recommended the establishment of small claims court machinery in Britain with a jurisdictional limit of £100. Interestingly, the concept of special tribunals handling small claims was expressly considered, and rejected, by the Council, even though the features of special tribunals and small claims courts were to all intents indistinguishable for this purpose.

The Consumer Council's proposals in fact had a rather lukewarm reception from the incoming Conservative Government. Nor did academic commentators give wholehearted support. Professor T. G. Ison thought that while small claims courts would use a procedure that was simpler than in the higher courts, they would still operate on basically the same principles:

The small claims judge tends to imitate his superiors in the adversary system. If justice is ever to be done in small claims, the approach must be far more iconoclastic. Indeed, almost every principle that a common lawyer has cherished must be abandoned. The adversary system, the rules of evidence, the dignity of the courtroom, the concept of the trial; all must go. And we must brace ourselves for such innovations as a judge speaking on the telephone to one of the parties in the absence of the other. Above all, the judge's function must be recognised as first and foremost the task of investigation, with adjudication being an ancillary role.[90]

In passing, the same sort of comments can be made about many special tribunals. While to some extent the rules of evidence and many of the trappings of the courtroom are abandoned, the basic adversary system (with all its attendant defects and limitations) remains.

The Conservative Government ultimately decided not to establish small claims courts or to set up special tribunals. Rather it thought that the problem should be solved within the existing judicial machinery. To that end, the Administration of Justice Act 1973 has given to the Registrars of the County Courts the power to arbitrate informally claims below a hundred pounds. And there the matter now rests. The comment can be made that it is perhaps sensible to deal with new problems through existing machinery, where at all possible, rather than to continue the process of diversification which has marked recent court and tribunal development.

The provision of a cheap, quick, flexible and accessible forum in which the citizen can pursue his consumer claim is plainly an important step forward in the achievement of an effective, equitable legal system. But it still leaves a lot to chance. The chance that the system will work well; and more especially, the chance that there will be enough aggrieved plaintiffs willing and able to litigate a sufficiently broad spectrum of consumer complaints to provide an effective overall system of control of manufacturers, wholesalers and retailers. No one consumer – nor indeed the totality of individual consumers – have the resources to detect the different, often subtle ways in which the freely struck bargain is loaded against him. The Minister for Trade and Consumer Affairs, in moving the second reading of the Fair Trading Bill, acknowledged as much when he pointed to 'continuing changes in the techniques of marketing and promotion, new ways of persuading the consumer to enter into a transaction, new ways of arranging the transaction and new ways of arranging payment for a transaction'.[91]

The minister also pinpointed one of the inherent defects of the legislative solution: it is usually one step behind the 'astute minority of traders' who 'devise new ways of outwitting the consumer'.[92] It was partly by way of attempt to overcome the slowness and other difficulties in enacting legislation which led to the introduction in the Fair Trading Act of the director general of fair trading. Though not described as such, his role was to be that of a kind of consumer Ombudsman in the sense that he would keep 'a continuing watch' on new developments which were likely to damage the consumer's economic interests.[93]

The Act gave to the director general the power to refer to a new statutory agency also established by the Act – the Consumer Protection Advisory Committee – the question whether any consumer trade practice specified in the reference adversely affected the economic interests of consumers. In certain categories of case the director general's reference could embody proposals for recommending to the Secretary of State that he should take action to prevent or limit the practice complained of. In any event, the advisory committee was to conduct its own investigation, reporting back to the director general and to the Secretary of State. The latter then had the power to make an order by statutory instrument embodying the committee's recommendations (modified or unmodified). The order would take effect when approved by a resolution of each House of Parliament.

The Fair Trading Act also gave the director general the power to require a written undertaking from any person who in the course of his business has maintained a course of conduct which is detrimental or unfair to consumer interests that he would refrain from continuing that course of conduct. Should such an assurance not be forthcoming or, if given, not be observed, the director was further empowered to bring proceedings against the recalcitrant trader in the Restrictive Practices Court. The Court, if finding the course of conduct complained of proved and if satisfied that it was likely to continue, could then make an order directing the discontinuance of that or similar conduct.

In explaining these new provisions in the Commons the minister stressed that it was expected that they would 'operate in the main by conciliation and voluntary response'.[94] That the enactment of legislative requirements of conciliation or informal procedures seeking undertakings can readily lead to an almost complete avoidance of formal hearing proceedings can be seen from New Zealand experience in the restrictive trade practices area. In that country a tribunal known as the Trade Practices Commission exercised a similar jurisdiction to that of the Restrictive Practices Court and, like the latter body, held hearings and gave final determinations regularly. In 1965, however, the New Zealand legislation was amended to enable the examiner of trade practices, an official holding a comparable position in the restrictive practices field to the registrar (now director general), to seek written assurances from parties to restrictive practices that they would voluntarily cease such practices. This has effectively encouraged the development of a bargaining process in which the worst excesses of trade practices are trimmed and collective agreements modified to the satisfaction of the examiner who ultimately refrains from taking a formal case to the Commission. The results have been quite spectacular – not one Commission hearing and determination has occurred under the cease and desist provisions of the Act since the new administrative procedures came into force.[95]

The New Zealand experience and the new machinery provided by the UK Fair Trading Act reveal the beginnings of a new sophistication in the employment of tribunal decision-making in public interest jurisdictions. The trend appears to be away from the establishment of tribunals as the agencies primarily concerned and towards the use of such tribunals at one or two stages removed from the initial confrontation or action. Thus, under the 'detrimental or unfair course of conduct' provisions just described, the Restrictive Practices Court is likely to exist for the most part simply as a back-stop which is called into play only when the director general fails to achieve his objectives through informal conciliation and negotiation. As such, the Court will nevertheless be important for the very possibility of resort to its formal decision-making processes will shape the settlement that the director general achieves and ensure his success through the bargaining process. Similarly, the role of the new Consumer Protection Advisory Committee, when juxtaposed against the initial investigative and referral powers of the director general and against the order-making powers of the Secretary of State, provides a useful intermediary function (and even, in this case, safeguard) by which the standards of the administrative proceedings will in part be determined.

(b) *Economic licensing*

The growth of the areas of activity which require a licence from the State or one of its agencies is one of the features of the modern welfare state.[96] Many of these areas have no direct economic significance as such and licensing requirements are based on other considerations such as physical safety (for example, motor car driving), prevention of public nuisance (processions, street pedlars) and public health (dairy operators, milk vendors). Some professions or callings are also in effect licensed (law and medicine, for example) in order to ensure the protection of the public that those professions serve.

In the economic sphere, licensing has proved a useful and flexible form of regulation and control. Import (and export) licensing, exchange control regulations and restrictions on office and industry location have been of major importance. In other areas, licensing has also enabled the avoidance of the worst excesses of competition, particularly where such excesses have had adverse non-economic consequences – for example, on safety or on labour conditions.

The most important instance is that of transport: here an

attempt has been made to maintain some kind of equation between supply and demand in a way which is consonant both with public service and reasonable operator margins. Street seems to suggest that licensing of transport services has been employed as the most stringent form of public control possible short of nationalization.[97] Whether this is so or not, one thing that may be said is that where licensing exists tribunals tend to be found. This is certainly most true of transport, both road and air, goods and passengers, where in all instances independent licensing authorities or tribunals have been responsible for determining the issue, renewal and revocation of licences. These tribunals have played a vital role in seeking the achievement of licensing objectives although continuing legislative change reflects the inherent difficulties of regulating the vast transport sector through a licensing system. The intractability of the problem and the basic impotence of the licensing tribunals to solve it can be seen by sketching a brief history of road transport licensing (goods and passenger services) and its administration.

The introduction of a licensing system for the control of carriage of goods on roads was the result of the problems which arose after the First World War from the vast increase of the use of the motor lorry for the carriage of goods. These problems have been described as falling into two categories.[98] First, the large number of motor lorries available ensured 'the use of road haulage for long-distance through traffic in preference to rail because it was cheaper and more able to offer such a service at short notice.'[99] Secondly, the fierce competition which existed in the road haulage industry itself often led to rate cutting with the accompanying evils of overworking of drivers and inadequate maintenance of vehicles. The Geddes Committee, which reported on *Carriers' Licensing* in 1965, doubted the extent to which these evils were in fact prevalent in the postwar period and suggested that the criticisms which had been made by road hauliers were exaggerated;[100] certainly, however, the Salter Committee in 1932 thought that the effects of excessive competition were bad enough to necessitate the establishment of a system of quantitative restriction of road haulage.[101] Danger arising from overdriving was in fact met in part by the Road Traffic Act 1930, which stipulated the hours for which a driver could operate, but the question of proper enforcement and the other problems remained.

The licensing of goods vehicles was established by the Road

and Rail Traffic Act 1933 (largely re-enacted by Part IV of the Road Traffic Act 1960, but now changed substantially by Part V of the Transport Act 1968). Under its provisions no goods vehicle could be used after October 1934 for the carriage of goods for hire or reward without a carrier's licence. A distinction between public carriers' licences (including limited carriers' and contract licences) and private carriers' licences was established from the outset. The latter were obtainable by manufacturers and traders for the carriage of their own goods as of right. The real area of dispute therefore concerned applications for public carriers' licences. The rule laid down by the Road and Rail Traffic Appeal Tribunal, which was the appellate body set up to determine appeals from the licensing authorities established to grant or refuse licences, that an applicant for the public carrier's licence must prove not only that he has prospective customers but that their work cannot for some reason be done adequately by other carriers already engaged in carriage (whether by rail or road)[102] ensured that applications for these licences were generally contested vigorously by other hauliers in the area. The jurisdiction of the road and rail traffic appeal tribunal was transferred to the road haulage appeals division of the Transport Tribunal in August 1951. Both tribunals were responsible, under a series of lawyer chairmen, for the important body of case law which through the years has guided licensing authorities for their administration of the statutory provisions relating to licensing.

Thus, except for the period during the Second World War when full licensing was suspended in favour of the issue of defence permits which were granted without public hearings and without any right of appeal, the licensing of road haulage services remained essentially the same as when it was enacted in 1933. However, the new 1968 Transport Act system of operators' licences and special authorizations for large vehicles has reduced fairly considerably the importance of licensing authorities and the Transport Tribunal in the overall determination and administration of transport policy.

The changes made by the Transport Act 1968 were as follows.[103] A person using a goods vehicle for the carriage of goods (a) for hire or reward; or (b) for or in connection with any trade or business carried on by him, had still to obtain a licence (known as an operator's licence) from the licensing authority. This requirement did not extend to the use of a 'small goods vehicle' as specially defined. On the other hand 'large goods vehicles', as defined, when on 'controlled journeys' required 'special authorization' from the licensing authority. The criteria which licensing authorities were to apply in the case of operators' licences were different from those applied in the case of special authorizations. In the case of the latter the licensing authority had to grant the application where no objection had been received from British Rail or from the National Freight Corporation. Where an objection had been received, the application also had to be granted if the licensing authority was satisfied that the provision of the disputed service by British Rail or the NFC respectively, as compared with its provision in pursuance of the special authorization, would be less advantageous for the person for whom the goods in question were to be carried. In relation to operators' licences, the former 'full discretion' of the licensing authority was also now very much more circumscribed. The authority was required to grant the licence if satisfied that (a) the applicant was a fit person to hold an operator's licence, having regard to his previous transport activities and to any convictions that he may have had in respect of goods vehicles; (b) the applicant's proposals as to a transport manager were satisfactory; (c) there would be satisfactory arrangements for ensuring that the requirements of the Act in relation to drivers' hours and the keeping of records of such hours would be complied with and that vehicles were not overloaded; (d) there would be satisfactory facilities and arrangements for maintaining the vehicles in a fit and serviceable condition; and (if the authority thought fit) (e) the applicant would have sufficient financial resources for ensuring that his vehicles were so maintained.

It is therefore fairly clear that the licensing authority's discretionary powers (and those of the Transport Tribunal on appeal) are now much narrower than previously. In a sense it might be said that much of the discretion by which goods services licensing has always been administered has now passed from the licensing authorities to British Rail and the National Freight Corporation whose attitude to any application made for a licence will in many cases be decisive. This is borne out by the dramatic decrease in the number of full appeals heard by the Transport Tribunal since 1968. From a busy tribunal jurisdiction transport licensing has become something of a tribunal backwater.

In the case of road passenger transport, licensing as it exists today was established under the Road Traffic Act 1930, now largely re-enacted in the Road Traffic Act 1960. Licensing of vehicles had in fact existed before 1930 but there was at that time no counterpart to the modern regulation of services. In the same way as the post-First World War period had opened up a whole new era of transport of goods by road, so too the defects which prevailed at this time in the use of rail for passenger transport ensured rapid expansion of the use of the motor coach. An operator needed only to obtain a licence from his local authority for his coach to be able to run it virtually anywhere, using the device of return fares if necessary to circumvent the requirements of other local authorities through whose territory his coach passed. The comparative lack of restrictions on operation eventually led to a demand for greater controls to combat the effects of excessive competition, in particular the irregularity of services, the wide variation of fares and the safety and comfort of the coaches. The establishment of the licensing of services was the solution provided by the 1930 Act. A tribunal of traffic commissioners was empowered to control services as a whole, thus eliminating most of the causes of excessive competition and enabling them to take into account not only omnibus services but also other forms of transport such as rail. The Act provided for appeals from the decisions of the traffic commissioners to go to the Minister – an odd contrast with goods services licensing but one which still remains today, despite criticisms made from time to time.

Just as the Geddes Committee reviewed the system of road haulage licensing, so the passenger transport licensing system was examined by an independent committee, the Thesiger Committee, which published its report *Licensing of Road Passenger Services* in 1953. Unlike the Geddes Committee, which recommended the abolition of licensing in road haulage, the Thesiger Committee was in favour of retaining, virtually untouched, the licensing of passenger services.

The apparent contradiction of providing a right of appeal from the traffic commissioners, an independent tribunal, to the Secretary of State was noted by the Thesiger Committee (who upheld the practice) and it seems even more anomalous in the light of the complete tribunal machinery operative in road haulage licensing. However, the Committee, with one dissent, expressed itself satisfied with the ministerial appellate structure and confined itself to recommending that a bulletin of selected appeal decisions should be published periodically (as in the case of the Transport Tribunal). There is, however, still no official bulletin though decisions given by the minister are available to the commissioners from the department. Counsel sometimes obtain access to them through the old-boy network but they are not readily obtainable by the public. It would seem to be the fear of the wider use of decisions as precedents which prevents the establishment of a systematic official publication.

The anomalous contrast of two transport licensing jurisdictions, the one presided over by an appellate tribunal promulgating case law in the form of precedents, the other controlled by the minister in a more arbitrary way, has not escaped comment.[104] It perhaps represents an outstanding example of the extreme pragmatism which has characterized the development and growth of tribunal administration in Britain.

3
Tribunals and the worker

The relationship of the worker to the law has not always been a happy one. While Professor Wedderburn's oft-quoted statement that 'most workers want nothing more of the law than that it should leave them alone'[1] bristles with difficulties of definition and begs all kinds of questions, it remains true that there have been continuing problems in accommodating traditional legal concepts and institutions to the changing factual position of employment.

Karl Renner provided the key to the difficulty when, writing at the turn of the century, he analysed the inconsistency which has developed between the traditional determination of the *legal* rights and obligations of the worker under the private law of contract and his *actual* employment situation which had come to be regulated and defined largely through collective and public organizations and bodies.

Renner described the situation which had developed as follows:

If the worker is accepted, at terms which are fixed beforehand and scarcely mentioned, he goes on the job. Formerly based upon contract, the labour relationship has now developed into a 'position'.... The 'position' comprises the claim to adequate remuneration (settled by collective agreement or works rule), the obligation to pay certain contributions (for trade unions and insurance), the right to special benefits (sickness, accident, old age, death) and finally certain safeguards against loss of the position or in case of its loss.

What is the meaning of this development from the contract of employment to the position of work and service? The private contract, by means of the complementary institutions of collective agreement, labour exchanges, social insurance and the like, has become an institution of public law.[2]

The major task facing reformers in the labour law field has really been the need to evolve new legal tools and institutions with which to match the changed factual situation in which employment conditions are regulated. The increasing use of special tribunals to administer new statutory laws passed to deal with particularly difficult areas of employment is an indication of the direction in which current reform is moving. It should not be assumed, however, that special tribunals, because of the improvements which they appear to be effecting, provide the whole solution. Assuredly they do not, for their effectiveness is determined very largely by the quality of the laws they administer. And in another respect their use to date, reflecting as it does a piecemeal and ad hoc approach to reform, contains the same ingredients of weakness as have existed in the common law and in the ordinary courts.

Special tribunals have assisted in the administration of labour laws, both as they affect the individual worker directly and as they control the conduct of labour relations generally. Their development and operation will thus be discussed according to this division here.

1. TRIBUNALS AND INDIVIDUAL EMPLOYMENT LAW

It has been stated that the contract of employment constituted the traditional basis of the worker's position and this still provides the framework by which his rights and duties are regulated. Increasingly, however, the common law is giving away to statutory provisions which, perhaps in acknowledgement of the inequalities and selectiveness of the labour market place, are granting new rights and protections to the worker.

(a) *Personal injuries*

This is not in fact a new process. It began with medieval legislation relating to the employment of apprentices and later evolved into general regulations of employment in factories. Restrictions

c

were imposed on hours worked and also on the conditions of work. The prime concern of legislators was to ensure industrial safety. A major consequence indeed of the Industrial Revolution was to expose workers to serious health and physical hazards. And it was here that the defects of the common law became most obvious. Not only did common law doctrines (contributory negligence, *volenti non fit injuria*, common employment) serve to prevent the injured worker from obtaining adequate compensation from his employer but the system of recovery through the courts was generally too complex, too expensive and too slow to ensure effective relief.[3]

Ultimately the Workmen's Compensation Act of 1897 was passed to mitigate the worst effects of the common law. However, while this legislation brought about a substantial improvement, the denial of compensation in the serious misconduct cases and the boundaries provided by the 'arising out of and in the course of employment' test left less than comprehensive coverage. And because the adversary system administered by the courts was in essence retained, the procedural barriers to recovery continued to cause dissatisfaction. The national insurance industrial injuries scheme which was introduced after the Second World War went a long way towards meeting this last objection by substituting more streamlined tribunal machinery in place of the courts; but it left substantially untouched the limitations of the workmen's compensation law.

The provision of compensation to the worker for personal injury (or, in the case of death, to his dependants) was in any event not enough. Something more was needed to cover the many other exigencies of life in modern industrial society. It was in this area that the national insurance system acted as a financial backstop by establishing benefits in respect of unemployment, illness and other such personal misfortunes. National assistance, or supplementary benefit as it later became, gave further support where the claimant was ineligible for national insurance payments or where such payments were inadequate.[4] But one of the major faults in the whole system was the inadequate regard paid to the *causes* of industrial injury. If the cure was not notably successful, neither were the accident prevention measures employed.

This is not to decry the individual efforts of the various departments, authorities and inspectorates charged with the enforcement of factories legislation in different industries. But, as the Robens Committee which reported in 1972 on *Safety and Health at Work* found, the division of responsibility between these enforcement agencies and the consequential fragmentation of administrative jurisdictions has led to a low level of efficacy in accident prevention.[5] The committee has recommended therefore that the entire administration of safety legislation should be vested in a national authority for safety and health at work which would be responsible for the provision of advice, information, research, training, collaboration with other agencies, inspection, advisory services and review of statutory provisions.

It is proposed that the new authority should accept broad policy directives from the appropriate minister, though its day-to-day management would fall under the entire control of an executive director. The obvious parallel is that of the Civil Aviation Authority established by the 1971 Civil Aviation Act. That Authority exercises functions which, in traditional terms, encompass the full range of legislative (rule-making), judicial or quasi-judicial (licensing) and administrative powers. Similarly, it is subject, on matters of broad policy, to ministerial directive.

There is of course a comparison to be drawn here between the proposed National Safety Authority and the Civil Aviation Authority, on the one hand, and the North American regulatory agencies such as the National Labour Relations Board, on the other. It is interesting to speculate that in Britain there may exist in these authorities the seeds of a development from single function tribunals or agencies exercising either administrative (enforcement) or judicial (licensing) or rule-making powers, which on their own have proved inadequate, to multi-function agencies providing comprehensive control in all its facets.[6]

It is possible in fact that the enforcement of industrial safety and the provision of compensation for personal injury will eventually all be swept up together under the aegis of a single central administrative agency. In December 1972 the Prime Minister announced in the Commons the setting up of a Royal Commission to inquire into the whole system of the recovery of compensation for personal injury (whether caused within or outside the course of employment).[7] Just as with the enforcement of safety legislation, there is considerable fragmentation of jurisdictions relating to compensation for personal injury. Thus, first there is the remedy in the courts of an action for damages in negligence or for breach of statutory duty; then industrial injuries compensation, obtainable through a network of insurance officers, national insurance appeal tribunals and commissioners and medical boards and tribunals. Ordinary national insurance and supplementary benefit (the latter obtained through the supplementary benefits commission and appeal tribunals) are also available in certain circumstances and even the Criminal Injuries Compensation board may provide an ex gratia payment if the injury is caused by a 'crime of violence'.[8]

The problem of compensation for personal injury, and of accident prevention, goes far beyond the employment situation as the terms of reference of the Royal Commission recognize.[9] The victims of motor accidents constitute a major social problem, as evidenced by the introduction in various States of America of no-fault compulsory insurance schemes. New Zealand has recently established a system of social insurance – or rather two systems, one covering the victims of road accidents and the other providing twenty-four hour insurance cover for earners – which is likely to influence the Royal Commission very strongly in its deliberations.

The New Zealand schemes were enacted by the Accidents Compensation Act 1972, following the recommendations of the Woodhouse Royal Commission Report on *Personal Injuries* in 1967. The schemes became fully operative in April 1974 and all existing remedies (statutory and common law, courts and tribunals) are abolished and replaced by the new machinery and scale of compensation provided by the Act. Significantly, a single Accidents Compensation Commission exercising adjudicative, rule-making and administrative powers is established. Its functions include overall responsibility for the implementation and co-ordination of accident prevention and industrial safety measures. Through its officers it also processes and determines all claims for compensation. In this last respect, however, its decisions are subject to appeal to independent appeal tribunals (and, on questions of law, on further appeal to the administrative division of the New Zealand Supreme Court).

The New Zealand social insurance and compensation scheme underlines dramatically Renner's thesis that the workers contract has become a concept of public law. In so far as that scheme in fact extends beyond injury arising at work, it is also illustrative of a wider thesis that the institutions of private law (courts) are to some extent being replaced or superseded by institutions of public law (special tribunals and agencies).

(b) *Statutory rights and the growth of industrial tribunals*

The establishment of statutory tribunals tends to go hand in hand with the increase of regulation by statute. In the labour law area the process of statutory encroachment on the common law has been a continuing one; but in recent years there has been a marked upturn in the use of tribunals in the administration of new jurisdictions. One of the reasons can be found in the tendency of judges to read statutes in the light of the common law and in their inability to break away from common law concepts.[10]

A recognition of this fact probably accounts for the dramatic growth of the industrial tribunals first established under the Industrial Training Act 1964 and for the high hopes that have been held out for them. Their original function was to determine appeals from assessments to levy made by industrial training boards. Subsequently their jurisdiction has been extended to cover:

(1) Redundancy payment appeals under the Redundancy Payments Act 1965;
(2) The determination of a worker's particulars of employment under the Contracts of Employment Act 1963;
(3) Compensation rights under certain legislation concerned with loss of employment and pension entitlement resulting from nationalization and denationalization of some industries or from the alteration of local government boundaries;[11]
(4) Appeals against the assessment of selective employment tax under the Selective Employment Payments Act 1966;
(5) The determination of disputes relating to the operation of the equal pay clause provided by the Equal Pay Act 1970;
(6) The settling of certain demarcation disputes under the Docks and Harbours Act 1966;
(7) Different new jurisdictions under the Industrial Relations Act 1971, including compensation for unfair dismissal and the enforcement of member rights against trade unions.

The principal jurisdiction to date of the industrial tribunals has been that under the Redundancy Payments Act 1965. The Act set up a redundancy fund (to which employers must contribute) from which a rebate could be claimed by any employer required by law to make a payment to any redundant worker. Generally speaking, any worker dismissed for redundancy was given a right to payment calculated according to the provisions of the Act, provided (*inter alia*) that he had not unreasonably refused an offer of re-engagement or suitable alternative employment from his employer. If an employer refused to recognize a worker's claim to a payment then the worker could apply to the tribunal for the matter to be determined. Either party could appeal to the Divisional Court from a decision of the tribunal on a point of law by virtue of the provisions of the Tribunals and Inquiries Act 1958 (now 1971) which grant such a right in the case of scheduled tribunals.

The industrial tribunals, as they were originally constituted, consisted of a lawyer chairman and two other members, one from a panel drawn up by the minister after consultation with the trade unions and the other from an equivalent employers' panel. Following the enactment of the Industrial Relations Act, the TUC announced a boycott of all institutions established by or operating under the Act. Trade union members of the tribunals consequently withdrew and the statutory regulations were amended to allow appointment of non-union nominees in their stead.

The tribunals have operated regionally with both full-time and part-time chairmen, one of whom acts as president of the industrial tribunals for England and Wales and another as president for Scotland. Sir Diarmaid Conroy, the president for England and Wales, has described the industrial tribunals as 'middle-of-the-road'[12] and they have been otherwise tagged by a tribunal official as 'poor men's courts'. Certainly, most commentators have been ready to accede to the procedural informality of these tribunals,[13] an impression which is readily confirmed by observation.

One of the distinguishing features of industrial tribunal hearings has been the comparative lack of legal representation, particularly in individual employment cases.[14] This has led to tribunal chairmen adopting a semi-inquisitorial role. Generally speaking, legal representation has not been welcomed. One tribunal referred to the irrelevant and 'complex, not to say sophisticated argument' led by counsel.[15]

Sir Diarmaid Conroy told the Birmingham Conference that counsel were frequently poorly prepared and that he was also against the extension of legal aid to industrial tribunals because of the increase in legal representation and inevitable formality that would result. Ironically, in the light of these comments, the industrial tribunals have been accused of taking too formal and too narrow an approach to their interpretation of the legal provisions which they administer. Dr Rideout has referred to the tribunals' 'utmost rigidity in applying the rules both to employee and employer', though elsewhere he says that in the sense that there are serious inconsistencies in the decisions given by different tribunals, the tribunals would appear to 'lack the quality of legalism'.[16]

To some extent it would appear that the industrial tribunals have been severely constrained in their legislative interpretations by rulings given in those cases which have gone to the High Court. Wedderburn and Davies go so far as to say that the existence of this appeal right is 'likely to prove an Achilles' heel' in the policy of using tribunals to determine industrial disputes of this kind, or of any other kind.[17]

Certainly it must be agreed that the High Court has given some unfortunate decisions. Two of these are mentioned by Wedderburn and Davies: *Morton Sundour Fabrics Ltd* v. *Shaw*[18] where the High Court reversed a tribunal's decision allowing a redundancy payment to a worker who had looked for and found new employment after he had been told by his employer that he would soon be redundant but before he had been formally dismissed, and *North Riding Garages Ltd* v. *Butterwick*[19] where again the High Court reversed a tribunal's award of a redundancy payment, this time where, on the change of ownership of a garage, the workshop manager was dismissed because he did not measure up to the new work standards required by the re-organization of the garage.

The tribunal had thought that this was a redundancy situation but the High Court disagreed: Wedderburn and Davies comment that the Court had simply replaced the tribunal's policy with its own,[20] given that alternative interpretations of the relevant statutory wording were possible. And of course, as a pure matter of interpretation (a question of law), it was open to the High Court to substitute its own ruling for that of the tribunal. From a legal point of view, no special expertise was involved in interpreting the meaning of the statutory words, and in the absence of any discretion given to the tribunal in the application of those words, the Court was fully entitled to overrule the tribunal's decision. In legal theory, the fact that the ultimate decision may not have advanced the broad policy behind the Act or may even have had a detrimental effect on industrial relations[21] was irrelevant.

The High Court ought not, however, to shoulder all the blame. The individual tribunals themselves have also on occasions opted for a strict literal approach to the legislation with little or no regard to the effect of their decisions on the known policy of the statute. For example, one of the principal aims of the Redundancy Payments Act has been said to be that 'unnecessary workmen should not be retained in any industry but should be released so as to be free to take employment elsewhere'.[22] The tribunal in *Hawkins* v. *Thomas Forman & Sons Ltd*[23] refused, however, to take account of this. In this case, a photogravure camera operator, on becoming redundant, had been offered alternative employment in his employer's photo-litho department. His refusal of the offer on the grounds that he would be underemployed was held by the tribunal to be unreasonable so that his claim for a redundancy payment failed. The argument that the tribunal's decision should be consistent with the policy behind the Act was rejected:

We take the view that matters of policy of this kind are not for the Tribunal. The Tribunal is here to decide whether a particular man's refusal of an offer of alternative employment was, or was not, reasonable. If an employer wishes to keep, against possible increases of work, an excess number of employees, it is not, we consider, for this Tribunal to say: 'No, that you cannot do. The policy behind this Act was otherwise and we, the Tribunal, will enter into the enforcement of policy in this regard.' The provisions of the Act lay down what the Tribunal is to do.[24]

Similarly, in the industrial training jurisdiction, an industrial tribunal has refused to entertain a complaint that the objects of the Industrial Training Act, viz 'to spread the cost of training more evenly between firms',[25] was not being fulfilled in particular cases.[26] Thus, in *St Mary's (Contractors) Ltd* v. *Construction Industry Training Board*[27] the employer of workmen occupied in the demolition of buildings was ordered to pay the full levy under the Act even though no theoretical courses were provided by the Training Board. Further, the employer did not qualify for a grant in respect of practical training given on the job because the men who were being so trained were not wholly unproductive. When the plea of injustice was advanced, the tribunal stated impassively that it was 'a creature of statute' and that the only powers and jurisdiction it enjoyed were those given to it by its enabling legislation.[28] This approach has been confirmed in a number of subsequent tribunal decisions.[29]

The industrial tribunals have been criticized also for inconsistency in decision-making.[30] Instances can certainly be found of cases where hairline distinctions have led to apparently anomalous results. Thus, in *Anderson* v. *National Coal Board*[31] a tribunal distinguished an earlier decision of 'somewhat similar facts' on the grounds that the claimant in that case had been employed prior to the closure of a coalmine 'mainly, not wholly, on piece-work' while Anderson, a miner in an otherwise identical position, had 'in practice, if not in theory, been wholly employed on piece-work'.[32]

The problem has been particularly acute in redundancy cases where tribunals have had to rule on the suitability of alternative employment which has been offered to redundant workers. Under the Act a redundant employee is not entitled to a redundancy payment if his employer has offered him alternative employment which is 'suitable employment in relation to the employee' and the employee has 'unreasonably refused that offer'.[33] One would have hoped that the tribunals would have taken a broad approach to this provision and, making use of the knowledge which the lay members on the tribunal have of jobs in industry and their relative importance in terms of status, conditions and wages, determined cases very much according to the merits of the individual situation. Unfortunately, however, different rulings have been given by different tribunals as to whether the reasonableness of a worker's refusal of an offer was to be judged on a subjective or objective basis.

The tribunals were agreed that the suitability of alternative employment must be measured against the needs and characteristics of the individual worker to whom the offer had been made, rather than according to any class of workers to which that individual may have belonged.[34] Where they differed was on the

C*

question of whether – given that an offer was suitable – a worker's refusal was to be judged according to his personal needs and circumstances (subjective) or according to the characteristics of the class of workers to which he belonged (objective).'[35] If the former, then matters such as family and personal (e.g. health) reasons for refusing an offer would constitute a major factor; if the latter, they would be irrelevant or at least only relevant to the question of the suitability of the job.

The confusion which was engendered perhaps reached its height in the Court of Session's decision in *Carron Company* v. *Robertson*[36] where an industrial tribunal was held to have erred in law. The Lord President thought that suitability was an objective matter concerning the nature of the job and that reasonableness of refusal went to personal factors. Lord Guthrie said that, in deciding suitability, 'one must consider not only the nature of the work, hours and pay, the employee's strength, training, experience and ability, but such matters as status in the premise of the employer and benefits flowing from that status'.[37] The reasonableness of the refusal, he said, depends on a consideration 'of the whole circumstances in which he would have been placed if he had accepted the offer. These circumstances include such personal matters as the demands upon him of his duties towards his family. They also . . . include the conditions of the employment offered.' Lord Migdale's view was that the 'question of suitability is mainly objective while the question of reasonableness is to be viewed subjectively'. The opinion that 'suitable employment in relation to the employee' must be measured objectively differed from the great body of English tribunal case law which had established that this involved subjective considerations. Nor did Lord Guthrie's dictum that the resonableness of a refusal included both personal factors and the conditions of the employment offered assist in resolving the confusion of the English tribunals on this point.

This confusion which has resulted in the interpretation of the alternative offer provision can be seen from contrasting the following two sets of cases. In *Rose* v. *Shelley and Partners Ltd*[38] the reasonableness of a worker's refusal to accept an offer of alternative employment was determined subjectively. The applicant had been quite in agreement with his employer's proposal to accompany the removal of the latter's north London factory to Huntingdon, but eventually refused to do so because his wife said she would not leave her friends in Tottenham. The tribunal said that he had not acted unreasonably in refusing the offer.[39] Subsequently, different tribunals have adopted an objective test to the question of reasonableness of refusal and this has resulted in a tougher line against workers unwilling to accept alternative jobs involving a minimal degree of hardship or inconvenience. Thus, in *Brown* v. *James Keiller & Co Ltd*[40] a redundant employee who rejected an offer of a similar job involving overtime, on the grounds that his wife worked in the evening and his young children would be left unattended during the period after his wife left and before he returned home, was held to be acting unreasonably. Then, in *Paisley* v. *Scottish Co-op Wholesale Sty Ltd*[41] a redundant laundry manager who refused to leave his friends and relations in the south of Scotland to move to the north was also held to be acting unreasonably. These two cases contrast noticeably with the earlier case of *Rose* where the tribunal bowed to the wishes of the wife who did not want to leave her friends.

One other set of cases that also makes the same point is *Gay* v. *The Commander US Naval Activities, United Kingdom*[42] and *McNulty* v. *T. Bridges & Co Ltd*[43] In Gay's case a London tribunal, in holding that a redundant employee was not unreasonable in refusing an offer of alternative employment, placed stress on the fact that his journeys by car to and from work would be 'considerably longer and more expensive'.[44] In fact, the employee's distance to work was to have increased from eight to thirteen miles and he was to have received an increase in salary of some ten shillings a week, sufficient at least to cover his higher petrol costs. In striking contrast to this decision, in *McNulty* v. *T. Bridges & Co. Ltd.* a different tribunal, sitting at Cardiff, dismissed as not being a 'serious factor'[45] a complaint that the new job offered to a redundant tunneller involved travelling sixteen miles to work as against nine miles in his old employment.

While the decisions under the Redundancy Payments Act have been somewhat disappointing to those who hoped for a more liberal interpretation from tribunal determination, the industrial tribunals have in fact shown greater flexibility and a better appreciation of legislative and policy objectives in some of their other jurisdictions. Thus, decisions given under section 51 of the Docks and Harbours Act 1966 on the question as to whether a particular kind of work is dock work or whether any place is in or in the vicinity of a port to which a labour scheme applies have shown a willingness to go beyond the surface and get to the root of the industrial dispute to which the case relates.[46] In *Hull Association of Port Labour Employers* v. *National Dock Labour Board*,[47] for example, the question was whether or not the driving of normal commercial road vehicles for the transport of cargo within the dock estate was dock work within the local definition of the labour scheme. The tribunal, in holding that this was not dock work, undertook a most exhaustive examination of not only the relevant law and the scheme itself, but also of the whole history of the Hull dock yards and the background to the dispute. Having given its decision which, as the chairman carefully pointed out, was done as a service to industry and with the assistance of two members on the tribunal who between them had ninety years of experience and service in industry, a short addendum was then provided setting out clearly and concisely a reformulation of the *effect* of the decision 'in a way that . . . [would] be understood by those in industry who read it, although it [was not the official decision]'.[48]

The general record of industrial tribunals in the administration of the Selective Employment Payments Act 1966 has also been good. There will be a full analysis of the SET cases in Chapter 6 and at this point it should simply be noted that a reading of those decisions does reveal a uniformly common-sense approach which fits the industrial facts that the Act sought to encompass. There is also a correspondingly different attitude shown by the High Court – seen in a reluctance to interfere with the decisions given by the tribunals which are regarded as expert bodies.

One naturally wonders why the industrial tribunals should have such a patchy record under the Redundancy Payments Act, while being so much more successful under the Selective Employment Payments Act. The answer lies in the nature of the legislation. The Selective Employment Payments Act embodied a document known as the Standard Industrial Classification which determined the rights and obligations arising under the Act. The SIC was, however, a flexible document whose wording could easily be bent – and was intended to be bent – to fit the industrial facts and the policy behind the legislation. The jurisdiction was therefore a very different one from that under the Redundancy Payments Act which provided, in the form of complex, legal wording, a legal straitjacket from which the tribunal could depart only with the greatest difficulty. No scope was provided for the application of policy considerations or for having regard to industrial realities. The High Court accordingly has not hesitated to substitute its own interpretations for those of the tribunals of the detailed and complex provisions of the Act. Under the legislation there is no question of a tribunal's being left with any degree of discretion to adjudicate, for example, according to need, justice or any other generalized criteria which would enable the formulation and application of a flexible policy relating to redundancy. Herein lies the fatal flaw which accounts for the middling record of the tribunals under the Redundancy Payments Act. Wedderburn and Davies have criticized the 'technical decisions' given by the tribunals – and so they can be criticized – but in fairness it ought to be emphasized that the fault of these decisions lies more in the scheme and wording of the Act than in the ability and willingness of the tribunals to adopt a more flexible and realistic approach.[49]

(c) *Industrial tribunals and the Industrial Relations Act 1971*

In a note in the *New Law Journal* for 1966, following the establishment of the redundancy payments jurisdiction, the comment was made under the heading 'Industrial Tribunals – Gathering Strength':[50] 'the spectacular growth of their jurisdiction does prompt the question how far we in this country have acquired a virtually distinct system of "labour courts" without knowing it'. The Ministry of Labour itself, in giving evidence to the Donovan Commission, also referred to the tribunals as they existed then constituting the nucleus of a Labour Court. And, during the second reading in the Commons of the Redundancy Payments Bill, the Minister of Labour (Mr Gunter) commented that he would not rule out the possibility that, as the tribunals became established and gained experience, further functions relating to industrial relations might be given to them. 'I believe that they will constitute a valuable experiement in our industrial relations system,' he said, 'and I hope that we can keep an open mind on the development of their role in future'.[51]

When the Donovan Royal Commission on *Trade Unions and Employers' Associations*[52] reported in 1968, it made sweeping proposals for the extension of the jurisdiction of the industrial tribunals (which it would have liked re-named labour tribunals).

The Commission thought first, that the tribunals' jurisdiction should 'comprise all disputes arising between employers and employees from their contracts of employment or from any statutory claims they might have against each other in their capacity as employer and employee'. This included the employee's claim for wages, holiday pay etc, for breach of contract, e.g. by wrongful dismissal, and for statutory payments such as those arising under the Redundancy Payments Act. It further included all such claims for damages for breach of contract as the employer may have against the employee.

On the other hand Donovan's view was that a number of existing jurisdictions should remain outside the purview of the tribunals. Into this category fell actions for damages arising from accidents at work, whether founded on breach of contract, negligence or breach of statutory duty. Actions for damages for strikes and other disputes and not founded on breach of contract in particular should also be left untouched. Similarly, disputes between employers or employers' associations and trade unions or groups of workers were properly settled by procedures of, or agreed through, collective bargaining rather than through tribunals which should also not handle any issues connected with the negotiation or interpretation of collective agreements.

Probably the most notable of the Donovan proposals for the industrial tribunals was the recommendation that workers who had been *unfairly* dismissed should be given compensation – and through the tribunal system. In making this recommendation the Commission was strongly influenced by the seriousness of dismissal to employees: 'in reality people build much of their lives around their jobs'. And in finding a need for a statutory scheme the Commission differed from a report on *Dismissal Procedures* published the previous year by a Committee of the National Joint Advisory Council appointed by the Minister of Labour to inquire into the subject.[54]

The apparent enthusiasm of the Royal Commission for expanding the work of the industrial tribunals must be seen against the background of a general attitude by the Commission that in the industrial relations field voluntary procedures for the settlement of disputes were preferable to legal determination and enforcement. It is clear from a reading of its Report as a whole that the Commission restricted its preference for tribunal decision-making to the settlement of individual employment disputes. The distinction between individual and collective, as we shall see, is not an easy one to draw; but there is no doubt that Donovan thought that a limited role only would be appropriate for tribunals in the whole employment area.

The Bill introduced by the Labour Government in 1970 (but not passed before the Government's fall) paid respect to the Donovan principles and the proposed unfair dismissal protection was accordingly to be entrusted to the existing industrial tribunals. So too was the similar protection given in the incoming Conservative Government's Industrial Relations Bill introduced later in the year. This new Bill, however, gave further functions to the tribunals than had ever been contemplated by Donovan or by the previous Labour Government. These included a power to adjudicate in certain disputes between a trade union and its members and also other kinds of disputes in the collective arena.[55]

But the most significant of the new jurisdictions was undoubtedly that relating to unfair dismissal. Many regard these new provisions as a milestone in the advancement of workers' legal rights. In the first unfair dismissal case to go to the Court of Appeal, Lord Denning, MR, underlined the significance of the new provisions:

The Act gives an employee a right in his job which is akin to a right of property. The employer can no longer give the legal notice and say: 'Out you go, without compensation'. The tribunal can enquire into the reasons for the dismissal. If the reasons are not sufficient to warrant it, the tribunal will hold it to be an unfair dismissal. The employer will have to pay compensation.[56]

Lord Denning had himself struggled in earlier years to establish a common law right of property in employment,[57] but the generally accepted consensus is that his endeavours lacked authoritative support.[58] It remained for legislation to establish indisputably a property basis for employment. In this respect the Industrial Relations Act, by providing compensation to the worker for 'loss of security in his job',[59] completed the task begun by the Redundancy Payments Act which had given 'compensation for long service'.[60]

The criteria laid down in the Industrial Relations Act as to what constitutes fair and unfair dismissal are perhaps rather more complicated than might have been expected. Once the fact of dismissal has been established, the employer is required to show the reason (or, if more than one, the principal reason) for the dismissal and that it either (a) related to the capability or qualifications of the employee for performing work of the kind which he was employed by the employer to do, or (b) related to the conduct of the employee, or (c) was that the employee was redundant, or (d) was that the employee could not continue to work in the position which he held without contravention (either on his part or on that of his employer) of a duty or restriction imposed by or under any enactment. Broadly speaking a dismissal will then be regarded as unfair if the employer cannot show that the reason fell within one of the above categories or was some other 'substantial' reason of a kind such as to justify the employee's dismissal. Where a good reason (whether falling within one of the said categories or not) is shown, the dismissal will nevertheless be regarded as unfair if in the circumstances the employer acted unreasonably in treating it as a sufficient reason for dismissing the employee. Finally, subject to the specific matters outlined above, the question of fairness or unfairness is to be determined 'in accordance with equity and the substantial merits of the case'.[61]

The process therefore requires the tribunals to classify the facts in accordance with the categories provided but then to form a value judgement based on such criteria as reasonableness, equity and the substantial merits of the case. Save in the most blatant of cases (where dismissal was clearly for the most trivial of reasons), it is plain that the tribunals were left with the widest of discretions in determining disputes as to dismissal. Equally it was obvious, given the inevitable development of the decision-making process in tribunals of this kind,[62] that this discretion would ultimately be delimited and defined through principles formulated in case law.

And so it has proved to be. Some cases have effectively decided themselves on their facts – as in the case of the canteen worker who simply refused to carry out his normal cleaning duties and who did not then appear before the tribunal to provide an explanation[63] – but others have provided the tribunals with particular situations which have called for a statement of principle.

In this respect by far the most important type of case that has been determined to date has been the dismissal which has not been preceded by the giving of an opportunity to the employee to state a case against dismissal. In public law terms these are what may be termed the breach of natural justice cases.

At common law not only was a master entitled on giving due notice (or in paying wages in lieu) to dismiss his servant without cause, but he was under no obligation to provide reasons (however spurious they might have been) for the dismissal.[64] Nor was he required to give his servant the right to be heard before dismissing him. While we ceased to speak of 'master and servant' some time ago, the common law has not changed its basic position on these points.[65] Undoubtedly the statutory protections now provided are a reflection of this failing.

On the other hand the courts have become increasingly concerned to formulate and apply procedural safeguards of their own wherever the particular employment had been put on a statutory footing or was in any other respect regulated by statute. Thus Lord Reid in the well-known natural justice case of *Ridge* v. *Baldwin*[66] distinguished the position in relation to 'a pure case of master and servant' from that of 'dismissal from office where the body employing the man is under some statutory or other restriction as to ... the grounds on which it can dismiss him'.[67] In the latter case, the court might readily imply obligations of natural justice such as the right to be heard before dismissal. The result has been that employees in the public sector, whose employment has in some respect or other been made amenable to legislative regulation or definition, have been granted procedural protection by the courts which have been denied to employees in private employment.[68]

The exciting possibility that arose after the enactment of the Industrial Relations Act 1971 was that it would now be open to import into the entire area of employment obligations on employers to allow hearings before dismissal and to give reasons in respect of dismissal. To the extent that virtually all employment and the right to dismiss in particular was now regulated by statute because of the unfair dismissal provisions, it could be argued that the principles applied in *Ridge* v. *Baldwin* were equally applicable. That conclusion was certainly not clear cut for in *Vidyodaya University Council* v. *Silva*[69] the Judicial Committee of the Privy Council had held that the presence of a statute might not affect the basic status of contract; it was necessary to show that there was a 'statutory flavour' to the

relationship of employer and employee. Nevertheless the possibility of such a conclusion was undoubtedly very real.

The matter came up fairly quickly in a number of tribunal
cases. First, in *Neefjes* v. *Crystal Products Ltd.*[70] it was held by a
London tribunal that an employee who had previously been
warned about his unco-operative conduct was not unfairly
dismissed after he subsequently assaulted another employee.
Neefjes' solicitor endeavoured to argue before the tribunal that
the dismissal was unfair because no opportunity was given to
allow him to confront his adversary and challenge the truth of his
complaint. It was also argued that the procedure adopted by the
employer did not match up to that provided in the Code of
Industrial Relations Practice.[71] The tribunal held, however, that
it was sufficient that Neefjes had been allowed to state his version
of the incident to the employer. Further that such breaches of
the code as had occurred did not in reality affect his dismissal.

The importance of the opportunity to state a case was affirmed
the following day when a tribunal in Leeds held that a full-time
district organizer of a trade union who had been dismissed for
working for another employer during his holidays and who had
not been allowed to appear before the executive committee of the
union had been unfairly dismissed: *Gibson* v. *National Union of
Dyers, Bleachers & Textile Workers.*[72] The applicant won a
pyrrhic victory, however, for the tribunal held that nominal
compensation of £10 only would be awarded because even if he
had been allowed to appear before the committee the most likely
result would have been that no reconciliation of their differences
would have proved possible so that dismissal would have been
inevitable.

Other tribunal decisions upholding the opportunity to state a
case were also decided[73] and the point then came before the
newly created National Industrial Relations Court, which had
taken over the High Court's appeal jurisdiction on matters of law
under the various statutes administered by the industrial
tribunals. The case was *Earl* v. *Slater and Wheeler (Airlyne)
Ltd.*[74] and the appellant had been dismissed because of incompetence. His dismissal had been effected by a letter of
dismissal setting out specific reasons and details of his shortcomings. He was not given an opportunity to rebut the allegations
before the dismissal took effect.

Before the National Industrial Relations Court, it was argued that the appellant should have been allowed to state his case either because the principle of *audi alteram partem* applied to all employment relationships as a result of the enactment of the 1971 Act or because certain sections in the Act, together with the Code of Practice, had directly imported a right to a hearing. On the first point, Sir John Donaldson (President of the Court) thought that an application of the *audi alteram partem* principle would lead logically to the conclusion that there had been no effective dismissal, although the fact of dismissal was of the essence of the claim.[75]

On the effect of the Code, however, he agreed that the appellant was 'fully entitled to rely upon paragraph 132 which provides that the disciplinary procedure should "give the employee the opportunity to state his case and the right to be accompanied by his employee representative"'. 'In any event', Sir John said, 'good industrial relations depend upon management not only acting fairly but being manifestly seen to act fairly'. This did not, he concluded, happen in the case of the appellant. The dismissal was thus found to be unfair but, because the tribunal had found that on the facts the allegations of incompetence were entirely well-founded and that the appellant therefore would have had no explanation or case to offer, the compensation payable should be assessed at nil.

The appellant Earl may be forgiven for thinking that there was something perverse about the Court's refusing him any compensation after it had found that his dismissal was unfair. As the Court itself said, while it was the appellant's own conduct or lack of capability which led to his dismissal, 'he in no way caused or contributed to its unfair character which is the essence of his complaint'.[76] It is in fact arguable that the holding of the Court that failure to allow an employee to state a case is unfair means absolutely nothing; for if the employee does not have an answer to make then he will be given no compensation and if he does then presumably in nearly every case his dismissal will have been unfair anyway.

The Earl case, perhaps more than most, underlines the uneasy compromise into which labour law appears to be settling. The continuing importation of statutory terms into the employment relationship – enforced for the most part through statutory tribunals – has moved the worker well along the road towards the status position that Karl Renner seemed to be claiming for him.

But the retention of private law concepts – in this case that of consequential loss – prevents the application to the entire area of employment the kind of all-or-nothing procedural standards such as *audi alteram partem* that are the strength and hallmark of public law. This is not to say that specific, existing public law remedies are always entirely appropriate; they may be too dramatic and may therefore require severe adaptation. But a failure to break away from many of the old common law concepts – loss as the measure of compensation, fault as determining liability, compensation or damages as the remedy and even contract as the basis of the whole relationship of employer and employee – reduces the effectiveness of the new statutory protections and the efficacy of the tribunals which administer them.[77]

2. TRIBUNALS AND COLLECTIVE DISPUTES

Writing before the passing of the Industrial Relations Act, Wedderburn and Davies expressed doubts as to whether industrial tribunals should be used for the settlement of employment disputes 'which, although individual in form, in reality clothe collective problems' :

If Britain is to see a greater use of legal sanctions in the handling of those disputes, the tribunals are bound to be utilized in the experiment. But in truth Britain has to choose between an uncertain experiment of that kind and new initiatives pursued with patience and perseverance within the patterns of negotiated procedure, voluntary arbitration, and public inquiry, where legal sanction and lawyers make their greatest contribution to industrial life by being self-effacing rather than obtrusive.[78]

(a) *Industrial tribunals and collective disputes*

Dismissal disputes fall clearly into the type of case discussed by Wedderburn and Davies. While employees have from time to time successfully brought wrongful dismissal actions in the courts, the much more common form of settlement has undoubtedly been through collective action taken by trade unions. On the other hand, the enactment of legislation in the past decade is to some extent changing this pattern. The Contracts of Employment Act 1963, the Redundancy Payments Act 1965 and the Industrial Relations Act 1971 have all extended the worker's legal rights and remedies in relation to dismissal and, more important, have provided new machinery in the form of comparatively cheap, quick and informal tribunals by which the realization of those rights is a practicable possibility.

The effect of this development it to bring about the removal of dismissals from the collective area (where trade unions play a major role) and to put them squarely back into the field of individual employment law from where, in a different form and context, they originally arose. The use of tribunals, which have been found to be more acceptable than the courts, makes this possible. On the other hand, multiple dismissals – for example, on the closedown of a factory – have continued largely to be dealt with by collective negotiation and settlement.[79]

Another type of dispute where an attempt appears to have been made to 'individualize' disputes by the use of the industrial tribunals is that between the worker and his trade union. While on the face of it these disputes may always have appeared to have been individual in nature, in very many cases the dispute was in fact not confined to the immediate parties but was extended also by union pressure to the employer. This was particularly the case where the union was seeking to enforce union membership in a closed shop situation.

The Industrial Relations Act attempts a number of different solutions to the problem of disputes arising out of union membership. It provides, first of all, an express statutory right for every worker, *as between himself and his employer*:

(1) To be a member of any trade union registered under the Act that he chooses;[80]
(2) Except in a closed shop situation which has been established in terms of the Act,[81] to belong to no trade union (registered or unregistered) if he so desires;
(3) Where he is a member of a registered trade union, to take part, at any appropriate time,[82] in the activities of the union and to seek or accept appointment or election as an official of the union.[83] Any interference[84] by an employer with the exercise of any of these rights is deemed to be an unfair industrial practice[85] and on complaint an industrial tribunal may award compensation to the aggrieved worker or make an order declaratory of his rights.[86]

The Act also endeavours to regulate directly as against the union the worker's rights to join and belong to a trade union. The denial of admission to, or the expulsion from, a trade union can lead to a loss of or failure to obtain employment.[87]

Concern had also been felt as to the exercise by unions of disciplinary powers generally against members.[88] Hence the Act has laid down a number of guiding principles by which trade unions (both registered and unregistered) must regulate their relations with their members. These include:

(1) A worker applying for membership of an appropriate union is not to be excluded from membership by way of any arbitrary or unreasonable discrimination, provided that he is reasonably well qualified for employment as a worker of the description of which the union, according to its rules, is intended to consist or of which it does consist;

(2) Every member of a union shall have the right, on giving reasonable notice and complying with any reasonable conditions, to terminate his membership at any time;

(3) No member of a union shall, by way of any arbitrary or unreasonable discrimination, be excluded from taking part in and voting at union meetings and elections; nor may he be prevented in this way from being a candidate or holding office or from nominating candidates;

(4) Voting in any ballot must be kept secret;

(5) Every member of a union, in casting his vote in a ballot, must be given a fair and reasonable opportunity of casting his vote without interference or constraint;

(6) No member of a union shall be subjected by the union to any unfair or unreasonable disciplinary action; and, in particular, no disciplinary action shall be taken against any member for refusing or failing to take any action which would constitute an unfair industrial practice under the Act either by him or by the union or by any other person;

(7) No disciplinary action may be taken (except for non-payment of any contribution required by the rules) by a union against a member unless (i) the latter has had written notice of the charges brought against him and has been given a reasonable time to prepare his defence; (ii) he is afforded a full and fair hearing; (iii) a written statement of the findings resulting from the hearing is given to him; and (iv) where the union rules provide a right of appeal, that

appeal has either been heard or the time for appealing has expired without that right being exercised.[89]

The taking of any action by a union in contravention of these principles (or a threat to take any such action) constitutes an unfair industrial practice under the Act[90] and, as such, may be referred to an industrial tribunal by the individual affected. Similarly, any action taken by a union in contravention of its own rules may be referred to a tribunal.[91] If the tribunal is satisfied that the complaint has been proved, it may, if it considers that it would be just and equitable to do so, either make an order determining the rights of the parties in relation to the action specified in the complaint or it may award compensation to be paid by the union to the complainant.

It remains to be seen whether the attempt to settle disputes in this particular area through the tribunal machinery will be successful. The Trades Union Congress strenuously opposed the new statutory provisions and saw them as constituting an unwarranted attack on union democracy. In accordance with a boycott policy adopted by the TUC against the procedures and institutions of the Act, the unions have not generally submitted to the jurisdiction of the tribunals in this type of case, though this has not stopped tribunals making orders against them in their absence.[92]

More to the point perhaps is the fact that many union member disputes clothe what are in reality demarcation disputes between one individual and another as to entitlement to membership. The individual worker, and sometimes also the individual employer, may be little more than a pawn or unwilling participant in many demarcation disputes, thus verifying in those cases the analysis provided by Wedderburn and Davies as outlined above. The collective nature of these disputes is reflected also in the insistence by the TUC and its constituent unions that the Bridlington rules should continue to determine all such disputes in preference to the provisions of the Industrial Relations Act.

The Rules contained in the Bridlington Agreement were drawn up at the annual conference of the TUC held at Bridlington in 1939. They established procedures which were to be followed in the transfer of a member of one union to another union and also provided a disputes committee of the TUC to deal with all inter-union disputes. The Bridlington Agreement received little recognition from the courts, however, which were unwilling to incorporate its terms into the contract of union membership.[93]

Bridlington has also suffered badly at the hands of the tribunals since the passing of the Industrial Relations Act. In *Phillips* v. *National and Local Government Officers' Association*[94] the applicant had resigned from NALGO and joined the National Union of Public Employees. Three months later NALGO notified NUPE that they did not agree to the applicant's transfer whereupon NUPE refused to continue his membership. A complaint was made to an industrial tribunal that both unions had committed unfair industrial practices against the applicant. The tribunal ultimately upheld the complaint against NUPE but dismissed that against NALGO. This time both unions appeared before the tribunal which remarked in the course of its decision that the official representing NUPE at the hearing had 'evoked the "Bridlington Agreement" as though it conferred some divine right upon himself and other union officials'.[95] Bridlington certainly had value, the tribunal concluded, but it was 'not right to fall back on one's own interpretation of the . . . "Agreement" when one has disregarded its clear terms or to call the agreement in aid when taking action against a person who has been accepted as a member and who has been a loyal member for several months'.[96]

It seems inescapable that conflict will continue. On the one hand there is the claim by the TUC that disputes of the kind discussed above are essentially collective in nature and that they are therefore appropriately settled through the rules and the internal machinery of the Bridlington Agreement. On the other hand there is the insistence of the tribunals that the individual has been given certain rights by Parliament and that Bridlington can at best operate as an aid to the enforcement of those rights through the statutory machinery. It is not easy to see a ready reconciliation.

(b) *The impact of the National Industrial Relations Court*

Throughout the 1960s the legislative solution of individualizing industrial disputes evolved in a piecemeal way. It was largely unplanned and to some extent represented a response to the failure of collective institutions and voluntary dispute solving procedures to handle adequately particularly troublesome areas of industrial relations. There was in fact nothing novel about supplanting voluntary methods with statutory machinery. This has happened before. For example, wages councils have been established in certain industries where trade unions are too weak to operate as effective bargaining units and their recommendations as to pay rates, holiday entitlement and other conditions of employment are binding on employers when effect has been given to them by order of the Secretary of State.[97]

What was perhaps different about the legislation of the 1960s, and also about the industrial tribunals which operate under that legislation, is the effect which it had of changing the nature of many kinds of dispute from having a predominantly collective aspect to one of individual bias.

As we have seen, many of the new jurisdictions contained in the Industrial Relations Act 1971 have continued this trend, whether intentionally or not. To this extent the description of the National Industrial Relations Court given by its President as a 'small claims court' is a superficially attractive one. But in reality it only provides a part of the picture, for the new Court is something more than just the body to which appeals from the industrial tribunals on questions of law now go. The Court, in addition to its small claims function, does also regulate and determine directly many industrial disputes which the legislators did not find themselves able to put on to an individual plane in the Industrial Relations Act. These disputes therefore remain fully on a collective level. The difference is that it is now intended that they should be settled through statutory institutions (principally the new Court) and according to statutory rules rather than by voluntary methods.

The difficult areas of industrial relations which it was thought necessary to regulate by law but not possible to individualize include recognition disputes, exclusive bargaining rights and closed shops, the enforcement and interpretation of collective agreements, and the settlement of strikes which have or may have serious repercussions for the national economy or security. Each of these disputes is legislated for in the Industrial Relations Act and in each the National Industrial Relations Court plays an important role.

The establishment of a special Court with far-reaching decision-making powers in the industrial relations field has been strenuously resisted by the trade union movement and lamented by supporters of collective bargaining as the principal technique by which industrial disputes are settled. Professor Kahn-Freund has provided what may be an explanation to union hostility to the new Court when, writing in general terms of union attitudes to law, he pointed out that historically the experiences of the unions with the courts 'toward at least certain forms of typical union action – the closed shop, secondary or sympathetic action etc – was such as not to encourage contact with the law if it could be avoided'.[98]

The Act provided that the new Court was to consist of judges from the High Court and Court of Appeal specially nominated to it by the Lord Chancellor. At least one judge from the Court of Session, nominated by the Lord President of that Court, was to be included. The Court was also to be composed of such members appointed by the Crown as have special knowledge or experience of industrial relations.[99] The Act made provision for one of the judges to be appointed as President of the Court; Sir John Donaldson, who had previously been one of the judges of the Commercial Court, was appointed to this position when the Court became operative.

No doubt the reputation of the Commercial Court for achieving a speedy disposal of disputes and for its flexibility and freedom from procedural and legal technicality was an important influence in the making of this choice. Nor, on this score, has the performance of the NIRC been anything less than excellent. Emergency or urgent applications have been handled at a moment's notice,[100] the rules of evidence have been dispensed with and indeed evidence has even been taken by telephone and amplified directly into the courtroom. Neither judge nor counsel are robed.

One of the claimed justifications for the Court was that its expertise and experience in industrial relations would enable it to deal more expeditiously with disputes and also to bring down decisions which were much more closely attuned to the realities and to the practical requirements of industrial relations. The use of the Court's expertise has, however, been kept within fairly tight bounds. The Court itself, when exercising its appellate jurisdiction, has been unwilling to do more than act as a pure court of review.[101]

On the other hand the Court has stated its willingness in its original jurisdictions, in view of the expertise of its members, 'to reach decisions not solely upon the basis of evidence, but upon the evidence weighed in the light of that special knowledge and experience'.[102] This has not meant that the Court can dispense with the ordinary requirements of evidence. Members of the NIRC can not from their own experience make good a deficiency in the evidence, said Buckley, LJ, in the Court of Appeal; they must reach their decisions on the evidence before them, 'no more and no less'. They are, however, he continued, entitled to weigh evidence and assess its cogency in the light of the special knowledge of the appointed members.[103]

In another respect the NIRC has been able to take a somewhat wider view of cases before it than the evidence and statutory rules applicable warrant. Under section 4 of the Act a Code of Practice containing 'practical guidance' for the promotion of good industrial relations, prepared by the Secretary of State and approved by both Houses of Parliament,[104] may constitute evidence in any proceedings before the Industrial Court (or an industrial tribunal) under the Act and, where relevant, must be taken into account by the Court. The Lord Chancellor at the report stage of the bill described the intended effect of this provision in this way:

It was thought appropriate that not merely should the Commission on Industrial Relations and the Secretary of State consider the principles and give effect to some extent to the code, and that the employers and trade unions should obey the moral injunctions of the code, but that in exploring this new field of jurisprudence the Court itself should pay attention to the common sense rules or practice which obtain in the best of industry now but which will, when the code is finally promulgated, be embodied in the code.

... the whole point of the code is that it is written in non-legal language. It cannot be construed as a statute. It is not intended to override that, but it is intended to be a guide both to those who wish to ensure for themselves compliance with the best standards at present obtaining in industry. The court and the industrial tribunals will have to consider, in making an order giving effect to people's rights in a dispute, whether or not the conduct of both parties has been in accordance with best practice.[105]

The Court has not taken the view that the Code represents the only means of development of canons or standards of industrial behaviour. Where the occasion has warranted it general state-

ments of what is proper from an industrial relations point of view have been freely made. Thus in *Harrison* v. *George Wimpey &
Co. Ltd.*[106] the Court, in dismissing a claim for redundancy pay, concluded its judgement with some general observations about the need of employer and employee to keep each other informed on matters of mutual concern. This was 'a matter of general industrial relations' the Court said, which it was hoped employers and employees would take note of 'in the general interest'.[107]

The summer of 1972 also saw the new Court sprinkling observations of general interest liberally through the pages of its judgements. This was the time in which the Court faced its greatest challenge from the trade union movement, a time when one of its key decisions was overruled by the Court of Appeal and later reinstated by the House of Lords in a tense and dramatic legal and political situation, when it made the first (and to date the last) cooling-off order under the Act, when it fined the largest trade union in the country £55,000, when it martyred five unofficial union leaders by sending them to gaol and when the whole country was averted from a national strike by the proverbial whisker.

The summer had started quietly enough. The Court had opened shop in February of that year and had received mild applause on most sides for the sensible decisions which it made in the first redundancy appeals which went to it. Industrial unrest was, however, high at this time because of the Government's incomes policy.[108] While seeking a voluntary limitation on pay increases by the observance of an unofficial norm of around eight per cent, the Government had endeavoured to achieve an acceptance of the policy in the private sector by using its position as employer, or in the case of the nationalized industries its influence, to restrain increases in the public sector. The policy had led to some major confrontations in the public sector. At first the Government had done well. The Post Office Workers' Union suffered a humiliating defeat after a lengthy and, to its members, costly strike in 1971. But the coal miners, who had left the pits in January of 1972, supported by a vigorous picketing campaign, had an unexpected victory when an ad hoc court of inquiry chaired by Lord Wilberforce recognized their claim as constituting a 'special case' and awarded them an increase of approximately twice that stipulated by the Government's norm.

The trouble with special cases is that you can't afford to have too many of them if they are to remain special and, when the railwaymen instituted a work-to-rule shortly afterwards in April as backing to a wage claim of nearly twenty per cent, the Government decided to go to Court.

Under the Act the Secretary of State had been empowered to apply to the Court where it appeared to him that in contemplation or furtherance of an industrial dispute certain conditions existed. These were that industrial action had begun or was likely to begin; that as a result there was or might be an interruption in the supply of goods or services so as to cause grave injury to the national economy, security or public order or danger to the lives or health of a substantial number of persons; and that in the circumstances it would be conductive to a settlement of the dispute by negotiation, conciliation or arbitration if the industrial action were discontinued or deferred. If satisfied on the evidence that the national economy etc was imperilled, the Court was required to order discontinuance or deferment of the industrial action for a period of not more than sixty days.[109]

In accordance with TUC policy the railway unions involved did not appear before the Court which ultimately made an order that industrial action be discontinued for a period of fourteen days.[110] This time the conclusion of Sir John Donaldson's judgement was more than of just general interest – it was of interest to the whole world:

In conclusion, I should like to return to the position of the court in relation to this dispute. We have from the very beginning been ready, able and willing to consider an application such as the present on the shortest notice at any time. That is no more than our duty and part of the service which Parliament wished us to provide. But it was not for us to take the initiative. That is and was the responsibility and duty of the Secretary of State. The Solicitor-General has been good enough to give the Secretary of State's reasons for applying at this particular moment of time. Now that the application has been heard and determined, and an order is about to be issued, a new situation has arisen. Great Britain is one of the oldest and most politically mature of the parliamentary democracies. The hallmark of such a way of life is compliance with, and respect for, the rule of law. In a free and civilised community this is not achieved by compulsion of authority, but by the intelligence of individual men and women. They recognise instinctively that without the rule of law there is no true freedom for anyone and licence only for the few who for the time being have the power to impose their will on the many. But the rule of law exacts its price. That price includes a willingness to comply with laws whether or not we agree with them, whilst reserving our fundamental right to campaign by every constitutional means for their repeal or amendment. This has always been the approach of the political parties, of the employers' associations, and of the trade union movement. It has also been the approach of every responsible citizen. We none of us believe that this has changed. This being the case, the community expects, and is entitled to expect, that the board, the union and the railway men and women will co-operate with one another in order to ensure the earliest possible restoration of normal railway services, and that they, and all others less directly concerned, will thereafter use their best endeavours to secure a settlement of the present dispute. With reasonableness and realism on the part of all concerned, this can be done. The whole country and, indeed the world will be watching. Let no one do anything which he may hereafter regret.[111]

After considerable speculation in the press the unions complied with the order; but at the expiration of the fourteen days the dispute remained. Under the threat of resumption of industrial action, the Secretary of State went again to the Industrial Court, this time seeking an order for the holding of a compulsory ballot of union members to ascertain the degree of support which the union leaders were being given. The statutory grounds which existed for such an order were analogous to those existing in the case of a cooling-off order[112] and, although on this occasion the unions were represented by counsel, an order was duly made (and later upheld by the Court of Appeal).[113]

The ballot was duly held and, not surprisingly by this stage, it resulted in an overwhelming vote (proportionately six to one) in favour of continuing strike action. Within a week the Railways Board had agreed on a pay settlement which was very favourable to the unions.

In retrospect there would seem little argument but that the decision to apply to the Court for these orders was a political misjudgement. More to the point, it also constituted a misuse of a tribunal for a purpose which went beyond the proper scope of its jurisdiction. The National Industrial Relations Court was not, and is not, an agency established to enforce government incomes policies. It should not have been used to achieve that objective.[114] Equally disturbing are the terms of the legislation which left so much to the subjective determination of the

Secretary of State and which, by exercise of his discretion, left the Court with no real powers of investigation and judgement. In the first ASLEF case Sir John Donaldson commented that in these emergency applications the Court was far from being a rubber stamp.[115] Many will find it hard to agree with him.

The Heatons and the Chobham Farm cases, which saw the Transport and General Workers Union fined £55,000 and which culminated in the imprisonment and then release of five dock workers, raised issues of a different kind. A detailed analysis of the sequence of events and of the various judgements which were given is beyond the scope of this book. But the point should be noted here that they constituted a direct challenge to the authority of the Court and raised the whole question of the enforcement of industrial legislation.

As in the ASLEF case Sir John Donaldson did not hesitate to pose the case in constitutional terms:

The National Industrial Relations Court is a court, but a court with a difference. All courts exist to uphold the rule of law. So does this court. All courts are concerned with people. So is this court. Without the rule of law and courts to enforce it, each one of us would be free to push and bully our fellow citizens and (which may be thought more important) our fellow citizens would be free to push and bully us. In a free-for-all none of us would hope to be the winner. The justification for law, the courts and the rule of law is that they protect us from unfair and oppressive actions by others; but if we are to have that protection we must ourselves accept that the law applies to us, too, and limits our freedom. In civilized countries nearly everyone accepts this and agrees that it is a small price to pay. There remain the few who want to use the laws which suit them and disobey those which do not. If the rule of law is to have any meaning, the courts must in the last resort take action against these few and impose some penalty.[116]

It is now history that the NIRC's decision was that the Transport and General Workers' Union was legally responsible for the blacking of container depots which had been organized by shop stewards; that the Court of Appeal overruled this decision; that as a consequence of that ruling proceedings were brought against named individual shop stewards and an injunction issued; that a warrant of committal was later issued by the NIRC but stayed by the Court of Appeal after intervention by the previously little-known Official Solicitor; that proceedings brought by another group of workers against the dockers' leaders did finally lead to their eventual imprisonment by the NIRC; and that they were released by the NIRC a few days later in the light of the changed circumstances of the issue of the House of Lords' judgement in the original Heatons case, a judgement which reversed the Court of Appeal and restored the £55,000 fine against the Transport and General Workers' Union.

The sequence of events was bewildering and in many ways bizarre. The original cause of the dispute – the laying-off of dockers by the encroachment of containerization – never seemed to emerge throughout the whole summer until finally it was settled (though not without difficulty) by negotiation between the Union's general secretary and a representative of the employers and Dock Board. It was perhaps this inability of the NIRC, and of the judicial process which it encompassed, to traverse the root issue which constituted the principal weakness of the Court. The limitations of the adversary system and its potential for determining the wrong issues provide a lesson which should not be lost sight of in the whole field of tribunal decision-making.

(c) *The Commission on Industrial Relations*

The Court is not, however, the only body under the Act which determines disputes. Other institutions have been re-established and their jurisdictions expanded; arguably they are of greater importance than the NIRC. Thus, an application for a recognition order or for sole bargaining rights is made initially to the NIRC which also makes the ultimate order; but the major investigation is conducted, at the Court's direction, by the Commission on Industrial Relations which is required to make recommendations to the Court for its final decision.[117]

The Commission on Industrial Relations was first set up by royal warrant in 1969 following recommendations by the Donovan Commission that an agency was needed to assist employers and unions to develop better and more orderly bargaining procedures. Its objective at that time was therefore to improve and support voluntary collective bargaining. The Industrial Relations Act, has, however, given the CIR a very different role and, while it continues to report on general questions of collective bargaining,[118] it must also now exercise the investigative functions relating to particular disputes entrusted to it by the Act. For this reason, trade union co-operation with the CIR was withdrawn at the time of the passing of the Act and George Woodcock, formerly secretary of the TUC, resigned from his position as chairman of the Commission.

The Industrial Relations Act established the CIR as a statutory body and provided that it was to consist of between six and fifteen members (full-time or part-time) appointed by the Secretary of State.[119] The Commission is said by the Act not to be regarded 'as the servant or agent of the Crown or as enjoying any status, immunity or privilege of the Crown'.[120] It is also empowered to determine its own procedure, though in this respect it must act in accordance with any general directions which may be given by the Secretary of State from time to time.[121] The Commission is therefore semi-autonomous in the sense that it operates independently of any government or other authority or agency though remaining subject to ministerial direction on general matters of procedure. It is also dependent on ministerial reference in respect of its general investigations into collective bargaining matters[122] and on reference by the National Industrial Relations Court with regard to its investigations of disputes. Comparisons can thus be drawn with the National Board for Prices and Incomes, the Civil Aviation Authority, the Monopolies Commission and other similar agencies described elsewhere in this book.

From a procedural point of view also the CIR is very close to these various agencies. The characteristic of its procedure is investigation by administrative inquiry rather than by judicial trial. Discussion, consultation, survey and report comprise the tools of trade of investigating officers. The inquiry sometimes in fact goes beyond mere investigation. In recognition disputes, which centre on the degree of support given by the work force to the union claiming recognition and on the strength of opposition from other unions, the CIR's officers, by their very process of investigation and determination of worker and union attitudes, undoubtedly exercise a considerable influence on the formulation and expression of those attitudes. This is openly acknowledged by Commission officials, who say that 'the whole style of the CIR is that of strategic mediation' or, as one official put it, 'pushing people in one direction or the other'.

The proceedings of the CIR clearly lack the drama and the display exhibited in the National Industrial Relations Court in particular and generally in other tribunals whose inquiries are of the judicial hearing kind. But, though less spectacular, the CIR is arguably more interventionist by nature, but in the best possible way. One of the most difficult problems faced by adjudicators of industrial disputes has always been to gain acceptance of their decisions: a process which includes mediation, explanation and persuasion is thus likely to achieve an ultimate result which will avoid the difficulties of enforcement so often encountered otherwise.[123]

3. SOME CONCLUDING REMARKS

Clearly labour law is on the move. Professor Kahn-Freund writing in 1968 said that a 'change has taken place in the attitude toward the role which law is called upon to play in the regulation of labour relations in Britain and this change affects the very foundations of the role of law in society generally'.[124] How much truer these words are today.

The Conservative Government in one sense was adding to a trend which was already well established when the Industrial Relations Act was passed. But they may have accelerated that trend and altered the institutional structure of industrial relations too quickly. The industrial tribunals have perhaps survived best and, whatever temporary setbacks they may have suffered from the trauma of the passing of the Act and the establishment of the NIRC, their position as arbiters of individual employment law is secure.[125] The future of NIRC, at least as a regulator of collective disputes, looks uncertain; that of the CIR rather more hopeful.

Industrial relations does not of course exist in a vacuum. Its condition at any time is often dependent to a large extent on the current state of the economy. To this extent prices and incomes policies, and the agencies which administer them, play a vital part. So too do the various ad hoc committees and courts of inquiry which so often serve to provide a respectable way out when regular methods and established machinery have failed. The NIRC may or may not have been a mistake; but the strength of the legal institutions operating in the area of industrial relations lies in their variety and in the alternatives that they provide for the solution of what are generally acknowledged as among the most difficult and intractable disputes known to mankind.

4

Tribunals and social welfare

1. INTRODUCTION: THE TWO SYSTEMS

Increasingly, social welfare is coming under attack in Britain –
both from the right, which is particularly concerned at abuses in
the system, and from the left, which regards the broad discretion
possessed by some state agencies (especially the Supplementary
Benefits Commission) as being incompatible with any concept of
welfare rights. This fact makes it difficult to assess the value which
special tribunals have played, and still play, in this area. While
these tribunals do have a distinctive function of their own as
providers of some measure of independent review, their performance and effectiveness are inevitably dependent upon the efficacy
of the social welfare system as a whole. It is probably fair
to say also that attitudes to the tribunals of those for whose benefit
they were established will be coloured by their view of the welfare
system itself. The claimant who is dissatisfied with the rejection of
his claim or appeal by a tribunal may feel aggrieved with the
personnel and operation of the tribunal itself or he may simply
believe that the rules, whether legal or administrative, which the
tribunal is applying are unjust. For this reason it is difficult to test
consumer reaction to welfare tribunal decision-making. It may be
possible to determine whether the claimant believes that he has
received a fair and unbiased hearing; but even then his feelings
are likely to be inextricably bound up with the result of his case.

One thing, however, is clear as to the part played by tribunals
in this field. This is that their operation, and more particularly
their own view of themselves, is determined by the nature of the
jurisdiction which they administer. This in turn is a reflection of

the entirely different philosophies of the twin concepts of social insurance and national assistance upon which social welfare in Britain is based. Social insurance in British terms, and as enacted in the national insurance legislation, is equated with legal entitlement arising from contribution. State or national assistance, on the other hand, has as its objective the provision of subsistence needs and is not concerned at all with the question of contribution.[1] In each case there is a direct correlation between the philosophy and the methods of decision-making adopted by the appeal tribunals. Thus, as we shall see, national insurance tribunals, both local appeal tribunals and the National Insurance Commissioners, are relatively formal bodies and might in many respects be compared with one of the lower courts of law (say magistrates' court in the case of local tribunals and county court in the case of the Commissioners). This is not to say that they are just like lower courts. They are not: the adversarial process is less marked, for example, because of the role adopted by insurance officers, and so the procedure works somewhat differently. But, in the sense of decision-making, the modus operandi is very similar. In particular they apply precedents in the form of published case-law and generally determine questions of legal entitlement based upon statutory rules. The area of discretion is thus fairly confined. By contrast, supplementary benefit (formerly national assistance) appeal tribunals are much more informal, both in a procedural and more especially in a decision-making sense. This marked informality, it is suggested, can be attributed directly to a general lack of legal entitlement under the supplementary benefits scheme. By comparison with the national insurance system, it is in fact a scheme dominated by discretion and where, arguably, the charity of the poor law to a considerable extent lives on. In other countries, the view has sometimes been put that where social security is regarded as a form of charity, a right of appeal may even be thought alien.[2] This view has not been taken in Britain but it is nevertheless noteworthy that certain characteristics of informality which mark supplementary benefit appeal tribunals – such as private hearings, a general lack of legal representation and a failure to give reasoned decisions based upon published principles or precedents – are not those normally associated with legal rights exercisable through a judicial appeal system.

The difference between national insurance tribunals and

supplementary benefit appeal tribunals is therefore measurable in purely functional terms. One of the National Insurance Commissioners thought that the distinction between legal right[3] (based, he said, on a contract between the State and the citizen) and discretionary power to confer benefit was such that it would be wrong to consider amalgamating the two jurisdictions under the cloak of one appeal tribunal, for the tribunals were doing different jobs. This was the view also of the Franks Committee, which commented that although national assistance (supplementary benefit) appeal tribunals were in form hearing appeals and therefore were exercising 'adjudicating functions', they were in practice acting more like 'an assessment or case committee, taking a further look at the facts and in some cases arriving at a fresh decision on the extent of need'.[4] The difference in function has also been described by Walter Freidlander, formerly Professor of Social Work at the University of California, Berkeley, writing without reference to any country in particular :

Social insurance benefits are financed either entirely or in part by contributions of the insured persons, by their employers in their behalf or by both. Thus, the beneficiaries have a legal as well as an economic and moral claim to the benefits when the contingency occurs. Eligibility and benefits are predictable. Social insurance benefits are a legal right of the insured person without regard to his personal economic need or financial situation; no means test may be required in order to qualify the insured for benefits. . . . The claim for social insurance is based upon the former occupation of the insured person, whether independent or employed, and not upon individual financial indigence. The insured, or his survivors, may use the benefits as they please. *This fact implies that the claimants of social insurance benefits are less subject to the discretion of the agencies which administer the social insurance plan than are the applicants for public assistance.*[5]

The existence and extent of discretion in the British supplementary benefits system has been a matter of much argument in recent years but, before discussing this, it should first be noted that the Beveridge Report, which laid the foundations of the present system, did not envisage that national assistance would form a major part of the whole system of social welfare. It is doubtful therefore whether Beveridge had in mind appeal tribunals, which reviewed and exercised wide discretionary powers, playing as important a role as the supplementary benefit tribunals in fact do today. A comprehensively planned social insurance scheme supported by a generous level of benefits would, he thought, put national assistance very much in a subsidiary, if necessary, position. Certainly Beveridge recognized that the State could not be excluded altogether from giving direct assistance to individuals in need because, however comprehensive an insurance scheme was established, some people through physical infirmity would never be able to contribute and others would 'fall through the meshes of any insurance'. But, he concluded, 'the scope of assistance will be narrowed from the beginning and will diminish throughout the transition period for pensions. The scheme of social insurance is designed of itself when in full operation to guarantee the income needed for subsistence in all normal cases.'[6] Unfortunately the expectation has not been fulfilled. As Professor A. B. Atkinson has shown, 'there has been a major departure from the principles of Beveridge' in so far as the levels of national insurance benefits have been set consistently below the subsistence standards established by the national assistance and supplementary benefit schemes. The result has been that the 'national minimum level of income has been provided not through social insurance as proposed by Beveridge, but by the means-tested National Assistance.'[7] Far from dying away, therefore, or from existing purely as a residual backstop, national assistance has played a significant part in the total system of social welfare. Atkinson shows that in December 1968 there were two and a half times as many households receiving assistance as there were in December 1948.[8] Of greater significance, however, is the fact that a substantial proportion of recipients of national insurance benefits also receive supplementary benefits. This can be seen from the following figures taken from the Annual Reports of the Department. They show the proportion (in percentages) of national insurance beneficiaries who are at the same time also receiving supplementary benefit:

	1968	1969	1970	1971
Unemployment benefit	20.2	22.5	19.5	23.4
Sickness benefit	14.5	14.2	14.3	12.6
Retirement pensions	28.6	27.7	28.0	27.7
Widow's benefit (excluding widow's basic pension)	21.9	16.3	16.7	15.0

From the point of view of those people who are driven by necessity to seek supplementary benefit it is clear that a concept of legal entitlement based on contract has no real meaning. There is also the unfortunate fact that the income received from the State by a substantial body of people is being determined under two separate and different administrative systems. It is true that to some extent the administrative reforms of the Ministry of Social Security Act 1966 (bringing the administration of supplementary benefits and national insurance together into a single ministry) were intended to provide some unification so that contributory and non-contributory benefits would be jointly administered 'without the sharp distinction which exists today and which is itself responsible for keeping some people away from the help that they should have'.[9] But within the ministry the Supplementary Benefits Commission officers and national insurance officers have operated independently of each other (and to some extent of the ministry). Further, at appellate level the dichotomy remains untouched. Consequently much confusion can be caused to recipients. Thus, the experience of the Cambridge Law Surgery (a voluntary legal advice centre) was that there were people who did not appreciate that they might need to make separate appeals against adverse national insurance and supplementary benefit determinations. There was, for example, the case of a man who had been dismissed by his employer on the grounds of ill-health which rendered him incapable of work. He had been sent separate notifications from the Department of Health and Social Security advising him that he had been refused national insurance and also supplementary benefit respectively. In each case he was advised in writing of his appeal rights but it was clear that he did not understand that he would have to file two separate appeals, even although he had made two separate claims (on instructions from the department on calling at the local office) initially.

2. THE SUPPLEMENTARY BENEFITS SYSTEM

We can now return to the debate surrounding the existence, and extent, of discretion in the supplementary benefits system. That it is largely a discretionary jurisdiction is not really in doubt, though when the national assistance system was reformed by the Labour

Government in 1966 much was made of the new concept of welfare 'rights' which the reforms were said to achieve. The Ministry of Social Security Bill of that year created a single Ministry of Social Security to replace the former Ministry of Pensions and National Insurance and the National Assistance Board. The latter had administered the system of national assistance, as it was then called, since 1948, having taken over at that time from the Unemployment Assistance Board which had been set up by the Unemployment Act of 1934. According to Miss Margaret Herbison, Minister of Pensions and National Insurance, two of the principal objectives of the 1966 Bill were (1) 'to establish new and clear rules for awarding non-contributory benefits, *as of right*, to provide a form of guaranteed income for the elderly' and (2) 'to improve the level of benefit available to the elderly and others who need help over a long period without detailed inquiries into their particular needs'.[10] The Joint Parliamentary Secretary to the Ministry, Mr Norman Pentland, went even further. The Bill makes it quite clear, he said, that 'any person whose financial circumstances warrant it has a *right* to claim supplementary pension or allowance and that there is to be no question of the Commission reducing the amount of any pension under any discretionary powers. *This is quite a new concept.*'[11] Mr Pentland's summation was that 'throughout the Bill the emphasis is placed under the claimant's right to benefit and in place of what has been to a great extent a discretionary system we shall have a benefit, to which there is a clear entitlement'.[12] For herself, the minister pointed to clause 4 of the Bill which, she said, was 'written in terms of entitlement to benefit' and which set 'the tenor for the rest of the Bill'.[13] It will be as well to set out the provisions of clause (now section) 4, the principal subclause (1) of which reads:

Every person in Great Britain of or over the age of sixteen whose resources are insufficient to meet his requirements shall be entitled, subject to the provisions of this Act, to benefit as follows, that is to say,
  (a) if he has attained pensionable age, to a supplementary pension,
  (b) if he has not attained pensionable age, to a supplementary allowance,
and, in a case falling within section 6 or 7 of this Act, to such benefit as is mentioned therein.

Far from setting the tenor for the rest of the Act, however, section 4(1) represents the high-water mark of legal entitlement from which subsequent provisions detract, rather than support. Even paragraph 1 of Schedule 2, which by virtue of section 5 determines a claimant's entitlement to benefit, and which provides that 'the amount of any benefit to which a person is entitled shall be the amount by which his resources fall short of his requirements', is to be read subject to paragraph 4(1) of that Schedule which says:

Where there are exceptional circumstances,
  (a) benefit may be awarded at an amount exceeding that (if any) calculated in accordance with the preceding paragraphs;
  (b) a supplementary allowance may be reduced below the amount so calculated or may be withheld;
as may be appropriate to take account of those circumstances.

Thus, although there is a basic floor of legal entitlement, it is movable by exercise of discretionary power, either upwards or (in the case of supplementary allowance) downwards according to the existence of 'exceptional circumstances' which make such a movement 'appropriate'. Further substantial discretionary modifications are to be found in sections 7 (single payments to meet exceptional needs), 11 (power to impose conditions that recipient be registered for employment), 13 (overriding discretion in cases of urgency) and 14 (payment in kind 'by reason of exceptional circumstances'). In addition, and in many ways a much more important factor, it is left to the Supplementary Benefits Commission (and to the Secretary of State as to 'the main lines of policy and ... the standards of benefit')[14] to determine what a person's 'requirements' are and whether, under section 4(1), his resources are insufficient to meet them. The area of discretion implicit in such general criteria as requirements and sufficiency is clearly very large indeed.

The divergence between the stated policy of legal entitlement to supplementary benefits and the real position pertaining under the Act has been commented on by Rosalind Brooke: 'If it is decided that entitlement rather than discretion is the order of the day, then surely we need to put this into practice'.[15] She complains in particular that 'it is difficult to find out what a person is entitled to if the way to assess it is based on rules in the A Code, available only to ministry officials'.[16] The 'A' Code – or, as it is officially called, 'Allowances and Pensions Instructions' – has been the subject of much controversy. It contains over nine hundred pages of administrative rules and directions to departmental officials as to how the various discretionary powers outlined above are to be exercised and as to how questions of requirements, resources and sufficiency are to be determined. The Code itself is supplemented by various other documents including 'A' circulars and an AX Code (which lays down procedures for investigating fraud).[17] Many of the provisions in the Code and in circulars 'have been designed precisely to ensure what one civil servant called "uniformity of discretion" '.[18] It is tempting therefore to conclude that in this respect the Department and the Commission are both having their cake and eating it too. Discretion is being largely restricted by administrative rules but these latter have no legal standing and therefore do not create legal entitlement. Now that in itself might not matter so much from the point of view of a claimant who is not over-concerned with jurisprudential terminology and the classification of norms; but what does matter is the fact that the claimant does not even receive *expectations* arising from the Code's directions because the Code is not published. On the other hand, it must be said that since the supplementary benefits handbook was first published in May 1970,[19] claimants and their advisers have been in a position to know much more than previously of the likely outcome of a claim. The handbook purports to give a 'detailed explanation of the scheme', setting out 'not only its basic structure but also the broad lines along which the Commission exercises its discretionary powers in day to day administration'.[20] But in many crucial areas of discretion the handbook gives little away.[21] Thus, on the subject of exceptional needs arising from emergencies, it is simply provided that 'the Commission's officers will be anxious to help in the task of relief' and that in particular the Commission can 'make use of its overriding discretion to make payments in cases of urgency to people who would normally be excluded from receiving supplementary benefit, e.g. because they are in full-time work'.[22]

It is claimed that the handbook 'provides in a readable manner the material of importance to claimants and their counsellors freed from the mass of procedural and other detail which is necessary in staff instructions such as the "A" Code, but which is largely unintelligible to the lay reader'. For this reason, it is said, the Commission decided that the 'A' Code was 'unsuitable for publication'.[23] It would seem a fair inference, however, from the following passage in the introduction to the handbook that the real reason for non-publication of the Code was that the Commission wished to retain control over the exercise of discretionary powers through the expedient of directions (as issued from time to time) to commission officers. The passage reads:

An exclusively legal approach to a non-contributory benefits scheme can only lead to a narrower not a broader concept of the 'rights' of claimants, since those rights are or should be social as well as legal. It will also tend to a more restrictive rather than a more generous or adaptable range of entitlement. Under a contributory scheme for example a person's rights are very precisely determined; if the appropriate contributions have been paid and the defined national insurance contingency exists then there is a clear right to so many pounds national insurance benefit, no less but no more. The distinctive feature of the Supplementary Benefits Scheme is its discretionary element, those powers vested in the Commission which enable it to consider the claims of individual circumstances. By definition no one can claim as of 'right' that a particular discretionary power should be exercised in his favour. But for the individual claimant the existence of these discretionary powers may be more valuable than a prescribed right because they give the scheme a flexibility of response to varying situations of human need.[24]

The point may be that publication of administrative directions would more easily enable supplementary benefit appeal tribunals to review and assess the Commission's determinations and in particular would enable appeal tribunals to rule on the validity and/or desirability of the directions themselves. In such a situation, there would be less flexibility, though possibly a much better basis for the exercise of discretion in a way which would achieve the objectives of the scheme. As it is, appeal tribunals operate very much in the dark when endeavouring to ascertain the rationale of a Commission officer's decision. Certainly tribunals may know what the Commission's policy underlying the decision is, either because it is set out in the supplementary benefits handbook or because the department's presenting officer has told the tribunal what departmental policy is. This is, however, very much a second-best affair and does not readily enable the tribunal to rule that departmental policy, as contained in instructions to officers, is wrong or unsound. This is not to say that a tribunal is bound by departmental policy – it is not[25] – but just simply that, as an appeal body, the tribunal may not easily be able to determine whether the initial decision is based on sound legal and social principles.

The use of the 'A' Code as the basis of administration of supplementary benefits was defended by the late Professor Titmuss (Deputy Chairman of the SBC)[26] who thought that the problem of discretion was best handled by administrative rules. He sought support for this view in the comment by Professor K. C. Davis that 'the creation of new law through either statutory enactment or administrative rule-making is much more desirable than creation of new law through either judicial decision or administrative adjudication'.[27] But nowhere does Professor Davis give his blessing to unpublished, secret administrative rules and indeed he has been a consistent champion of openness in government and administration.[28] There is, however, the matter of wider principle discussed by Professor Titmuss. A state of confrontation exists, he said, between those (like himself) who support the present system of supplementary benefits which allows 'flexible responses to human needs and to an immense variety of complex individual circumstances'[29] and those (the 'New Diceyists') who abhor discretion and who demand 'income-maintenance rights, judicialized appeal systems and equality of access to material facts contained in files or office procedural books' (including 'so-called "secret" code As').[30] Titmuss sees the Ministry of Social Security Act as laying down 'a minimum standard in financial terms, with discretion given to the Commission to vary these where circumstances warrant it and a right of appeal if the claimant is dissatisfied with the Commission's decision'.[31] His opponents, he said, are on the other hand all for calling in lawyers and basing welfare decisions 'on a massive body of precedent and case-law' as a means of abolishing 'personalised discretion in giving or withholding cash grants'. Claimants would thus be represented by lawyers, appeals 'judicialized', access to the courts made available; and the adversary system would then replace the inquisitorial tribunal method.[32]

Now all this, in my view, overstates the case of those who seek a greater measure of legal entitlement and a better form of review of discretionary decision-making. Professor K. C. Davis himself, it should be noted, believes in formalizing discretion and in so removing elements of personalized arbitrariness.[33] And to argue for a greater knowledge of 'expectation', it must be said, is not necessarily inconsistent with administrative rule-making. Nor does it necessarily mean an advocacy of case-law and precedent simpliciter. Paradoxically one of the features of administrative rule-making is that it may lead to greater rigidity and less flexibility (in individual cases determined under the rules as they exist at any given time) than a system of case-law. But it need not do so, provided that the rules are stated as principles and so long as the scope of remaining discretion is clearly referable to basic legislative objectives. Neither, however, do case-law and precedent of necessity lead to absolute rigidity. In so far as they consist of the sum total experience of interpretation of general principles contained either in legislation or in the application of other rules, case-law and precedent can in fact serve to maintain flexibility and to develop those principles to meet changing conditions. This is a matter which will be returned to in Chapter 7 but the point might be made here that at least in theory interpretation according to reasoned case-law does overtly seek to fulfil legislative objectives; administrative rule-making may in many instances lack the discipline of the constant review provided by a case-law system and may therefore tend more readily to arbitrariness.[34] The view will be expounded later, however, that a 'hybrid'[35] approach, combining the best of generic rule-making with individualized case determination may provide the best of all worlds.

(a) *The operation of supplementary benefit appeal tribunals*

We have seen that Professor Titmuss has argued against 'judicializing' the supplementary benefits appeal system which he took to mean (*inter alia*) the encouragement of legal representation in the context of an adversarial contest. The antithesis that he described is that of a lay inquisitorial tribunal operating without the assistance (or hindrance, according to taste) of legal advocacy. This is in fact a correct summation of the present method of inquiry which is undoubtedly characterized by an absence of what might loosely be called legalism. Legal representation is rare; indeed in a substantial proportion of cases the claimant himself does not appear. (One writer puts that proportion at more than half.[36]) There is also the fact, already noted, that supplementary benefit appeal tribunals do not have published precedent decisions to which they can refer. Nor are regular conferences or meetings of chairmen, of the kind organized by the President of the Industrial Tribunals, held. Procedure at hearings is very informal and, after the preliminaries have been completed, can easily fall into a round-table type discussion in which members of the tribunal, the claimant (if he is present) and the presenting officer freely participate. When a claimant does not appear and is not represented, hearings are normally very perfunctory with (regrettably) little effort made by the tribunal to press the presenting officer to justify the original decision.

Supplementary benefit appeal tribunals owe their origins to the Unemployment Act of 1934.[37] By that Act, appeal tribunals consisted of 'a chairman and two other members'. The chairman was a ministerial appointment and the other members were selected by the Unemployment Assistance Board from panels, one comprising persons nominated by the minister and representing 'work-people', the other comprising persons representing the Board.[38] Procedural rules were made by the Board and were (typically of the time) sparse. The 1948 National Assistance Act, institutionally, did little more than change the name of the Unemployment Assistance Board to that of the National Assistance Board (though of course with a much expanded jurisdiction). The 1948 Act did, however, put the power of appointment of all the members of the appeal tribunal into the hands of the minister. One member was still to represent 'work-people', another was to be chairman, but there was now no provision for the third member to represent the Board. This last fact perhaps revealed a growing concern that appeal tribunals should provide a genuinely new and independent review of the original decision. The composition of the appeal tribunals as then provided has been continued under the 1966 Act, though procedural rules are now no longer made by the Board (or Commission as it now is) but are promulgated by the minister after consultation with the Council on Tribunals.[39]

The current procedural rules are the supplementary benefit (appeal tribunal) rules 1971.[40] These are scarcely much fuller than the original rules and, in general, leave the procedure in connection with the consideration and determination of any matter to be determined by the appeal tribunal in such manner as the chairman determines.[41] The claimant is, however, entitled to be present at the hearing and 'to be heard, to call persons to give evidence and to put questions directly to any other interested person who is present and to any person who gives evidence'.[42] In addition he may be accompanied by not more than two persons either or both of whom may represent him at the hearing, whether they have professional qualifications or not; such persons may also represent a claimant who chooses not to appear at the hearing himself.[43] Tribunal hearings are not open to the public[44] but the 1971 rules provide a most worthwhile innovation in permitting the attendance of not more than two persons 'who are genuinely engaged in research connected with appeals to Appeal Tribunals' or who 'have other good and sufficient reasons for being present'.[45] The final provision of any note is that appeal tribunals must 'record every determination and provide a statement of the reasons therefor in writing'.[46]

According to the published figures of the Department of Health and Social Security, 4803 supplementary benefit appeal tribunal sittings were held in 1971 in which 22,434 appeals were dealt with.[47] In the same year, as a result of certain administrative reorganizations, the number of appeal tribunals in England and Wales was reduced from 151 to 120. As far as supplementary benefit appeals were concerned (as against other minor jurisdictions exercised by the tribunals),[48] the results were as follows:[49]

	Rate or decision confirmed	Rate increased/ benefit allowed	Rate reduced/ benefit disallowed	
	per cent	per cent	per cent	
1971	17,638 (78.6)	4,135 (21.4)	10	–
1970	18,336 (76.7)	4,563 (23.3)	12	–
1965	7,385 (78.7)	1,932 (29.1)	31	(0.4)
1960	5,596 (77.7)	1,726 (22.3)	7	–
1955	11,387 (83.7)	2,237 (16.3)	8	–
1950	6,759 (75.5)	2,236 (24.5)	6	–

The proportion of appeals which have been successful has thus been fairly consistently around twenty-one to twenty-three per cent. This is comparable with the national insurance appeal success rate.[50] But, in a jurisdiction which confers much greater discretion than does the national insurance legislation, one wonders whether the success rate should not in fact be higher than it is. Particularly disturbing is Professor Herman's revelation, from the Department's own files, that less than half of appellants appear at the hearing.[51] The further absence of legal representation – certainly a common feature in many tribunal jurisdictions – aggravates the problem and it is yet to be shown that non-lawyer representatives as a class are effective at presenting all the relevant facts of a case to the tribunal and in testing the presenting officer's contentions. Herman in fact says that supplementary benefit appeal tribunal members to whom he spoke felt that appellants with lay representation were worse off than those who had none because the tribunal in such cases felt that it could not be so active in eliciting information. There is also the fact that, unlike national insurance officers who are normally quite scrupulous in this regard, presenting officers in supplementary benefit appeals do not always see their function as including that of revealing the weaknesses as well as the strengths of their cases.[52]

As has been said, it is difficult to assess the merit of supplementary benefit appeal tribunals. The nature of the jurisdiction, the administrative rules operated at first instance by the Supplementary Benefits Commission and its officers and the lack of readily ascertainable legal principles all tend to compound the picture. There are undoubtedly some unsatisfactory procedural features and equally there are inconsistencies in decision-making, a matter which will be returned to later. But perhaps the principal value of the appeal tribunals lies in their independent existence. There is in this respect a very telling passage in an article by a lecturer in sociology who was from 1960 to 1963 an executive officer in a local office of the National Assistance Board.[53] Based on his observations at that time, he pointed out that the filing of an appeal was one of the more effective forms of control exercisable over the actions and decisions of the Board's officers. An appeal

created a situation in which the original decision had to be re-scrutinized in order that it might be justified before an Appeal Tribunal. More appeals were withdrawn than ever went to the Appeal Tribunal, largely because an appeal would provoke the revision of a harsh or hasty decision. During much of the time the author worked at the Area Office the local Appeal Tribunal had as chairman a man who was very critical of the Board and who regarded some of the common interpretations of the Act by the Board as unreasonably harsh. Since the Manager disliked continually losing appeals the tendency was to anticipate the tribunal decision whenever an individual appealed.[54]

The comment may be added that there should be further justification for the existence and continued operation of appeal tribunals other than that mentioned above, however admirable that may be in itself, if tribunals are to play a really active part in the administration of our laws and policies.

3. THE NATIONAL INSURANCE SYSTEM

Beveridge saw his proposals for social or national insurance as an extension of existing compulsory and voluntary insurance schemes. Insurance, he said, was what the people of Britain wanted. In particular he pointed to 'the strength of popular opposition to any kind of means test', an objection which sprang 'not so much from a desire to get everything for nothing, as from resentment at a provision which appears to penalise what people have come to regard as the duty and pleasure of thrift, of putting pennies away for a rainy day'.[55] The National Insurance Act and the National Insurance (Industrial Injuries) Act of 1946 both, therefore, required compulsory contributions. In this respect they were not breaking new ground because the National Insurance Act of 1911 and later the Unemployment Insurance Acts of 1920–34 had established the principle of benefits for sickness and unemployment based on insurance contributions. This legislation had also set up the adjudicatory machinery (insurance officers, courts of referees and umpires)[56] institutions of insurance officers, local appeal tribunals and Commissioners.

Entitlement to benefit under the National Insurance Act 1946 was dependent upon the requisite number of qualifying contributions having been made but this was not the case under the industrial injuries scheme. Here, benefit was paid in respect of personal injury caused by accident 'arising out of and in the course of employment' (the same criterion used in the earlier workmen's compensation legislation) and also for certain prescribed 'occupational' diseases occurring in particular jobs. For both these kinds of industrial misfortune three main classes of benefit were provided: injury benefit which covered the first 156 days from the accident or onset of the disease; disablement benefit which covered personal afflictions; and death benefit which was payable to certain dependents following death by industrial accident or disease. There were in addition various additional allowances, the most important of which was the special hardship allowance which was (and is) a complex provision and which, according to the Chief National Insurance Commissioner, has been the principal cause of certain delays in the hearing of appeals.[57] It should be noted that initially industrial injuries claims and appeals were dealt with under separate machinery, though normally the personnel of local national insurance tribunals and local national insurance (industrial injuries) tribunals were the same and the National Insurance Commissioners also acted as National Insurance (Industrial Injuries) Commissioners. There were some differences in procedure – for example, legal representation before national insurance tribunals was not permitted but was allowed with leave of the chairmen in the case of industrial injuries tribunals.[58] The Franks Committee thought that the functions of these tribunals were not 'sufficiently cognate to permit of complete integration'[59] but amalgamation was nevertheless eventually effected by the National Insurance Act 1966. This followed the transference of the appeal functions of the Family Allowance Referees to national insurance local tribunals in 1959.

The principal legislation was consolidated in 1965[60] and remains today of direct importance and application to millions of people. In 1971 nearly fifteen million claims were made for benefits under the National Insurance Act and a further number just under a million under the Industrial Injuries Act. The full picture is given in the table on the next page, showing 1970 figures for comparison.[61]

By way of comparison the total number of supplementary benefits of all kinds in 1971 was 6,428,000 (1970: 6,087,000) and new family allowances claims totalled 575,000 (1970: 593,000). In nearly all the national insurance and industrial injuries claims set out above decisions were given by the national insurance officers who, under the legislation, are constituted adjudicators at first instance. There was a small number of claims (1971: 553 national insurance and 39 industrial injuries) which were referred to local appeal tribunals without decision by the insurance officer. The total numbers of claims dealt with on appeal (or reference) by local tribunals in 1971 was 24,031 (national insurance) and 4,661 respectively.[62] By way of further appeal the Commissioners adjudicated in 1,546 (national insurance) and 624 (industrial injuries) of these.[63] Under the legislation Commissioners' decisions are final, though there has been a very small trickle of industrial injuries cases which have been reviewed in the High Court through the prerogative orders for error of law and breach of natural justice.[64]

	1971	1970
All national insurance benefits:	14,655,000	16,069,000
Retirement pensions	697,000	780,000
Widows' pensions and widowed mothers' allowances	5,000	60,000
Attendance allowances	120,000	not applicable
Sickness or invalidity benefits	8,801,000	10,632,000
Unemployment benefits	3,570,000	3,159,000
Maternity benefits	865,000	901,000
Death grants	527,000	537,000
All industrial injuries benefits:	894,000	1,014,000
Injury benefit	729,000	822,000
Disablement and death benefits	165,000	192,000

It will be seen that the insurance officer is the focal point for the determination of the great majority of national insurance and industrial injuries claims. Initially all claims go to him, though certain special questions relating to a claimant's contributions must then be referred to the Secretary of State for determination.[65] In addition certain industrial disablement matters must be referred to a medical board for decision. (Medical boards comprise two medical practitioners[66] and there is a right of appeal from their decisions to a medical appeal tribunal which consists of a chairman[67] and two medical practitioners.[68] There is also now a further appeal, with leave, on questions of law.[69])

Insurance officers

Insurance officers are appointed by the Secretary of State for

Health and Social Security, subject to the consent of the Treasury as to number 'to act for such areas or otherwise as the Minister directs', and (in the case of national insurance claims only) may include officers of the Department of Employment appointed with the concurrence of the Secretary of State for that department.[70] The insurance officers are, however, in an interesting position: they claim to act independently of either department and, according to one senior department man with whom I spoke, the Chief Insurance Officer is punctilious in instructing officers to preserve this independence. There is here, therefore, a direct analogy with the Supplementary Benefits Commission which was 'a direct step to establish *within the Ministry* independence in adjudication' (as it was put by the Minister of Pensions and National Insurance when the Bill creating the Commission was debated).[71] Just why it should be thought desirable to have an 'independent' sub-department of the department is difficult to see. In relation to the Commission the minister during the course of the parliamentary debate laid great emphasis on putting responsibility for determining awards of benefit on 'a group of independent people with an extensive knowledge of the kind of persons with whom the new scheme is concerned'. On the other hand, it was said, responsibility for 'the main lines of policy and for the standards of benefit' was the Minister's.[72] This raises important constitutional questions which are allied also to the position of truly independent special tribunals, a matter which will be discussed generally later.[73] For the moment it will be sufficient to say that there are special difficulties with regard to decision-making agencies or officials such as the Supplementary Benefits Commission and national insurance officers who claim to possess independence 'within' a ministry or department.

Insurance officers also stand in a strangely ambivalent position in so far as they exercise decision-making functions at first instance and then appear as respondents or quasi-litigants on appeals which go to the local tribunal. More will be said about this shortly. As far as their powers to determine claims are concerned there has been a ready acceptance by the department of the fact that insurance officers have no special training or skill in judicial decision-making and for that reason certain specific limitations have been put on their powers of investigation. The most important of these is the fundamental requirement that they should, while having regard to all the facts known to them (including any which have occurred since the claim was made),[74] give a decision 'on the papers'. Personal contact or discussion with claimants is discouraged, for fear that judgements will be formed on the basis of demeanour or credibility. For this reason, some local departmental offices go to great lengths to isolate the insurance officer: in addition claimants are encouraged to post their claims to the department rather than to call in person. This, it is said by the department, serves to prevent any possible encounter between the claimant and the insurance officer which might be regarded as tantamount to a hearing.

When the application has been received by the department it prepares a dossier consisting of a statement of the facts, the relevant legal provisions and precedent decisions of the Commissioners and any other material that is relevant and then submits the dossier to the insurance officer for decision. The insurance officer must satisfy himself that he has been provided with all the relevant facts and information : if he thinks that any further information would be of assistance, he will request the department to get it for him. He does not conduct investigations himself, whether by interviewing the claimant or witnesses or by writing to them. The department accepts this responsibility and will do whatever is required; for example, it will write to the claimant's employer to obtain further facts or to seek corroboration. Sometimes the department will write to the claimant and ask him to call at the local office with further information or, more likely, ask him to post a reply. In the case of information obtained from extraneous sources, the claimant will in proper cases be advised of the information which has been so acquired and given an opportunity to comment. Thus, on a claim for unemployment benefit, the former employer will probably be asked to explain the circumstances surrounding the claimant's dismissal and, if the reply is unfavourable, the claimant will be asked to comment.

Although this procedure is clearly designed to preserve the independence and impartiality of the insurance officer, it would seem doubtful whether it really does have this effect. It is surely naive to suppose that claimants really make the distinction between the department's officers as fact-gatherers and go-betweens and the insurance officers as decision-makers or judges. To the claimant it is the department that he deals with and surely it is the department that he sees as making the determination. The reliance which the insurance officer, and sometimes also the claimant, must place on the department's officers can put the insurance officer in an invidious position as well. In those cases where there is personal contact between the department's officer and the claimant there is a danger that information elicited from the claimant over the counter will be interpreted and transcribed to the dossier in a way which misrepresents the claimant's position. In such cases the insurance officer will simply be giving a decision on incorrect information. There is also the danger that wrong or misleading advice will be given to the claimant by junior departmental officers so that the wrong benefit is applied for or, worse, no application is made at all. The department regards these cases where 'duff information or advice' is given very seriously and on occasion will make an ex gratia payment.[75] But the point is that inadequate fact-gathering or wrong advice given by departmental officials may in many cases be reflected in the decisions given by insurance officers and thus in the general reputation which they acquire for fairness and impartiality.

Finally, it should be mentioned that the façade of independence often breaks down in any event once the insurance officer has given his decision. An applicant who has received an adverse decision and who calls at the department's offices may simply be told by the department to file his appeal if he wishes but equally the insurance officer may be produced at this point to explain personally to the applicant the reasons and the effect of his decision. There are of course no rules about this procedure – it is completely informal – and it is not universally employed throughout the country nor is it always used in any particular office. But according to senior departmental officials it is recognized in the department as a useful procedure, especially when there is a backlog of appeals waiting to be heard. The department is in fact very keen to elevate this 'dissatisfaction procedure', as it is called, on to a formal plane. There is in fact already one formal dissatisfaction procedure provided under the national insurance legislation but this exists only in the case of potential contribution disputes (which are minister's questions) and not in pure benefit disputes. This is to be found in regulation 5(1) of the National Insurance (Determination of Claims and Questions) Regulations 1967[76] which provides:

Where an insurance officer has decided any claim or question on an assumption of facts as to which there appeared to him to be no dispute, but concerning which, had a question arisen, that question would have arisen for determination by the Minister, it shall be deemed to be a sufficient compliance with the requirements of section 69(1) (appeals to local tribunals) of the Act as to notification to the claimant to give him notice in writing informing him of the decision and of the reasons therefor and that, if he is dissatisfied with the decision, he should reply to that effect, giving the reasons for his dissatisfaction.

It is only where the claimant has replied to that notice and remains dissatisfied 'after any appropriate investigations and explanations have been made' that the decision of the insurance officer (if not reviewed) is to be treated as adverse to the claimant so that he must then be notified of his right to appeal to a local tribunal.[77] Alternatively, if it appears to the insurance officer that the sole ground of the claimant's dissatisfaction is a challenge of the facts assumed by the officer, thus raising a contribution question, the claimant must be notified of his right to apply for a determination of that question by the Secretary of State.[78]

In cases of this kind, therefore, quite a number of people are now dealing directly with insurance officers. As a result the department approached the Council on Tribunals to seek the Council's agreement to extending the provisions of regulation 5 to all national insurance claims. The Council refused on the grounds that this procedure was tantamount to a cutting down of notification of the appeal rights possessed by claimants.[79] Undaunted, the department pressed ahead with similar provisions in the National Superannuation and Social Insurance Bill introduced into Parliament in 1970. In the case of certain determinations and decisions to be made by the Secretary of State and by insurance officers respectively, the Bill provided that regulations should provide for the prescribed person to be informed of his right to appeal against a determination if he has notified the Secretary of State or the insurance officer within the prescribed period of his dissatisfaction with the determination *and* if it was not explained to his satisfaction or reviewed under the express powers given to that effect.[80] The Bill lapsed with the dissolution of Parliament at the general election of 1970. The Social Security Bill introduced by the Conservative Government in 1972 had no comparable provision in it.

There are obviously definite advantages in the use of dissatisfaction procedures, particularly if they help to prevent the appeal tribunals from being overloaded with appeals. The holding of an oral hearing is after all an expensive business: at one extreme there is the example of the thirty-nine appeals from decisions of medical appeal tribunals heard by the National Insurance Commissioners in 1970, the administrative cost of which was £36,000. The total amount of benefit at stake was £6,000.[81] On the other hand there is no evidence that serious delays are occurring in the hearing of appeals by local national insurance appeals. The number of appeals being heard does not appear disproportionate (see below) and, as George has shown in his work on *Social Security*,[82] there has in fact been a steady decline in recent years of the proportion of cases going to appeal. His figures, given as the percentage of appeals and references as a proportion of all cases dealt with by insurance officers, are as follows:

	Insurance benefits	Industrial Injuries	Family allowances
1952	0.5	0.8	–
1960	0.25	0.7	0.2
1965	0.2	0.7	0.2
To which may be added:			
1971	0.17	0.45	0.11

It is clear that the introduction of formal dissatisfaction procedures would accelerate this trend. It is possible that these figures reveal that there is already more informal dissatisfaction discussion occurring than I have been able to indicate above. If so, then in my view the situation is alarming. While in other contexts informal (or even formal) negotiation is highly desirable as a means of avoiding an over-use of formal decision-making institutions, social security is not an area where the bargaining process is at all appropriate. The welfare claimant is in all too weak a position altogether: his appeal rights are therefore valuable and should not be subject to the possibility of either not being explicitly brought to his attention or of being prejudged by explanation or advice, however sincerely intended.[83]

Appeals

Local national insurance appeal tribunals, which hear appeals from the decisions of insurance officers, consist of a chairman, selected by the Secretary of State, and two other members. The latter are drawn from two panels, one representative of employers and insured persons other than employees, the other representative of employed persons.[84] The chairman is nearly always a barrister or solicitor; the researches of one writer revealed that regional offices of the department are instructed that a person not so qualified should not be considered or interviewed for appointment 'without the prior approval of headquarters'.[85] Unlike supplementary appeal tribunals, national insurance tribunals conduct hearings of appeals in public, though the chairman of the tribunal has a discretion to hold a hearing in private 'if he is of the opinion that intimate personal or financial circumstances may have to be disclosed or that considerations of public security are involved'.[86] Often, however, a hearing is not held because neither the claimant nor the insurance officer has attended, the latter being content in some cases simply to make written submissions.[87] Where a hearing is held, the familiarity of the tribunal with the subject matter, as one would expect, 'helps to speed the whole process up'. In the words of one writer it 'would not be necessary for counsel to spend half a day outlining the most elementary principles of the industrial injury system as happened when a recent case was taken to the House of Lords'.[88] This may be a fairly obvious point but it is worth emphasizing because familiarity with the law which is pertinent to the jurisdiction is one of the distinctive features of special tribunals and marks one of their most important differences from courts of law (at whatever level) exercising general jurisdiction.

Another reason for the expedition of the hearing lies in the fact that the tribunal will already have a good idea of the issues in the case beforehand. It is the duty of the insurance officer who gave the decision which has been appealed from to prepare full written submissions and to forward these, together with copies of the factual evidence and information upon which his decision was based, to the members of the tribunal (and to the claimant) in advance of the hearing. Included in these submissions will be any second thoughts (sometimes favourable to the claimant) which the insurance officer may have had about the case since giving his decision. In addition, the tribunal may have acquired a report from a local referee, though normally local referees are only used where the claimant cannot be present at the hearing and it is thought desirable to interview him: in short, the local referee's report is used as a substitution for the tribunal hearing.[89] Where a hearing is held it will very likely appear to the casual observer to be of a cursory nature (this is true also of hearings held by National Insurance Commissioners on further appeal). The explanation is partly to be found in the previous acquaintance of the tribunal with the facts of the case, as explained above, partly in the knowledge which the tribunal has of the jurisdiction but partly also in the general lack of legal representation of claimants. The lack of legal representation may be particularly dangerous in those cases where the members of a tribunal have prejudged the case on the papers, a phenomenon which is not unknown. One is tempted to conclude generally that the hearing held by local national insurance tribunals in most cases is little more than a show of justice, a ritual which must be observed for the sake of appearances. Even where the claimant is present the difference from, say, a magistrates' court hearing is discernible. The unrepresented defendant appearing before magistrates is still faced with an adversary situation to which a set order of judicial procedure attaches: the unrepresented national insurance claimant is in much less of an adversary setting and the proceedings are designed to clarify facts already known rather than to inform *de novo*.

Some lawyers have been severely critical of what one of their number referred to as 'the medieval aspects of the trial of claims' before local national insurance tribunals.[90] It has been claimed, with considerable degree of truth, that 'adequate cross-examination is almost unknown in these cases' and also that written submissions are more likely to be accepted by the tribunals than oral testimony.[91] But, for all that, most tribunals do 'everything possible to make claimants feel at ease'.[92] In this respect proceedings are fairly informal though the decision-making process itself is very formal as far as tribunals generally go. This is partly because of the emphasis which is put on the written case which is submitted by the insurance officer beforehand, partly because of the effect which the precedent decisions of the Commissioners have and partly because of the detail of the legal rules of the jurisdiction itself. The apparent casualness of the hearing itself has to some extent diverted attention away from this formality of decision.

The existence of the Commissioners is of course a feature of the national insurance jurisdictions not to be found in most other areas where special tribunals operate. The Franks Committee had thought that an applicant should 'normally be allowed two attempts to convince independent bodies of the soundness of his case'[93] but it is clear that in laying down this principle they were envisaging a situation where the first independent tribunal was the body responsible for the initial decision (for example, transport licensing authorities). The initial decision on national insurance claims is of course made by the insurance officer so that National Insurance Commissioners in effect constitute a further appeal tribunal hearing appeals from the local appeal tribunals' decisions.[94] On the other hand there is no further appeal from Commissioners' decisions on questions of law (as provided generally in the Tribunals and Inquiries Act)[95] though as we have seen there have been a few cases reviewed by certiorari in the High Court. The absence of an express right of appeal on law to the High Court was the result of a direct recommendation to that effect by the Franks Committee, which was impressed by the high legal standing of the Commissioners.[96] The Commissioners are barristers or advocates of not less than ten years' standing[97] (and are often senior counsel), they are headed by a Chief Commissioner and are nine in number. They sit in London where they hear appeals on questions of law from decisions of medical appeal tribunals. In 1971 the Commissioners heard 1,546 national insurance appeals and 624 industrial injuries cases.[98] The department's annual report does not give separate statistics for appeals from medical appeal tribunals but, as previously mentioned, thirty-nine such appeals were heard in 1970.[99]

Procedure before the Commissioners is not unlike that before a local appeal tribunal except that the insurance officer does not appear in person but is represented by a senior legal officer from the department (another instance incidentally where the façade of insurance officer independence comes under strain). As already pointed out, insurance officers are not regarded as necessarily opposing claimants but are rather more in the nature of *amici curiae*. The department's legal officers take a similar view of their role but the fact that they are not defending a decision taken personally, and also their legal knowledge, more readily leads to their taking a different view of the case on appeal so that not infrequently appeals before the Commissioner are supported by the department. It should be noted also, when considering Commissioners' hearings, that there is no statutory power at this stage to appoint local referees to inquire and report; the Commissioners therefore often ask the insurance officer's representative to obtain any additional information that is required. This may be the only practical course where, for example, a hospital has refused to supply a medical report to the claimant directly, even though it may be favourable to his claim. Commissioners are not slow either in using other informal methods of fact-finding. They often write to employers for information and, on medical questions, where there is a conflict of evidence, will use assessors or obtain an extra report from a specialist at the close of the hearing. In the latter event the report must of course be disclosed to the claimant and to the insurance officer or his representative unless they agree (as they apparently often do) to waive disclosure.

Unlike local appeal tribunal hearings, legal representation before the Commissioners is not uncommon. As one would expect the points of law involved are often more complex, or at least are seen to be more complex, and there have been cases where legal argument (by counsel) has lasted for two or three days. Any party to an appeal to the Commissioners may request an oral hearing which will be granted accordingly 'unless, after considering the record of the case and the reasons put forward in the request for the hearing, [the Commissioner] is satisfied that the appeal can properly be determined without a hearing, in which event he shall so inform the claimant in writing and may proceed to determine the case without a hearing'.[100] In practice the power to refuse a hearing, when one has been requested, is exercised 'very sparingly' and normally only where the case is 'clear-cut' or 'completely unarguable'.[101] Wherever an issue of fact is involved a hearing will always be given.[102] Any hearing which is held will be in public 'except in so far as the Commissioner may otherwise direct if he is of the opinion that intimate personal or financial circumstances may have to be disclosed or that considerations of public security are involved'.[103]

In cases involving difficult questions of law, the Chief National Insurance Commissioner or an appointed deputy may direct that the appeal shall be heard by a tribunal of three Commissioners.[104] The original object of the tribunal of three was to obtain a consensus of opinion of the Commissioners where difficulties or inconsistencies existed. Now that the number of Commissioners has increased to nine, a tribunal of three does not, it is said, form quite the same consensus as formerly but still comprises an invaluable aid to the resolution of difficult points. In fact in 1971 no tribunal of three was constituted at all and the tendency seems to be to make less use of this device than previously. (In 1960 a tribunal was constituted on eleven occasions; in 1965 on four.)

One final point which should be emphasized is that selected decisions of Commissioners are printed and published as a series of reports;[105] as such, they are binding on insurance officers and local appeal tribunals.[106] It has already been noted that this has effectively helped to establish the national insurance jurisdictions as being fairly formal decisionally, notwithstanding informal procedural methods.

4. SOME CONCLUDING REMARKS

As attention focuses increasingly on the area of the law which has come to be called poverty law, social security tribunals of one kind and another have come under close scrutiny.[107] Opinions range from that of one tribunal chairman who thought that Britain 'has the best system in the world – and we ought to say so' to that of one welfare rights group which said of supplementary benefit appeal tribunals simply that 'these tribunals are incredibly bad'.

Certainly it is the supplementary benefits machinery which has been criticized more strongly. Undoubtedly the discretionary nature of the jurisdiction has been a contributing cause but the fact that these tribunals sit behind closed doors has not assisted their reputation. Legal representation, or representation of any kind, has been rare in the supplementary benefits forum but groups such as the claimants' unions and Child Poverty Action Group are rapidly changing this picture. The decision of one appeal tribunal has even been called into question and quashed in the High Court.

By contrast, national insurance tribunals, composed as they are at Commissioner level of eminent barristers, have received more praise than criticism. No one could deny that proceedings are generally conducted in an orderly and 'fair' manner and that, despite delays from time to time in particular types of case, the system works more smoothly than any of the comparable courts systems. And yet there is the disturbing suspicion that many people are not pursuing their appeal rights and indeed are not even fully aware of their appeal rights. Or, that if they are, the legal rules of national insurance are so complicated and have become so overladen with the precedents of the Commissioners that many give up rather than attempt to proceed unassisted.

5

Tribunals and rented housing

Rent control and regulation have been an everyday feature of English social and economic life for some while now and yet, as a distinguished economist has said, any discussion in mixed political groups whether large or small of the subject quickly arouses passions and debate of the most vehement kind.[1] Through the years controls have increased or diminished according to the persuasion of the Government of the day and, in a way which has most interesting parallels with the continuing changes in transport licensing controls, the changes have continued to be rung and doubtless will do so for many years to come. The political manoeuvring and debate on just one of the Rent Acts (1957) were sufficient to enable one scholar to gain considerable insights into the whole workings of the political and legislative processes.[2] Inevitably the political and economic arguments for and against rent control and regulation as such affect any assessment of the part which rent tribunals (in the case of furnished premises) and rent assessment committees (unfurnished premises) have played in the enforcement of the controls which Parliament has provided in the housing field. The tribunals and assessment committees are of course judged by many according to individual likes and dislikes for rent control *per se*. This is in a sense only to be expected for it is the machinery of the law which provides the point of contact with the substance of the legal rules.

1. HISTORY AND JURISDICTION OF THE RENT CONTROL AGENCIES

(a) *Rent tribunals*

Rent tribunals (with power to fix reasonable rents for furnished premises) were first established in Scotland in 1943[3] and in England and Wales in 1946.[4] Previously the Increase of Rent and Mortgage (Restrictions) Act 1920 had made it a criminal offence for a landlord of furnished premises to charge an 'extortionate' rent. Prosecutions were brought in a court of law of course and in any action brought for recovery of rent in the county courts the landlord was not able to recover any extortionate part of the rent. Proposals for the use of rent tribunals were considered in 1931 in the Ministry of Health Interdepartmental Committee Report on the Rent Restriction Acts but were rejected by that Committee.[5] Thus, it was not until Scotland had given the lead and a further Interdepartmental Committee had reported in 1945 (the Ridley Report)[6] that England adopted the tribunal system.[7] The Furnished Houses (Rent Control) Act 1946, which established the tribunals, was in fact temporary legislation only and was originally intended to expire at the end of 1947. It was, however, perpetuated from year to year by the annual Expiring Laws Continuance Act. Eventually, the Council on Tribunals drew attention to what was clearly an unsatisfactory situation[8] and the provisions of the 1946 Act (with modifications) were finally made permanent by the Rent Act 1965.

The jurisdiction of rent tribunals is generally understood to comprise the assessment of the rent (of furnished premises) which the tribunal thinks 'in all the circumstances' to be reasonable. As we shall see, there are many other questions which arise for determination in the making of this apparently simple assessment but the jurisdiction is expressed in these terms. There are of course definite limits specified to the type of premises over which the tribunals have jurisdiction. Thus, only those rented houses, flats or rooms which are not regulated[9] and the rateable value of which does not exceed £400 in Greater London or £200 elsewhere will be covered and then only if (a) they are let at a rent which includes payment for the use of furniture or services or (b) they are let under a contract in which the tenant has exclusive occupation of any accommodation and, in addition, the use in common with the landlord of other living accommodation, such as a kitchen, even though no furniture or services are provided. An application to the rent tribunal for the fixing of a reasonable rent may be made either by the landlord or the tenant or by the local authority. In giving its decision the tribunal may either approve the contract rent or reduce it to a reasonable sum. It cannot increase the rent except where it has been previously registered and there has since been a change of circumstances which justify an increased rent.[10]

Of equal importance to the actual function of rent tribunals of determining reasonable rents is their power to grant security of tenure to tenants. The 1946 Act had provided that, on every reference to a rent tribunal which had been made before a valid notice to quit had been served, the tenant would be entitled to security of tenure for a period of three months from the date of the tribunal's determination of the rent (whatever it might be) unless the tribunal thought that this period ought to be shorter for any reason. The Landlord and Tenant (Rent Control) Act 1949 later allowed a tenant who had been given three months' tenure and who had then received a notice to quit to reapply to the tribunal for an extension of a further period of three months. The tribunal was given a discretion to make an order to this effect and to grant further extensions where the tenant made the appropriate applications subsequently. Under these statutes a tribunal could not help a tenant who had received a valid notice to quit before an application for the fixing of a reasonable rent had been made but the 1965 Rent Act removed this limitation and at the same time doubled the period of tenure to six months.[11] Thus a tenant was expressly permitted to use the machinery for the determination of a reasonable rent as a means of forestalling a landlord who had served a notice to quit on him. It is interesting to note that in 1964 (the year preceding the 1965 Act) the total number of cases decided by rent tribunals in England and Wales was 5,318 while in 1966 the number had jumped to an incredible 12,197.[12] Any assessment of the role of rent tribunals must therefore take account of the fact that since 1965 at least one of their principal uses has been that of preventing tenants from being evicted summarily from rented premises, irrespective of whether the reason for this was connected with any application for the fixing of a reasonable rent. The tribunals do of course possess a discretion which would probably not be exercised in favour of a tenant who has wilfully or carelessly disregarded his obligations[13] but, that apart, the present provisions do provide an important extension of legal and social protection to tenants.

Professor Street, in his Hamlyn lectures,[14] has emphasized another aspect of the jurisdiction of the rent tribunals which is often overlooked – namely the rulings on difficult questions of law which the tribunals are constantly forced to make. As we shall see, there is no express statutory requirement for a lawyer to be appointed as chairman of a rent tribunal and the accepted view is that the fixing of a reasonable rent is not a task that needs a lawyer's knowledge and experience. But inevitably a tribunal will have to ask and answer difficult legal questions before examining the rent. Professor Street lists some of these. Has the tribunal got jurisdiction? (This question raises the further one of 'who are the parties to the contract?', the answer to which is complicated by the widespread failure of landlords to record particulars of the contract in a rent book or to update those particulars in the case of changes arising from multi-tenant lettings.) Is the contract covered by the terms of the Act? Is any notice to quit that may have been served by the landlord valid in law? What are the contractual provisions relating to services?[15] Many rent tribunal determinations of these legal questions have been challenged in the High Court. Thus, to take a recent reported example, the Court of Appeal had to rule on the tricky jurisdictional question which arises when a reference to a tribunal is withdrawn 'before the tribunal have entered upon consideration of it'.[16] It is clear from the Act that a valid withdrawal will oust the tribunal's jurisdiction to fix a reasonable rent but the problem is at what point is the tribunal deemed to have 'entered upon consideration' of the reference? In the Court of Appeal[17] Lord Denning, MR, rejected arguments directed towards showing that the tribunal had entered upon a consideration of the reference as from the time when the tribunal's clerk began considering the case – that is, when he first received the application and perused it or when he sent out notices for the hearing. 'It is the tribunal themselves', said Lord Denning, 'and not their clerk who have to approve the rent, and to reduce it, or to dismiss the reference'.[18] However, the Court of Appeal also rejected the argument that the tribunal did not enter upon consideration of the case until the three members of the tribunal had met together as a tribunal, either for the purpose of hearing the submissions of the parties or (prior to that) for the purpose of making the preliminary inspection of the premises.[19] The crucial moment was ultimately held to be that time when the members of the tribunal had variously begun to read the case papers which had been sent to them by the clerk. Thus on the facts it was held that a withdrawal which had been received after the tribunal members had started to read the papers but before they had met together for the inspection was too late to prevent the tribunal continuing with its inquiry and making a determination. Many non-lawyers would find this distinction incomprehensible and indeed Lord Denning himself ackowledged that the rival arguments were 'nicely balanced' and that it was only the informality of the rent tribunal which tipped the scales one way rather than the other. The Court of Appeal itself, he said, would not be held to enter upon a consideration of any case until the members of the Court had actually come into the courtroom and the case had been called.[20]

The conclusion which seems inevitable from this case and also from the examples given by Professor Street is that even the simplest tribunal jurisdiction, based to all intents and purposes upon a broad discretionary direction to the tribunal to do what is reasonable or just or expedient, will reveal legal problems. Some of these may be tangential or may be avoidable in one way or another. Sometimes, where the parties are both unrepresented, a tribunal will take a chance, as it were, and simply not take a point relating to, say, the form of the contract or the notice to quit. By way of illustration only I would mention here one case which I observed where the chairman clearly was worried by the form of a notice to quit but ultimately left the point alone when neither the landlord nor the tenant (both unrepresented) reacted to the tentative doubts which he expressed. Nevertheless there are some points of law and jurisdiction which simply cannot be brushed under the carpet. We may regret the fact that sometimes apparently irrelevant legal points seem to hamper the tribunals in their 'real' work. But it is an inescapable feature of our legal system that jurisdictional boundaries do always exist and that they do play a prominent part in the administration of that system. Unfortunately, as we shall see shortly, we occasionally compound these problems by dividing into two or more jurisdictions that which might profitably be kept together as a single jurisdiction, thus giving ourselves unnecessary legal complications to untangle.

(b) *Rent assessment committees*

The Rent Act 1965 broke new ground in a number of ways. In the area of unfurnished premises it established a completely new system of rent regulation (administered through new tribunals known as rent assessment committees) to take over from the earlier methods of rent control which had been employed.[21] Rent control itself had in fact been diminished considerably in scope by the Rent Act of 1957 which had removed controls for all but premises of low rateable value and then only while they remained occupied by the current tenant or his successor. Premises controlled by the provisions of the 1957 Act could after 1965 cease to be controlled and instead become regulated under the 1965 Act by various means, including the ending of the original tenancy and the letting to a new tenant. Otherwise, the 1965 Act applied regulation to all tenancies of dwellings with a rateable value of not more than £400 in Greater London or £200 elsewhere. There were certain exceptions – principally lettings at ground rents, lettings with board, furnished lettings (which of course came under the jurisdiction of the rent tribunals), houses where a business was combined with accommodation, houses let with agricultural land or as part of an agricultural holding.[22]

Where security of tenure had been provided under rent control, it continued to apply after the 1965 Act but it was to be enforced through the courts and not by the new rent assessment committees. The rent assessment committees have been concerned only to fix a 'fair rent' for the premises. When it has been fixed, it is registered and generally speaking this then becomes the maximum recoverable rent. On any change of circumstances, or in any event three years after registration, a new fair rent may be sought by either party. If a joint application is made, a new rent may be fixed before the expiration of the three-year period.[23] Rent assessment committees are very similar to rent tribunals in many ways and indeed, as we shall see, the same people often sit on both bodies. We shall also find that there is little but a semantic difference between the determination of a 'reasonable' rent (rent tribunals) and the fixing of a 'fair' rent (rent assessment committees). There is, however, one important structural difference between the two different bodies. Rent tribunals have original jurisdiction – that is, the application for the determination of a reasonable rent goes straight to the tribunal – whereas rent assessment committees are appellate tribunals and have no original jurisdiction. An application for the determination and registration of a fair rent goes initially to the rent officer – a new official created by the 1965 Act. Rent officers exist throughout the country and are appointed by the clerk to the relevant local authority in accordance with schemes establishing registration areas drawn up by the Secretary of State after consultation with the local authorities.[24] From the rent officer's decision there is a right of appeal by either landlord or tenant to the rent assessment committee.

The work of rent officers will be examined below but it should be said here that one of their most important tasks is to act as conciliator between landlord and tenant and if possible to obtain agreement between them on a fair rent. Perhaps more important, they also endeavour to ease the friction which frequently has developed between them, whether as a result of the application for registration or otherwise. The landlord-tenant relationship can be a very abrasive one and rent officers tend to bear the brunt of the rather unpleasant consequences. The rent assessment committees themselves and, more particularly because of their original jurisdiction the rent tribunals, also see a great deal of bitterness, friction and even persecution and must do their best to cope with it. The occasion of the inspection of the premises by the tribunal or committee, in particular, is often seized by the parties, or one of them, to bombard individual members with stories of the other party's manifold wickedness and failings. Where both parties are present, an open argument may break out between them and continue after the tribunal has left the premises.[25] It is difficult to offer any generalizations about how effective rent tribunals are in carrying out a peace-making role. From observation while accompanying one rent tribunal on its inspections, the members of the tribunal seemed most agile in fielding pleas for sympathy and understanding from one party or the other in relation to the shortcomings of the other without losing the confidence of both. One of the members of this particular tribunal remarked after a particularly stormy encounter, during an inspection, between an Indian landlord and an African tenant that often the root of the friction is one of race relations so that the tribunal members are forced into the role of race conciliators.

(c) *Jurisdictional or demarcation problems*

The establishment of separate rent assessment committees under the Rent Act 1965 to determine applications in respect of unfurnished premises gave rise to considerable controversy. Why was this jurisdiction not entrusted to the existing rent tribunals, thus preventing difficult demarcation problems and general confusion in the public as to the administration of the Rent Acts? In fact this is not an entirely new problem for it existed (though perhaps not in such an acute form) before the 1965 Act when unfurnished premises were governed by the Rent Restriction Acts. But if the premises were let with certain services, they might also come within the terms of the Furnished Houses (Rent Control) Act 1946 in which case a jurisdictional difficulty arose. This had to be sorted out according to a complex provision in the 1946 Act[26] and before a rent tribunal could claim jurisdiction it had to be satisfied that it complied with the terms of this provision. Nor surprisingly, the task proved to be a difficult one and in *R. v. Paddington and St Marylebone Rent Tribunal, ex parte Bedrock Investments Ltd.*[27] a determination by a rent tribunal was upset by the Court on the grounds that the tribunal had no jurisdiction. The 1946 Act, the Court said, was supplementary to but not destructive of the Rent Restrictions Acts and this meant, according to one commentator, that the sorting-out provision showed 'quite clearly that interlocking pieces of the jigsaw must be fitted together as they are, and not forced into place by altering the shape of either'.[28] Perhaps, but then jigsaw is not always an easy game.

When the new system of rent regulation of unfurnished premises was provided by the Rent Bill in 1965 the then Minister of Housing and Local Government, Mr Richard Crossman, rejected the idea of handing over the task of determining a fair rent to the existing rent tribunals. 'I think that we must do better than that', he said. In his view, the furnished rent tribunal system seemed 'far too rigid'. The minister outlined his intention to appoint much larger panels to serve larger areas, a factor which together with publicity would lead to consistency as between decisions. The result, he claimed, would be that the rent assessment committees' decisions would set the tone for rent levels over wide areas and (would) help rent officers, landlords and tenants in subsequent cases'.[29] Well then, why not widen the area of the operation of the existing rent tribunals and thus remove the objection to their taking on the new jurisdiction provided by the Bill? This was effectively the question put to the minister by the Council on Tribunals who protested vigorously at the separate systems of tribunal administration that were being established. The Council later reported its objection in these terms:

It seemed to us that it would be in many respects unsatisfactory to have two different systems of rent adjudication operating side by side. There would be problems of deciding which tribunals had jurisdiction and there would be competition between the tribunals for staff. The Bill appeared to present a golden opportunity to make a fresh start with one properly constituted system for the adjudication of residential rents which would have jurisdiction over furnished and unfurnished properties alike. We put forward this view very strongly to the Ministry of Housing and Local Government and the Scottish Development Department and suggested that, even if amalgamation could not be affected immediately, power should at least be taken in the Bill to carry out amalgamation of the old Rent Tribunals and the new Rent Assessment Committees ... at an appropriate time.[30]

The minister's reply was that the timetable laid down for the Rent Bill did not allow for the amendments necessary to bring about amalgamation. One amendment was, however, made to the Bill at the report stage in the Commons to enable the president of a rent assessment panel (from which committee members are drawn) to exercise the minister's power of appointment of the chairman and other members of a rent tribunal wherever that tribunal's area was wholly comprised in the area of the panel.[31] This amendment, the minister said, would 'ensure that personnel of rent tribunals and rent assessment committees are able to intermingle. There is no reason why somebody on a tribunal should not be a rent officer as well. These are not separate functions.' Without reference to the prompting he had received from the Council on Tribunals, he continued: 'Having studied furnished rent tribunals, I am certain that the kind of work which they do, and the qualifications held by the people who would serve on them, equips them to carry out the kind of work we have in mind here'.[32] The minister, in an amazing about-face from his original pronouncement on the need for separate systems of administration, even went so far at this point as to say that there would ultimately be further legislation which would 'fully integrate the law on furnished and unfurnished dwellings, not making them identical, but at least bringing them under the same system of tribunal control'.[33]

Subsequently the Council on Tribunals followed up their initial protest by writing to the Lord Chancellor and to the Secretary of State for Scotland without, however, receiving encouragement from either quarter. A further discussion with the minister, however, did bring forward a reaffirmation of his desire to assimilate the two systems 'as soon as possible'.[34] The following year the Council reported that outside the London area steps had been taken by the ministry to integrate the membership of the tribunals and the committees under the provisions of the amendment referred to.[35] Tribunal areas were adjusted where necessary to bring them wholly within those covered by rent assessment panels and rent officers were instructed to deal with inquiries about furnished lettings and to assist in the completion of application forms.[36] The integration of membership in the London area was not completed until two years later.[37] In the meantime the Council on Tribunals continued to press for total amalgamation but, although the demarcation problems had become sufficiently serious for the ministry to find it necessary to issue a complicated circular of guidance to rent officers on the dividing line between furnished and unfurnished lettings, nothing was done.[38] By now, dissatisfaction with the situation was being expressed in the legal profession. In a leading article in the *Solicitors' Journal* in 1968 under the heading 'Dual Controls Superfluous', the view was put forward that there was an 'unsatisfactory area of no man's land between our two parallel systems of control'. The leader writer reported confusion among lay people as to the differences between the two systems, a situation which had been aggravated by the 1965 Act establishing two parallel sets of tribunals 'with confusingly similar names'.[39] This article provoked agreement from correspondents[40] and later others, including Professor Street in his Hamlyn lectures, voiced similar views.[41]

In March 1971 the Francis Committee reported on the situation in some depth. The Committee rejected the suggestion that there should be complete assimilation of the furnished and unfurnished codes on the grounds that this would lead to a 'serious reduction in the supply of furnished accomodation for letting, without any compensatory addition to the supply of unfurnished accommodation for letting'.[42] The Council on Tribunals had not of course gone so far as to suggest that the substantive law of the two systems should be integrated but had merely stated that there should be a unified system of administration. And here the Francis committee proved to be in full agreement: 'we do not think that the perpetuation of the present dual system can be justified', it was firmly concluded.[43] The Committee was particularly concerned at the confusion and waste of time which can result from an application being made to the wrong body[44] and by the fact that in some cases members of rent assessment panels were not full rent tribunal members and were gaining little experience of sitting on a committee or tribunal because of the low level of objections to rent officers' decisions.[45] The recommendation made therefore was that all applications should go in the first instance to the rent officer who would have jurisdiction to fix the rent except where a notice to quit had been served and a question of security had thus arisen. In security cases the application should be referred straight to the panel office so that the questions of both rent and security could be dealt with by a second tier tribunal which would also hear appeals from rent officers' decisions.[46]

The dual system has continued to survive the Francis Committee's Report, however, and since then the Housing Finance Act 1972 has added to the complexity by adding a third type of rents tribunal – the rent scrutiny boards. The Housing Finance Act, certainly no less controversial than any earlier rent or housing legislation, *inter alia* requires local authorities to bring the rents charged for council housing up to a 'fair rent'. The principles which are to determine what is a 'fair rent' are in similar terms to those provided in the case of private regulated housing under the Rent Acts of 1965 and 1968.[47] In the case of council housing, the new Housing Finance Act provides for a system of rebates to meet the increases which the Act will bring about but this is a matter which is dealt with separately from the assessment of the fair rents. Such assessments are to be made in the first instance by the local authority itself, and not by the rent officer, though the latter may be consulted by the authority.[48] The machinery is as follows.[49] The local authority must provisionally assess a fair rent for each dwelling house coming under its Housing Revenue Account. It must publish its provisional assessments within six months of the coming into force of the Act and must also give notification in writing to each individual tenant. If within two months the authority receives written representations from a tenant concerning the assessment made on his house, it must consider those representations and 'according to the circumstances may re-assess the rent of the dwelling and of any other dwelling the rent of which in their opinion should in consequence also be re-assessed, or confirm the rent previously assessed'.[50] At

E*

this point the rent scrutiny boards effectively take over. Not later than four months from the publication of the original provisional assessment the local authority must submit that assessment (with amendments, if any) to the rent scrutiny board for its area.[51] The board must then consider the provisional assessment and either confirm the rents assessed or substitute other rents for them.[52] In so doing it is 'not obliged to consider individually the rent of any particular dwelling to which an assessment relates'; in other words, it may review the local authority's assessments on a representative or sample basis.[53] Rent scrutiny boards are left with a very wide discretion as to how they will come to a decision[54] but they must apply any directions made to them by the Secretary of State relating to the exercise of these discretions.[55]

From the last fact it would seem clear that the rent scrutiny boards lack at least one vital characteristic normally associated with tribunals[56] – they do not have guaranteed independence in their decision-making. They also lack further important characteristics in that there is no provision for the holding of a hearing and tenants, as the individuals ultimately most affected by their decisions, have no legal right to object to the local authority's assessment or to make submissions to the board on the subject.[57] These features led one speaker in the Commons to say that the administrative powers given to the rent scrutiny boards would make George Orwell's *Nineteen Eighty-four* look as though it had occurred in 1972.[58] Several Opposition speakers in fact saved some of their most vehement comments for the rent scrutiny boards. On the second reading of the Bill, Mr Anthony Crosland complained: 'the whole process of rent fixing under Part V of the Bill is arbitrary and authoritarian'.[59] In the Opposition's view there were actually two aspects to this issue. One was the lack of tenants' rights of appeal and objection before the rent scrutiny boards; the other was the fact that it was the latter who would be taking the final decision. The result of the boards' having the final decision, said Mr Crosland, was that the 'elected local authorities' would lose to 'an appointed body' their autonomy over rents for their own area. 'Instead', he said, 'we are to have rents by Whitehall direction'.[60] Other speakers returned to the same themes.[61] Mr N. McBride, for example, lamented the lack of accountability of the rent scrutiny boards and thought that tenants should at least have the right to seek review of their decisions by way of certiorari proceedings:

There is a bestowal of authoritarian powers on these boards, constituting them courts of administrative tribunals, consequent upon clause 55 ...
Surely we have departed from British justice, from the sense of fairness, of extending to the subject the natural justice which is his right? ...
In Part V of the Bill there is a dangerous infringement of the right of the subject to obtain legal and natural justice. This is exacerbated by the vesting in the Secretary of State of absolute legal powers. If this is considered coldly it must be conceded that the tenants, half the population of the country, must have some right of appeal against such boards which are not publicly accountable and not elected.
    Because of the close relationship between the Secretary of State and the rent scrutiny boards it is imperative to insert legal checks so that impartiality can be achieved, so that the local authority tenant may judge whether the decisions are acceptable. That is entirely right and just....
    Surely the boards are not setting themselves above the law? If this is persisted in Ministers are saying that such boards, with no public accountability and making decisions affecting millions of tenants are to be above the law. It would enable the local authority tenant to feel that justice was his of right as a higher court could quash the decisions of this minor administrative tribunal.[62]

    Beneath the rhetoric, there is a valid point or two. Certainly, the 'close relationship between the Secretary of State and the rent scrutiny boards' has been underlined by the composition of the boards provided by the Act. It is there stated that the panels for the constitution of rent assessment committees established by the 1968 Rent Act are also to be the panels for the constitution of rent scrutiny boards for the same areas.[63] The Secretary of State is empowered to add persons to the panels and each scrutiny board is to consist of a chairman and at least six other members, at least two of whom must be drawn from those so added by the Secretary of State.[64] Finally, it is perhaps unfortunate, given the criticisms of this kind which the boards will inevitably attract, that the rent assessment committee panels should be implicated. It is doubtful whether many people will be able to confine criticisms to the proper sector now that we have three different tribunals exercising broadly similar functions and in many cases sharing the same personnel.

2. CONSTITUTION AND PROCEDURE

(a) *Rent officers*

There has been some argument about the status and position of rent officers. A former chairman of the Greater London Council's Housing Committee referred in a letter to *The Times* to rent officers 'appointed by local authorities'[65] and was thereupon soundly rebuked by the Senior Rent Officer for an Inner London registration area who stated that the rent officer is a 'statutory tribunal of first instance' who was free from 'central and local government direction or control' and thus 'immune to political pressures'.[66] The final word was had by another *Times* correspondent who correctly stated that rent officers are appointed by the clerk to the relevant local authority in accordance with schemes establishing registration areas drawn up by the Secretary of State after consultation with the local authority.[67] Rent officers were in any event creations of the Rent Act 1965 which provided that where a rent officer was not satisfied that the rent specified in an application for registration was a fair rent (in cases where the application had been jointly made by landlord and tenant or where one party had made an application without objection from the other) or where written objection to the registration of the proposed rent had been received, the rent officer was to notify both parties of a time and place at which he would consider 'in consultation with the landlord and the tenant, or such of them as may appear at that time and place, what rent ought to be registered'.[68] The parties were entitled to be represented legally or otherwise at this consultation[69] after which the rent officer would determine the fair rent and notify the parties accordingly.[70] From that determination, there was of course a right of appeal by either party to the rent assessment committee.[71]

In the debates on the Rent Bill of 1965 the Minister of Housing and Local Government – at the time Mr Richard Crossman – placed great emphasis on the conciliatory role which rent officers would be expected to play. As we have seen, the landlord-tenant relationship is a difficult one. The National Citizens' Advice Bureaux Council, in giving evidence to the Francis Committee, instanced various examples of harassment ranging from locking the tenant temporarily out of his flat and withdrawing essential services to assaulting the tenant with knives and throwing petrol bombs through his letter box.[72] The Council was quick to point out also that harassment can work both ways and that there were quite horrifying stories reported of tenants terrorizing landlords, particularly if the latter were elderly women living on their own.[73] The Rent Act of 1965 was therefore designed, according to Mr Crossman during the second reading of the Bill, 'to provide to the good tenant real security in his home, while bringing him and the landlord together in a new climate of conciliation'.[74] The Act would enable the tenant to negotiate on equal terms with the landlord, he said, 'and that must take the bitterness out of his heart' with a resulting 'new and better relationship between landlord and tenant'.[75] Central to the achievement of this objective was the establishment of the new position of rent officer. The latter, the minister said, was being introduced for the very special reason that landlord and tenant should 'agree a rent wherever possible instead of fighting it out before a tribunal'. There were, he felt, 'quite a lot of people who are actually discouraged by the existence of a tribunal from making any real effort to sort out their differences themselves'.[76]

The rent officer proposal did not, however, receive unqualified acceptance from the Opposition. In the parliamentary debates several speakers aired misgivings. Fears were expressed that acceptance of the rent officers' decisions would be the exception rather than the norm and that the rent assessment committees would consequently be swamped by appeals.[77] More than one speaker doubted the ability of rent officers to determine a fair rent, or to achieve a settlement between the parties, in the absence of specific statutory criteria as to what was to constitute a fair rent.[78] But, in the minister's view, 'the best thing to do is not to smother them in detailed legal and statutory instructions, but to define their job and then rely on their powers of judgment'.[79] Rent officers (and landlords and tenants) would in any event, he stressed, be guided by the decisions of the rent assessment committees which would 'set the tone for rent levels over wide areas'.[80] Quintin Hogg, however, seemed to doubt that the rent committees would have any more idea about fixing a rent than the rent officers. His view was that landlord and tenant would find it difficult to come to an agreement without knowing 'the kind of thing which is likely to be decided in the absence of agreement',[81] a matter on which rent officers would presumably be unable to advise competently. It is certainly the case that lawyers negotiating settlements of common-law claims do so against a background of judicial pronouncements in similar cases so that the area of debate as to the quantum of damages in a motor accident claim, for example, is fairly confined. In short, the precedents of the court work downwards and permeate through the negotiating process. In the fair rent jurisdiction, however, the Secretary of State for Scotland thought that a completely opposite process would take place – that is, precedent would effectively work from the bottom up. The rent officers' consultations with landlords and tenants would, he said, provide experience of the kind of rent which people on either side would be prepared to accept. 'This will help the rent assessment committees in dealing with cases', he concluded.[82]

Much was said also of the qualifications which rent officers would require. Rent officers would not simply be performing a conciliatory function, as Mrs Margaret Thatcher pointed out, but would be adjudicating as well on the vital issue of fair rent.[83] Further, in the case of a person intending to erect a new house or block of flats or to convert any premises for letting purposes, a rent officer could be called upon to issue a certificate of fair rent, specifying that which would in the opinion of the rent officer be a fair rent.[84] This was a task where the conciliation factor was absent and, as Mrs Thatcher said, some considerable valuation skill and knowledge of building might well be required to assess the fair rent, when the project was only in the planning stage.[85] For this reason she and many others wished to see a statutory requirement that only experienced valuers should be eligible for appointment as rent officers.[86] For his part the minister had merely emphasized the required quality of practical experience and the ability to 'size up a problem and size up human beings, as well as being prepared to go out and see for themselves the conditions in the properties with which they are dealing'.[87] He instanced trade unionists, local authority officials, professional people, housing managers and those who are 'getting on in life, or retired, and would like a half-time job'.[88] In pointing to the need for expert knowledge, Mrs Thatcher agreed that such people with their 'experience of human nature' could probably handle the conciliation aspect of the job, but, she said, the Opposition did not accept that that was the limit of what the rent officer would have to do. It was only one part of his whole job. 'Indeed, if he is to bring about conciliation between disputing parties, his efficacy will be decided by whether the parties think that he is competent to do the job, apart from whether he has a knowledge of human nature.'[89]

One of the problems, as Mr Crossman was later to acknow-ledge, was the shortage of qualified valuers available to take on the new position of rent officer,[90] though he thought in any event that a knowledge of building and housing could be obtained in many kinds of local government experience.[91] In its 1971 Report the Francis Committee after a full study of the operation of the system since its inception in 1965 agreed that it was not essential for a rent officer to be an expert in valuation.[92] In fact, as the Committee found, almost a quarter of the rent officers appointed are qualified valuers. Many of the remaining officers come from local government (housing, public health, welfare) and a good number were retired senior members of the police force or, occasionally, HM Forces.[93] The preponderance of rent officers with some degree of housing or valuation experience perhaps underlines the fact that in reality the 'scope for conciliation is limited'.[94] Ultimately, as seen above, the rent officer is responsible for ensuring the registration of a fair rent within the terms of the Act and conciliation must necessarily take second place to this explicit statutory duty. The Senior Rent Officer for Hackney went so far as to say to the Francis Committee that 'he found it impossible to perform a conciliatory role, consistently with his statutory duty'.[95] Then too, some people were simply not amenable to conciliation, particularly, it seems, certain land-lords in London stress areas.[96]

The Francis Committee produced some interesting figures

	Rents registered by rent officers	Appeals to rent assessment committees	Percentage of appeals
1966	21,861	3,215	14.70
1967	35,132	3,855	10.97
1968	45,219	2,512	5.55
1969	48,665	2,497	5.13
1970[98]	43,066	3,196	7.42

showing a decline in the percentage rates of appeals against rent officers' decisions over the years 1966–70 (see previous page).[97]

The Scottish percentages were even more impressive, ranging as follows: 1966 (24.3 per cent); 1967 (8.3 per cent); 1968 (5.7 per cent); 1969 (10.2 per cent); 1970 (7.9 per cent). Further, the 1970 figure for England and Wales was adversely affected by a very high return for Yorkshire (23.26 per cent) caused by large block single ownerships which, if removed from the table, gave an annual average of around 4.5 per cent both for Yorkshire and nationally.[99] To some extent these figures would appear to support the view that rent officers, perhaps with the guidance provided by rent assessment committee decisions, have achieved a reasonable measure of uniformity and that the rent levels fixed have been generally acceptable.[100] On the other hand the Francis Committee did find that of the determinations made by rent assessment committees over half differed from the initial decision made by the rent officer.[101] As against that, the percentage difference in the rents fixed was only four, a mere £10 per annum in monetary terms.[102] It is difficult to say whether this remarkable proximity is the result of rent officers' following the guidance given by rent assessment committees in similar cases or whether, as predicted by the Secretary of State for Scotland in the debates on the Rent Bill, the rent assessment committees have been guided by the rent officers' decisions reached often in consultation with the parties.[103] The true answer is probably that, in a jurisdiction of this kind where (for whatever reason) there is widespread acceptance of the initial determination, precedent works both upwards and downwards. In other words, there is an inseparable inter-dependence of primary and appellate decisions in terms of precedent effect. This is perhaps not surprising when it is realized that there is an unusually high degree of communication and liaison between rent officers and the panels of rent assessment committees in the form of regular conferences and meetings.[104]

On the debit side the Francis Committee reported that there has been a rather low level of applications to rent officers[105] and a high rate of withdrawal of applications made.[106] The latter, which applied also to appeals withdrawn prior to the hearing by rent assessment committees, is reflected by the following figures:[107]

Total applications for registration (1966–31 March 1970)	Total withdrawn or not entertained	Total appeals to rent assessment committees (1966–31 March 1970)	Total withdrawn or entertained
206,830	27,620 (13 per cent)	13,064	1,265 (9 per cent)

The Francis Committee found it difficult to determine the exact reasons for these withdrawls but suggested that in many cases the tenant would withdraw his application voluntarily where he had reached agreement with the landlord about the rent or where an ulterior objective had been realized by the application – for example, where the tenant was merely forcing the landlord to carry out repairs for which he was responsible and the making of the application achieved that purpose.[108] On the other hand the Committee acknowledged that it would be naive to suppose that there was not in many cases some form of pressure on the tenant by the landlord to withdraw his application and that in some cases this might even amount to harassment.[109]

With respect to the low level of initial applications to rent officers, it was found that the total of regulated tenancies at the end of 1969 was approximately 1.2 million and the number of applications to rent officers represented fourteen per cent of that figure.[110] The Committee examined principal reasons under these headings:

(1) *Ignorance of the rent services and of rights under it:* the Committee agreed that a large proportion of tenants in low-income groups were probably ignorant of the nature and extent of their rights under the Rent Act but thought that the great majority would be aware 'in a general way' of the existence of the service. Acknowledgement of the publicity given by the Ministry of Housing and Local Government was made and it was recommended that this should be backed up by local authorities publicizing rent services in areas of housing stress and by rent officers opening sub-offices in areas of acute stress to serve mainly as contact points.[111]

(2) *Fear of the landlord:* This factor was thought to be a substantial one in stress areas though in localities where the tenant was able to afford the rent, even if excessive, the desire to live on amicable terms with the landlord was said to be stronger.[112]

(3) *Sense of moral obligation to stand by one's agreement.*[113]

(4) *Fear that the rent officer will put up the rent:* the Committee pointed out that eighty-five per cent of tenants' applications result in a reduction of rent and suggested that steps should be taken to disabuse the minds of tenants suffering under the misconception that an application was likely to end in an increase of rent.[114]

(5) *Overriding concern of the tenant to have repairs carried out by the landlord:* many tenants apparently feel that an application to the rent officer resulting in a reduction of rent would simply weaken the resolve of the landlord to carry out repairs.[115]

(6) *Satisfaction with the existing rent:* the Committee commissioned a special tenants' survey which revealed that a very high proportion of tenants expressed themselves as satisfied with their rents, whether registered or unregistered.[116] Although expressing some doubts about the subjectiveness of this survey,[117] the Committee nevertheless concluded that this was the most important single factor in accounting for the low level of tenants' applications to rent officers.[118]

(b) *Rent tribunals and assessment committees*

Rent tribunals in both Scotland and in England and Wales comprise a chairman and two other members.[119] Unlike many other tribunals, the chairman need not be a lawyer and in the *Paddington Rent Tribunal case* (above) this was held to indicate Parliament's intention that tribunals should not have the power to reduce the standard rent applicable to any premises.[120] Increasingly, however, lawyers only are appointed as chairmen, though there seems to be some uncertainty as to what proportion of chairmen acting today are lawyers. The Council on Tribunals reported in 1959 that the 'great majority' now possess legal qualifications[121] and similar views have been expressed by Yardley and Street.[122] In a very recent survey undertaken by the Institute of Judicial Administration of the west midlands area, on the other hand, it was found that slightly under half the chairmen were lawyers.[123] The position with rent assessment committees is very similar, particularly since the completion of the integration of the membership of the tribunals and assessment committees into common rent assessment panels. Each panel has a president and one or more vice-presidents, all of whom are appointed together with other chairmen by the Lord Chancellor. Other members of the panel are appointed by the Secretary of State.[124] There are no formal qualifications required for appointment as an ordinary member of a panel. In practice the membership of tribunals and assessment committees is comprised, wherever possible, of lawyer chairman, valuer (or land agent with valuing experience)[125] and layman who will often be a person with some experience in local body affairs. There is an interesting provision which in the case of rent assessment committees enables the president of a panel, if he thinks fit, to direct that the chairman may sit alone if the parties agree to this course.[126] The London panel has made use of this provision on nine occasions; in each case the application was said to have been disposed of expeditiously and without any subsequent complaint.[127] It is perhaps a pity that this practice is not more widely employed, though it should be noted that in many areas it is not uncommon for a hearing not to be held and for the parties to make written representations only. The Francis Committee found that some twenty-five per cent of the appeals decided by the Thames Valley Assessment Committees were disposed of on the basis of written representations alone, but in every instance an inspection of the premises was still held.[128]

The procedure of rent tribunals is regulated partly by the Furnished Houses (Rent Control) Act 1946 and partly by statutory regulations made under that Act and setting out various procedural steps in some detail.[129] Subject to the steps prescribed, the tribunal is master of its own procedure[130] and indeed it has been judicially held that even the express procedural requirements laid down in the regulations are directory only and not mandatory.[131] All this can and does lead to a certain lack of uniformity as between different tribunals. The Council on Tribunals commented in 1959 that 'each tribunal appears to have evolved over the years its own methods of procedure' with resulting variations in practices relating to the giving of reasons, the retirement of the clerk with the tribunal when decisions were being considered, the presence of the clerk during inspections, the time of inspections, disclosure of information received and the conduct of the hearing.[132] The position in relation to rent assessment was for a long time even more disorganized. Although the minister was given power under section 46 of the Rent Act 1965 to promulgate procedural rules, it was not until halfway through 1971 that this was actually done.[133] Before that the Council on Tribunals had pressed repeatedly for the enactment of rules.[134] There were actually procedural rules of a kind in existence from the early days of the operation of the rent assessment committees but these had no legal standing. They were simply 'notes on procedure to be followed in cases referred to a rent assessment committee'[135] and were prepared by the late Sir Sydney Littlewood who was the first president of the London Rent Assessment Panel. The 'rules' provided for a procedure 'similar to that followed by inspectors of the Ministry of Housing and Local Government when holding a public inquiry on a planning appeal'.[136] They were much more detailed than the statutory rules which eventually superseded them and at least one writer complained that they were applied too slavishly.[137]

The procedures followed by rent tribunals have been strongly criticized from the very beginning. An anonymous writer in the *Solicitors' Journal* for 1946 had this to say:

Novelty characterises the procedure rather than the substantive law. Those who have had anything to do with the working of the Act may well feel that the statute and Furnished Houses (Rent Control) Regulations, 1946, must have been drafted by someone who had just read *Bleak House*, and taken its lesson very, very much to heart. A more scientific explanation may be, though this is not brought out clearly in the language of the enactment, that the proceedings are essentially inquisitorial rather than accusatorial. Thus it is that there is no writ or plaint note or even application, no plaintiff and defendant or even applicant and respondent, and where the word 'party' occurs it is part of the phrase 'party to a contract', not to the proceedings. And it should be borne in mind that the 'reference', as the proceeding is called, may be instituted by the local housing authority.[138]

The standard answer to such an objection is of course that rent tribunals do not conduct trials but are simply concerned to fix rents. At least one writer, however, denies that this is so: frequently there is a conflict of evidence, he says, as to such things as what services were included in the contract, what furniture was contained in the letting, when was the notice to quit (if any) served, what were the other facts surrounding the giving of the notice to quit, and so on. An exhaustive inquiry of these matters is called for, he concludes, and cross-examination based on the knowledge of the other party may be the only effective means of making such an inquiry.[139] The real truth is that a rent tribunal's inquiry (and also that of a rent assessment committee) partakes of all these characteristics. The tribunal does have to determine disputed questions of fact and also, as we have seen earlier, difficult questions of law but in addition it is an expert body with its own experience and knowledge of values of similar premises.[140] As such it will gain little assistance from many of the procedural provisions present in, say, a county court – what use would a plaint note be to a rent tribunal? In any event it is arguably the inspection rather than the hearing which provides the most important part of the tribunal's proceedings.

The inspection normally takes place on the same day as the hearing. Before that, the clerk to the tribunal will have checked to make sure that all the papers are in order and that any information which the tribunal may require from the landlord has been obtained. The landlord must give such information as the tribunal may reasonably require regarding certain prescribed particulars relating to the contract.[141] These particulars are set out in the procedural regulations and include details of the furniture and services provided, the date on which the landlord became the owner of the premises (if such be the case), the price he paid, mortgage interest details, etc., the rent payable to any superior landlord, rates payable, whether board is supplied, and so on.[142] If any party to the contract of letting desires to be heard, the tribunal must give each party not less than seven clear days' notice in writing of the time and place of the hearing[143] but there is no obligation to give notice to or hear any superior landlord.[144] In the case of rent assessment committees, each party is sent a copy of any document on the file of which he does not already have a copy and is asked whether he wishes to make oral representations or merely written submissions. The parties are also asked to nominate dates within a specified period which would be convenient to them for a hearing; once a date is fixed it will not be changed except in the case of illness.[145] In evidence given to the Francis Committee the president and vice-presidents of the Thames Valley Panel said: 'Whilst not presuming for a moment to influence the parties to elect for the written representations procedure, we would certainly, in the light of our experience, not do anything to discourage them from choosing this alternative'.[146]

As stated above, the premises are always inspected irrespective of the form in which representations (if any) are made. Where an oral hearing is held, the inspection may take place either before, during or after the hearing.[147] There is some argument as to which is the better course. Sir Sydney Littlewood instituted the practice in the London area of rent assessment committees inspecting on the afternoon of the morning in which the hearing was held. The object of this inspection, he said, was to get the true value of the evidence which he had been given.[148] The difficulty with this practice is of course that the inspection may reveal features of the case which the parties had not brought out in their evidence earlier in the day. But under Sir Sydney's instruction no further representations or discussion with the parties was permitted while the inspection was being made[149] (indeed one or both parties might not even be present at that stage) so that it was important, he said, that 'every point the parties wish the committee to take into consideration should be brought out in evidence'.[150] The result of course was a circular one to which there was no easy solution. The new procedural rules have gone some way to meeting the problem by providing that the committee could reopen a hearing where an inspection had been made after the hearing.[151] In recent years, however, the more common practice has been to conduct the inspection *before* the hearing.[152] Sometimes, and particularly in the London area, a member of the panel staff known as a referencer will inspect the premises and prepare a detailed survey and plan for the committee and the rent officer too may prepare a report on the condition of the premises and send it, together with a plan, to the committee.[153] Where there are multiple applications affecting a large number of similar properties owned by, say, the National Coal Board, a selection only of typical properties will be made for inspection.[154]

If an oral hearing is held, it is normally conducted in public. Under their procedural rules, both rent tribunals and rent assessment committees may hold a private hearing if for some special reason a public hearing would be undesirable.[155] (Sir Sydney Littlewood's notes on procedure simply prescribed that all committee hearings should be in public.[156]) In both rent tribunals and assessment committees, a party may appear in person, or by a representative (legal or otherwise).[157] Sir Sydney's notes had even directed that the parties were to be told, when they were notified of the hearing date, that they had the right to be represented.[158] A right of representation may of course be worth little if a party cannot afford a lawyer or other competent representative. The Lord Chancellor's Legal Aid Advisory Committee on the Seventeenth Report of the Law Society on Legal Aid and Advice 1966–7 found that twenty-one per cent of landlords were represented at assessment committee hearings by a solicitor and a further twenty-one per cent by a surveyor. The equivalent figures for tenants were seven per cent and two per cent respectively.[159] The Lord Chancellor's Committee did not, however, recommend the extension of the legal aid scheme to rent tribunals or to rent assessment committees[160] but thought that a poor man's surveyor service would satisfy the needs of tenants who could not afford professional representation. Some faith was expressed in the pilot Surveyors' Aid Scheme which at that time had just been instituted in the Greater London area by the Chartered Land Societies' Committee and under which a surveyor would be provided to people on very low incomes without realizable capital for fees ranging from ten shillings to fifteen pounds.[161] The Francis Committee, reporting in 1971, found however that only about eight per cent of rent assessment references involved applications for assistance under the surveyors' aid scheme, despite the undoubted high proportion of cases in which tenants did not have representation. Because of the low use of the scheme the Chartered Land Societies' Committee had decided not to extend it to provincial areas; nor was it envisaged that the very low income eligibility limits should be raised while no public funds were available for the scheme.[162] Neither the Francis Committee nor, it seems, the members of rent tribunals in rent assessment committees themselves favoured legal aid being made available in rent cases. The Committee thought that legal aid would cause delay and would militate strongly against the informality of the proceedings. ('Direct communication between the members of the Committee/Tribunal and the party is a good thing. It makes it more interesting for both and helps to put the unrepresented party at ease and enables him to tell his story in his own way (within limits)', the Committee said.) There is in any event little scope for advocacy, the Committee thought,[163] which is an interesting comment in so far as it reveals the Committee's view of the lawyer's role. Criticisms of lack of legal aid in rent tribunals (and in other tribunals also) have, however, continued[164] and at the time of writing the Lord Chancellor's Advisory Committee is reconsidering the subject.

In arriving at a decision a rent tribunal or rent assessment committee will make considerable use of its own knowledge of values of comparable premises. Rent officers also of course are guided by what the committee determine in similar cases and in the London area at least officers prepare lists of 'comparables' based on registered rents. The panel office too normally has its own lists of comparables taken from committee decisions and in particular cases copies of the lists are forwarded to each of the parties.[165] This technique for determining rents is consistent with that envisaged when the Bill was in the Commons. During the second reading Mr Crossman had said: 'We need to ensure consistency so that the public at large and other rent assessment committees know of decisions that committees are making. The decisions will set the tone for rent levels over wide areas and will help rent officers, landlords and tenants in subsequent cases.'[166] This matter was in fact vigorously debated. It was felt by many that the criteria provided by the Bill for determining a 'fair rent' were far too vague,[167] although it was the very lack of specific standards which the minister said would guarantee flexibility. The only relevant criteria provided by the Bill (now section 46 of the Rent Act) read as follows:

(1) In determining for the purposes of this Act what rent is or would be a fair rent under a regulated tenancy of a dwelling-house regard shall be had, subject to the following provisions of this section, to all the circumstances (other than personal circumstances), and in particular to the age, character and locality of the dwelling-house and its state of repair.

(2) For the purpose of the determination it shall be assumed that the number of persons seeking to become tenants of similar dwelling-houses in the locality on the terms (other than those relating to rent) of the regulated tenancy is not substantially greater than the number of such dwelling-houses in the locality which are available for letting on such terms.

(3) There shall be disregarded –
    (a) any disrepair or other defect attributable to a failure by the tenant under the regulated tenancy of any predecessor in title of his to comply with any terms thereof, and
    (b) any improvement carried out, otherwise than in pursuance

of the terms of the tenancy, by the tenant under the regulated tenancy of any predecessor in title of his.[168]

There have in fact been several different methods adopted by rent assessment committees for arriving at a fair rent within the meaning of the section. Sir Henry Littlewood listed the more common of these. One, he said, was extrapolation which was an attempt to remove the scarcity value prohibited by the Act (subsection (2) above). This involved an assumption that the most expensive dwellings covered by the Act (i.e. premises with a rateable value of £400) had no scarcity value so that the market rent was also a fair rent. As one moved down the scale of rateable values, one would deduct a proportionately greater sum for scarcity though at some (undefined) point, Sir Sydney admitted, the system broke down. The second common method which he mentioned was to arrive at a market rent before the Act was operative, to determine a figure for scarcity value and then deduct that figure from the market rent. A third (fairly unsound) technique was to use a fair return on capital as a means of arriving at a fair rent.[169] Another writer lists other methods or rather factors which committees have taken into account – for example, cost of construction of recently built property, the landlord's liabilities to manage and repair the premises and certain losses incurred by the landlord.[170] It would seem, however, that as the committees have gained experience they have tended to rely more on their knowledge of comparables than on any of the above methods, which is an interesting example of the use of precedents assuming a decisive role in the decision-making process.

The rent tribunals too have their own methods of arriving at a 'reasonable rent' in the case of furnished premises. Under section 73(1) of the Rent Act 1968 (and its predecessor in the 1946 Act[171]), the tribunals were merely directed to approve the rent payable under the contract or reduce to such sum as the tribunal may 'in all the circumstances' think reasonable. The Council on Tribunals found on investigation that there were three different methods of assessment used by rent tribunals. The first was to ascertain the gross annual value of the property and to reduce this amount according to the proportion which the part let bears to the whole property; the figure arrived at was then multiplied by an agreed numerical factor and an allowance made for a reasonable profit on the estimated value of furniture and services provided. Another method, used in relation to newer property, was to take a fixed percentage of capital value and then add an approved profit. The third method was to ascertain the unfurnished letting value in the light of comparables and other factors and then to add on a sum for furniture and services.[172] This last technique, which is the most common of those used today, underlines the similarities between the concepts of 'fair rent' and 'reasonable rent'. In theory they are of course quite different if only because the Rent Act provides expressly that there was to be no scarcity value taken into account in the fixing of a fair rent. But in 1952 the Court of Appeal in *John Kay Ltd.* v. *Kay*[173] held that a market rent which was inflated by a temporary shortage of the particular type of property was 'unreasonable' within the terms of the Leasehold (Temporary Provisions) Act 1951. By analogy the view has since been accepted that a reasonable rent for furnished accommodation should discount any value attributable to scarcity. In 1966 the department circularized all panel presidents and tribunal chairmen to this effect[174] and this has no doubt helped to increase the popularity of the method outlined above of deciding what would be a fair or reasonable figure for the premises if they were unfurnished and adding to that an amount for furniture and services[175] This is a development which must surely be relevant to the question as to whether the substantive law relating to furnished and unfurnished premises ought to be assimilated, although of course the security provisions of the two codes remains quite distinct.

Finally, it should be noted that, although the rent tribunals and assessment committees fall within the provisions of the Tribunals and Inquiries Act so that they must supply reasons for their decisions on request, there was in practice a great deal of inconsistency between different tribunals and committees in so far as they chose to give reasons as of course or so far as the content of the reasons given was concerned.[176] This perhaps explains the somewhat unusual provisions relating to reasons enacted by the 1971 rent assessment committee procedural regulations. These provide that the committee's decision is to be recorded in a document signed by the chairman. This document must contain the reasons for the decision (whether requested or not) and a copy must be sent to the parties and to the rent officer. There is, however, to be 'no reference to the decision being by a majority (if that be the case) or to any opinion of a minority'.[177] The need for reasons to be coherent was referred to by Widgery, J, in *Metropolitan Properties Co. (F.G.C.) Ltd.* v. *Lannon*;[178] if they were not, he said, 'the right of appeal to this court upon a point of law[179] may become ineffectual, or at least the proceedings may become extremely lengthy, complicated and difficult'.[180]

3. CONCLUSIONS

In many ways rent tribunals and assessment committees epitomize all that is wrong with English tribunals generally. They give all the appearance of arbitrariness. Three factors in particular contribute to this: (1) the lack of specific statutory direction as to how they are to operate; (2) the failure of the tribunals and committees to publish and to make known both to the public generally and to each other any guidelines and principles by which they reach their decisions (though the admirable practice of some rent assessment committees sending the parties lists of 'comparables' detracts considerably from this criticism); (3) the lack of adequate representation of one or both parties. As we have seen, they also pose awkward demarcation problems, many of which could be avoided by the amalgamation of the tribunals and committees. There seems to be almost a fear of a system of a comparatively small number of high-powered tribunals; it is true that pragmatism and flexibility have been the two planks of the floor upon which the tribunal growth in England has proceeded, but an excess of diversification is surely now causing stress in the basic structure. The Housing Finance Act 1972 has done nothing to repair this situation. Finally, rent tribunals and rent assessment committees all too seldom articulate reasons for their decisions which will make any kind of sense to the parties. When all that is said, however, it must be acknowledged that rent tribunals have now operated for more than a quarter of a century; assessment committees, while much younger, seem to go from strength to strength. At its lowest, the very survival of these bodies without radical change suggests that they have won at least grudging support from both political parties which have governed at different times since their inception. Given the considerable controversy which surrounds the jurisdictions that they administer,[181] this is no mean feat.

6

Decision-making and tribunals 1: SET. A case study

1. LEGISLATIVE OBJECTIVES

Legislators are wont to make pious speeches about the reforms which they propose. Goals are usually expressed in the most general terms: 'to remove injustice', 'to achieve a more equitable society', 'to restore and maintain human dignity', 'to raise the standard of living'. The regulation of economic activity in particular may be designed to achieve any or all of these goals. But, as we have seen in Chapter 2, the machinery by which a capitalist society is regulated is extremely complex and by its very nature is unable to encompass goals which are at once so far-reaching and so vague. Regulatory agencies therefore need specific and unambiguous objectives if they are to make a contribution towards the achievement of the wider goals of the legislators. The task of the latter is thus to provide laws which are sufficiently well defined to enable the agencies to know what it is that they are charged to do. This is not to say that such laws must spell out in the minutest detail every facet and provide for every contingency of the legislators' policy so that there is a ready-made solution available for every conceivable case coming before the agency. In this sense discretion and justiciability are mutually compatible, provided only that objectives are sufficiently clear to indicate the basic principles by which discretion is to be exercised.

If the regulatory agency is a tribunal with power to take decisions which are both binding on the relevant department or minister and also given independently of it, the necessity to state explicit objectives becomes even more important. For in this case it will not be possible for the department to reject or modify an agency determination which does not accord to the policy as it is understood in the department.

The burden is not of course entirely the legislators'. The most beneficial or enlightened policy may be worth naught if it is not faithfully and accurately implemented. Legislative objective and administrative reality may in many cases be poles apart and the fault for failure may not therefore be properly attributable to the legislators. It is thus necessary, in assessing the success or otherwise of a legislative measure, to examine it on two counts – one according to the merit of the objectives and the extent to which they are adequately recorded in the legislation, the other according to their implementation and administration. In so far as special tribunals are established to carry out or play a part in the implementation of the legislation, both these matters will clearly be relevant to an appraisal of the worth of tribunals.

It is perhaps fortuitous that the rise and fall of selective employment tax in the United Kingdom in the years 1966–73 provides an excellent opportunity for examining the part which a special tribunal has played in the implementation of a legislative measure whose objectives were directed towards a better regulation of economic activity. Fortuitous because the comparatively short time-span concentrates the role of the tribunal in this field and because the measure itself was sufficiently important to ensure a full political account of its objectives. On the debit side is the difficulty, if not the impossibility, of assessing the ultimate success or failure of SET at the end of the day, judged in terms of those objectives. But, as with so many major economic reforms, the imponderables and the contaminating external effects prevent the forming of any pure judgement.

The Labour Government's intention to introduce selective employment tax was first announced by the Chancellor of the Exchequer (Mr James Callaghan) in the budget speech of May 1966 and in a White Paper presented at the same time.[1] The proposal was apparently a complete surprise, for under the editorial heading 'The Extraordinary Budget', *The Economist* commented on the complete lack of any previous public or academic suggestion or discussion of such a measure. 'Mr Callaghan's Selective Employment Tax springs, fully horned and tailed, straight from the inmost recesses of the Treasury, ready for immediate implementation', it said, a fact which was 'at once the small charm of its novelty and also its biggest danger'.[2]

There seems to be some disagreement as to what the Government hoped to achieve through SET. That it was a revenue-raising device is, and always has been, undoubted. The Chancellor made it clear in his budget speech that SET was to provide the 'new source' of 'extra taxation' which would be needed in view of the economic conditions then prevailing.[3] SET was, however, more than just a tax, for the Chancellor expressly rejected the possibilities of increasing excise duty, purchase tax and income tax. Measures of that kind, he said, would 'provide no positive incentives to bring about structural changes in the economy; and some of them, if used in present circumstances, might merely depress manufacturing output, check productivity, shatter industry's confidence and halt investment and modernisation.'[4] The White Paper was more explicit. The tax, it said, was designed to achieve two main objectives. First, although a revenue measure, it would improve the structure of the tax system by 'redressing the balance between services and manufacturing'. Services (including distribution), it pointed out, 'have hitherto been lightly taxed as compared with manufactured products, which are subject to excise duties and the purchase tax'.[5] Secondly, and as we shall see this proved to be the more controversial of the economic objectives stated, the tax would in the long term encourage economy in the use of labour in services and thereby make more labour available for the expansion of manufacturing industry.[6] An annex to the Paper showed that during the period 1960–5 a total of 1,330,000 new workers (including 423,000 released from sectors of declining employment – principally agriculture, mining and the armed forces) was added to the labour force but that only just over ten per cent of this number had gone into manufacturing industries. On the other hand over eighty per cent had gone into various service industries, including distribution and construction. Broadly speaking, as explained below, the objective of SET in this respect was to halt or even reverse this trend.

The stated objective of boosting manufacturing at the expense of services was, however, later played down considerably by Professor W. B. Reddaway, who was commissioned by the Labour Government to report on the effects of SET after it had been operative for some while. Professor Reddaway's first – the second came in 1973 – report was published in 1969 and was concerned with SET in the distributive trades.[7] On the subject of government objectives, he had this to say:

During the course of our research, the point has been put to us time and time again that 'S.E.T. has failed miserably in its basic objective of moving labour out of the service trades, and become nothing but a device for raising government revenue.' We have been left in no doubt that the unpopularity of S.E.T. is in large measure accounted for by the widespread impression that S.E.T. was 'put across' in 1966 *primarily* as a device for moving people out of the service trades and into manufacturing, with its revenue-raising effect kept well out of the limelight – and by the accompanying view that the influence of the tax on the distribution of labour has been very small, leaving the revenue raising as the major result *in fact*. I do not regard it as part of my task to explain how this impression about the Government's objectives came to be so widely held, even by a very large number of generally well-informed people; but the general attitude to a tax is important for an understanding of its consequences, and our study of S.E.T. would be incomplete without a very firm statement about the unfortunate consequences of this impression, on which there is no doubt in my mind whatsoever.[8]

With respect, however, this view would not seem to accord with the emphasis which the Government at the time placed on the objective of redeploying labour into the manufacturing sector. Certainly, on budget night the Chancellor stressed the importance of 'shaking out' labour from the service industries and of giving manufacturing a boost. 'Despite some hoarding and waste of manpower', he said, 'it is still true that the growth of manufacturing output has been seriously impeded by labour shortages; and this has hampered the growth of productivity'. To some extent, he continued, the necessary labour might even be obtained from the services sector: 'If manpower can be saved in the service industries, whether through a slower rate of growth in demand for services or through greater economy of manpower, extra labour might well become available for manufacturing, giving it greater scope for growth'.[9] For this reason, therefore, a universal payroll tax was not the answer; rather what was needed was a differential tax which would 'increase the cost of labour in services and reduce the cost of labour in manufacturing'.[10] This would thus serve to encourage 'the redeployment of labour'.[11] *The Economist* too, in the editorial already referred to, devoted considerable space to a critical examination of the basis of the selection adopted.[12] This was true also of academic comment at the time.[13]

One matter referred to by Professor Reddaway was certainly true: SET was unpopular and, as embodied in the Selective Employment Payments Bill, it received a hostile hearing in both Houses of Parliament. One member of the Commons claimed that, in his fifteen years' experience in the House, he did not think that a government measure had been so bitterly attacked from all quarters of the House and from behind the Treasury bench in particular.[14] The tax received the predictable parliamentary description of 'silly, ill-thought-out, and nonsensical'[15] but also (in the Lords) a literary comparison that was not altogether favourable. 'To me', said Baroness Asquith of Yarnbury, 'some of [the Government's proposals] have that quality of . . . inspired irrelevance and inconsequence only to be found in the pages of *Alice in Wonderland*. In fact, I myself feel rather like Alice confronted by a Government of Mad Hatters and March Hares and one poor little Dormouse who has been firmly stuffed into the teapot.'[16] Some years later, two economists were to confirm that SET had 'engendered more acrimony and controversy than any other form of taxation imposed in recent years'[17] and *The Economist* also was to refer to the 'odium' which it had attracted.[18]

2. THE PARLIAMENTARY DEBATES

Selective employment tax was provided for in the Finance Bill of 1966 and it was a tax on *all* employers – that is, there was no differential provided in *that* Bill as between employers in one sector and employers in another sector. The key differentials were introduced by the Selective Employment Payments Bill of that year. This provided that those employers who were engaged in manufacturing activities would be entitled to a refund of the tax which they had paid *and* a premium of thirty shillings per male employee over the age of eighteen years (together with lower amounts in respect of women, girls and males under the age of eighteen). There was to be no refund for employers in service industries (including construction) but certain other employers upon whom the tax was intended to have a neutral effect (for example, road hauliers and bus and coach operators) would receive a straight refund. The tax was to be charged on civil employment in both central and local government but the White Paper had previously made it clear that by various means this would be offset or refunded so that effectively there would not be a tax in the public sector.[19] With what was described by one journal as 'political crassness',[20] it was provided that nationalized industries should also receive refunds in respect of all their activities except those (such as railway hotels) which were directly comparable with those in the private sector.[21]

Of the many general and detailed questions that were asked in the parliamentary debates, four of the more important have particular relevance here. These were: (1) What is manufacturing and how is it distinguished from services (including distribution, construction and transport)? (2) How appropriate was the use of the Standard Industrial Classification (which had been adopted by the Bill as the means of classification) as an instrument for determining that question? (3) What criterion of economic or social utility justified the selection of manufacturing for special or favourable treatment? (4) Why were rights of appeal as to entitlement to rebates and/or premiums entrusted for determination by special tribunals and not by the ordinary courts of law? In fact not a great deal of attention was given to this last question, even although it was extremely relevant to the problems posed by the first two questions. The Bill had provided that the existing industrial tribunals which had been established under the Industrial Training Act 1964 but whose principal jurisdiction was provided by the Redundancy Payments Act 1965 should be used to determine disputes between the Department of Employment and Productivity and employers as to entitlement to a refund of SET and/or a premium. The government spokesmen in both Houses justified the choice solely on the grounds that the industrial tribunals were experienced in hearing appeals against levy assessments under the Industrial Training Act as well as other industrial matters and would therefore be 'well qualified' to deal with SET cases.[22] The then Leader of the Opposition, Mr Heath, protested at the choice of administrative tribunals to hear appeals in preference to the courts; unfortunately he did not explain the reasons for his objection though he did add that he thought it 'a little odd' that the tribunals chosen should have been those set up under the Industrial Training Act.[23] It is of course not quite correct to say, as Mr Heath did, that 'there is no power to appeal to the courts' because, although the Bill provided for a full appeal to the industrial tribunals on the question of entitlement to rebates and/or premiums,[24] there was and is, by virtue of the Tribunals and Inquiries Act, machinery for a further right of appeal to the High Court (and hence to the Court of Appeal and to the House of Lords). These further appeal rights are limited to questions of law only and, in so far as the ordinary courts are not entitled to examine questions of fact relating to an employer's activities, the Opposition's criticism retained some point.

Several speakers in the debates on the Bill raised the question of the difficulty of drawing the line between manufacturing and services. One speaker went so far as to claim that it was 'impossible to decide what is manufacturing and what is distribution'.[25] Is it not the case, he said, that a motor car show room anywhere in the country is just part of the manufacturing chain involved in turning rough metal into cars? With this example he undoubtedly placed his finger on one of the central problems which was later to dominate cases coming before the industrial tribunals – at what point does the manufacturing process end and the distributive (or construction or other service) process begin? Another pertinent example was provided by Mr John Peyton:

Let me take the case of a mixer truck which carries ready-mixed concrete and continues the process of manufacture while in transit and right on to the site. Is the driver regarded as in manufacturing or transport? I have not the slightest idea. Whichever side of the line he happens to be dropped on, it will be just luck or bad luck. There cannot be a really well-founded argument that would be the official justification for putting the man on one side or the other. If he is treated as transport, will he be able to claim that he is taking part in a manufacturing operation? One would say that this was disastrously unlikely. Taxation should not be made the field for such processes of lottery.[26]

It was not, however, just a matter of the Government leaving the question of what is and what is not manufacturing to be decided according to the ordinary everyday meaning of the word. A criterion or test was provided by the incorporation of the Standard Industrial Classification into the legislation. The classification had been used for some time by the Ministry of Labour for statistical purposes and its adoption for the economic purposes envisaged by the Bill was widely criticized both in and out of

Parliament. Before these criticisms are set out it will be useful to look briefly at the composition of the classification.

The Standard Industrial Classification (SIC) was divided into twenty-four orders or categories. Each order contained a number of 'minimum list headings' which set out examples of the category concerned. Thus, order III was entitled 'food, drink and tobacco' and contained thirteen minimum list headings (numbered from 211 to 240).[27] One of these headings was 'cocoa, chocolate and sugar confectionery' and it itself contained various paragraphs listing examples: for example, '2. Sugar confectionery – manufacturing boiled sweets, toffee, caramel, marzipan, liquorice, chewing gum and all other types of sweets'. Under the Bill the manufacturing industries were listed in the SIC as orders III to XVI inclusive.[28] Order XVII was titled 'Construction' (no refund), order XVIII concerned the distribution of gas, electricity and water, order XIX was transport and communication (which except for miscellaneous transport services and storage (heading 709) received a refund but no premium), XX distributive trades, including wholesale and retail distribution and dealing in various goods (no refund); XXI insurance, banking and finance, XXII professional and scientific services, XXIII miscellaneous services and XXIV public administration and defence (all no refund). Finally, order I (agriculture, forestry and fishing) and order II (mining and quarrying) qualified for a refund. The various minimum list headings were mutually exclusive in the sense that every industrial activity would, under the legislation, fit within one, but only one, heading. This solved the problem of an activity which might feasibly be classified both as a manufacturing industry qualifying for a refund and premium and as a service industry not qualifying for a refund. The duty of the industrial tribunals was to fit such a case into the more appropriate of the possible alternative headings.[29]

The tribunals were thus guided by a very long list of different types of industrial activity, broadly categorized under the order titles. If a particular activity were deemed by the SIC to be manufacturing, under one of the minimum list headings contained in the manufacturing sector, then that concluded the matter. There was therefore no question of a tribunal having to determine whether bacon curing, for example, was manufacturing, because bacon curing was expressly mentioned in minimum list heading 214 under order III and as such was deemed to be a manufacturing activity. The only difficult cases that would remain would be those which did not fall exactly within one of the named industries. Although it was predictable that there would be a great number of these borderline cases – and there have been – it is undoubtedly the case that there have been infinitely fewer such instances than there would have been if the terms 'manufacturing' and 'service' had been left completely undefined. This acknowledgement apart, however, it should be noted that two objections still remained. The first was whether the SIC provided adequate criteria to enable the tribunals to make the correct classifications in the many cases where gaps remained. The second problem was whether the categories of manufacturing provided by the SIC would in fact promote the kind of growth that the Government saw manufacturing as providing. These two questions were partly inter-related and to some extent answers can be found in the analysis of the tribunals' decisions given under the Act. But there was also the fundamental policy question as to why manufacturing (however defined or classified) was thought to be so beneficial. Government spokesmen in Parliament were surprisingly reticent on this vital question, beyond pointing out that there had been a shortage of skilled labour throughout the whole of the postwar period and that the great bulk of what additional labour there was had gone to the service industries.[30] The White Paper simply said: 'It is upon (the manufacturing) sector that the growth of the economy and its ability to meet competition primarily depend'.[31] The view that the manufacturing industries provide 'the principal source of potential expansion of output and improvement in productivity' has been expressed elsewhere[32] and may be correct. But if economic growth and increased productivity provided the rationale of SET, then it was important that the definition or classifications of manufacturing which were adopted should advance that goal.

It was hardly surprising therefore that during the parliamentary debates the SIC should have been in the firing line. Mr Geoffrey Rhodes, for example, asked what he termed the 'ultimate question': 'is the purpose of this Standard Industrial Classification sufficiently exact to be used for this type of legislation, which has a different purpose?' He answered his own question in the negative because, he said, the 'statistical value of the Standard Industrial Classification is quite unrelated to the purposes of the Bill. Although it is a convenient device, unfortunately it is a device that it also pregnant with anomalies of all kinds.'[33] Mrs Margaret Thatcher made the same point in a more homely way: what the Government is really doing, she said, is using machinery for a purpose for which it was never designed. In her view it was 'as absurd to use the Standard Industrial Classification for the purpose of the selective employment payments as it would be to use a clothes washing machine for washing up crockery'.[34] Doubts were also expressed in the Lords about the utility of manufacturing as compared with services. Baroness Asquith recalled the substantial part which the 'invisibles' have contributed to Britain's balance of trade and asked why tangible goods should be preferred to them. She also highlighted the role which transport, insurance and credit facilities play in the export of manufactured goods and suggested that they too deserved rewards rather than penalties.[35] All these points were in fact made by Mr Rhodes on the second reading of the Bill as follows:

Under the Bill, the criteria which will determine whether an employer pays the tax without refund, is repaid in full or receives a premium in addition depend not on the economic or social merits of the service being performed but on the place which it happens to occupy in the Standard Industrial Classification.

My Hon. Friend makes a distinction between manufacturing, distribution and services, which is a difficult distinction to make in some cases. But even the Standard Industrial Classification formula does not make the distinction in many instances. . . . The Standard Industrial Classification is not an economic or social priority yardstick. The purpose of that classification is as a means of comparability and the tabulation of official statistics in the United Kingdom.

My Hon. Friend the Member for Bilston (Mr Robert Edwards) put a question to the Parliamentary Secretary to the Ministry of Labour on that very point on 13th June. She replied:

'This classification does not attempt to distinguish between industrial groups on the basis of their importance to the national economy'. (Official Report, 13th June, 1966; Vol. 729, c. 220–1). If it does not make that distinction and we use it as the major instrument of classification under this Bill, it cannot carry out effectively the economic and social purposes behind the Selective Employment Tax, because it is not related in its classification to economic priorities.[36]

The Economist also voiced similar doubts as to the use of the SIC in relation to economic and social objectives. SET did not make social sense, it said, in so far as it had not been made to discriminate against overfull employment areas in favour of unemployment areas; nor did it make economic sense in so far as it did not provide reimbursement to export industries as such. (Preferential treatment for export industries was really what the Chancellor wanted, *The Economist* claimed, but he was too scared of GATT to implement it.)[37] Professor Reddaway too, in a paper published in the *London and Cambridge Economic Bulletin* in June 1966,[38] referred to the difficulties involved in the concept of 'establishment' by which the nature of the employer's business was determined in accordance with what the majority of his employees there were doing. It would seem, therefore, if the various critics of the Selective Employment Payments Bill were correct, that the economic objectives of SET were likely to be frustrated because (1) the policy of preferring manufacturing was economically unsound; (2) the SIC did not in any event embody an adequate definition or criterion for determining what was or was not manufacturing; and (3) the industrial tribunals would not be able to determine properly the many borderline cases that the deficiencies of the SIC would reveal. The soundness or otherwise of (1) must be left to the economists and politicians but some assessment of (2) and (3) can now be made in the light of the administration of the Act by the tribunals.

3. THE EARLY DECISIONS OF THE TRIBUNALS

In the 1967 volume of the Industrial Tribunal Reports, which covers the first nine months of disputed cases decided under the Selective Employment Payments Act, there are seventy-three SET decisions recorded. In reading them one quickly sees that the tribunals were forced to grapple very early with the use of the SIC as the instrument for determining whether an industry activity was manufacturing, distributive, etc. and that this, as the principal issue with which the tribunals have been concerned,[39] was not without its difficulties. In the first reported case coming before a tribunal – *J. & R. Darracott Ltd.* v. *Minister of Labour*[40] – the question for decision was whether the preparation and sale of packets of postage stamps fell within either of two possible categories specified in the manufacturing sector of the SIC. These categories were minimum list headings 483 which provided (*inter alia*) for 'All other establishments manufacturing paper goods' and 499(2), the miscellaneous catch-all category, which simply provided 'all other manufacturing industries not elsewhere specified'. If the collecting, cleaning, sorting and packaging of stamps could be said to be either manufacturing 'paper goods' or 'manufacturing' packets of stamps, then a refund of SET and premium would be payable. But if, on the other hand, this activity was regarded as wholesale distribution (heading 810(5) 'Wholesale dealers in paper products'), no refund would be payable. The tribunal, chaired by Sir John Clayden, pointed out that normally the term 'manufacturing' connotes the preparation of some article 'which differs from what existed before'.[41] In the instant case 'nothing new' had been created: the packet was simply a container which would be discarded. The tribunal thus concluded that 'this collection of saleable things into a container is not an operation which can properly be described as manufacture'.

If that seemed a rather easy case, a more difficult one shortly afterwards came before a tribunal chaired by Mr M. Butt, QC. This was the case of *G. Walsham & Sons Ltd.* v. *Minister of Labour*[42] and the tribunal displayed great dexterity in the use of SIC as the means of defining manufacturing. The company carried on the business of weighing, filleting, skinning and heading of fish (including the preserving of the fish on ice or in refrigerators prior to distribution). Under the SIC, this activity would qualify for manufacturing if it came within the heading 'Fish Products – quick freezing and otherwise preserving fish' (214). The alternative distributive heading, for which there would be no refund, was 810(2) which read: 'Wholesale dealers in fish'. Now, a literal reading of the words in 214 'otherwise preserving fish' might well lead to the conclusion that the refrigeration of fish by Walsham & Sons was, *under the SIC*, if not in ordinary parlance, a manufacturing process. But the tribunal in effect held that these words must be interpreted in a manufacturing sense because manufacturing was the 'basic concept lying behind the granting of premium (and rebates) under the Act'. The manufacturing process took place when the activity in question could be said to result 'in some change in the character or description of the commodity'. Thus, in this case, it was necessary to show that a stage had been reached when the commodity had lost its character of fresh fish and had become in character a different thing, namely preserved fish.[43] In short, the categories provided by the SIC were to be interpreted in a manufacturing sense if a rebate were sought. But equally manufacturing was to be defined in terms of the SIC. As another tribunal was later to say: 'Parliament has not said that if you are a manufacturing concern, or if you are a factory, you get your tax back; if you are not you do not. Parliament has adopted ... the Standard Industrial Classification'.[44] Then too, Lord Parker, LCJ, confirmed in one of the first appeals to go from a tribunal to the Divisional Court that SET cases were not to be decided on dictionary meanings, whether of 'manufacturing' or of 'dealers'.[45] But nor were the words of the SIC completely definitive. The correct approach was to interpret the SIC with an appreciation for or understanding of the principal feature of manufacturing as normally understood, namely 'some change in the character or description of the commodity'.

Once it was conceded that this hallmark of manufacturing was relevant to the interpretation of the activities listed in the SIC, it was a short, though important, step to the consideration of other features of manufacturing. Thus, it was recognized that assembly is normally regarded as part of the manufacturing process: 'The manufacture of a motorcar consists of collecting the various parts which go to make up a motorcar and assembling them into a motorcar'.[46] And where the disposal of what is made is done by the manufacturer himself, this will be regarded as part of the manufacturing process, even although, subcontracted, such disposal would be regarded as part of the distributive process.[47] These attributes were in fact those which industry itself recognized and acknowledged. As such, the manufacturing component or sector of any particular industry, as viewed by that industry, might well differ in comparison with that in some other industry. Thus in *Book Centre Ltd.* v. *Minister of Labour*[48] a tribunal chaired by Sir John Clayden held that a company which contracted with book publishers to store and sell and deliver books to retail booksellers was itself engaged in 'publishing' which qualified under heading 489 of the SIC for a rebate and premium. On normal criteria one might have thought that such an activity was distributive but, as the tribunal found, storing and dealing with orders are considered part of the publishing process itself within the industry. In this case it was not material that the activity was being performed by a company other than that which had originally issued the books if only because Book Centre Limited was a co-operative company fully owned by its publisher customers and making no profit itself. It was in that sense merely doing what the latter would otherwise have had to do themselves in order to publish their books.

An apparent contrast is provided by the case of *Shorey Hodgkinson and Cover Ltd.* v. *Minister of Labour*,[49] decided by a tribunal also chaired by Sir John Clayden. A company contracted with various importers of foodstuffs to collect the produces (cereals, dried fruit, rice) from the docks, clean the goods and then repack them into smaller saleable containers for delivery to the retailers, with the latter's labels on the containers. The tribunal held that this activity did not fall within heading 218 (manufacturing foodstuffs) but came under heading 899 (miscellaneous services). The activities of the company, the tribunal said, did not alter the goods in any way. 'The rice comes to it as rice, in large quantities, uncleaned; it leaves them as rice in smaller quantities, cleaned. And so it is with the dried fruits and other materials with which it deals.'[50] Wholesale dealers buy the unsaleable food in the form they do, knowing that they will be able to do the cleaning and packing which makes the food saleable themselves as part of the process of distribution. The company, said the tribunal, was merely providing this service for the wholesalers.

The point is really that cleaning and repacking of imported foodstuffs, being generally part of the distributive trade, could not become manufacturing merely by one of the distributors subcontracting this work to another company. In the publishing trade, on the other hand, storing and delivery of books was not generally part of the distributive trade at all but was regarded by publishers as an integral part of the publishing process. Subcontracting, at least to a co-operative company, did not alter this fundamental industrial organizational fact. The manufacturing and distributive sectors in different industries were thus viewed by the tribunal as industrial facts. There was no reason why these facts should not vary from one industry to the next and in view of the different organizational bases on industries, it would have been surprising if there had been no variation. Each industry would have what was perceptively described by one tribunal as its 'traditional demarcation'.[51] This approach provides the key to the successful implementation by the tribunals of the SIC and

F*

accounts for the remarkable consistency which they have displayed not only in their interpretation of the SIC but also in providing a relevance to the manufacturing component of each individual industry which by itself the SIC did not give. In this way the SIC has been made directly referable to the general policy of the Act's promoters of encouraging manufacturing as an industrial activity. The tribunals, in other words, have taken the worst of the sting from the criticisms made in the parliamentary debates on the bill of the choice of the SIC as the criterion of selection under the Bill. The knowledge of industry and industrial expertise which these tribunals have is undoubtedly a factor in this respect, though it is one which it is easy to exaggerate.

4. THE MANUFACTURING PROCESS – START AND FINISH

Whether any industrial activity is or is not part of the manufacturing process depends partly on who does it. Where an activity which might otherwise be regarded as distributive is performed by the manufacturer himself, it will be easier to view it as merely a continuation of the manufacturing process than if it is carried out by some other party.[52] But there are limits to how far manufacturing can be extended in this way, as Rank Xerox and Fisher-Bendix found to their cost. Rank Xerox manufacture copying machines at a factory in Mitcheldean and hire them to customers. From another establishment at Haydock they provide a repair service to these customers. It was held by a tribunal that this latter activity could not be regarded as part of the manufacturing process begun at Mitcheldean.[53] Fisher-Bendix were also manufacturers (of washing machines) and they too set up separate establishments to look after repairs and other after-sales services. This case eventually went to the Court of Appeal which held that these latter activities were not manufacturing but fell within heading 820(5) (Retail distribution – household goods).[54]

In fact, of greater importance than who does the work is what is the work that is done. And here the approach effectively taken by the tribunals (and later by the courts on appeal) has been to seek two cutting-off points or lines. One is drawn at the beginning of manufacturing as such; all work done prior to that point is then viewed as mere preparation to manufacturing and hence is classified as something else. The other is drawn at the end of the manufacturing process and all work done subsequently is then regarded as distributive or otherwise non-manufacturing. It is vital to appreciate that the tribunals have consistently drawn these lines to accord with the organizational and technical facts of the particular industry under examination. If this point is not recognized and acknowledged, the various decisions of the tribunals in the SET cases will appear arbitrary and difficult, if not impossible, to reconcile. As we shall see, the courts have generally appreciated this fact when reviewing the decisions of the tribunals.

One common activity where the distinction between manufacturing and preparatory work has arisen has been that of designing. The question as to whether the designing of a product was properly part of the process of manufacturing that product first arose in the case of *G. C. Phillips (Coventry) Ltd.* v. *Minister of Labour*[55] where a tribunal held that a company which designed machines and machinery in a wide range of industry for firms which consulted and engaged them for that purpose was not carrying on manufacturing activities but was properly classified as performing a scientific and technical service. A mere five days later a Scottish tribunal was to come to an opposite conclusion in what appeared to be a similar case, that of *Reliant Tool Company* v. *Minister of Labour*.[56] The Reliant Company designed machines and tools which were of a specialized kind and, unlike the Phillips Company, did so only on a contract basis for certain manufacturing companies such as Rolls Royce, Singer, Remington and Massey Ferguson. '*In this case*', the tribunal said, 'the specialised machine tools could not be made without being designed. The designing was a necessary stage in the manufacture.'[57] The Court of Session affirmed the tribunal's decision on appeal and the Lord President in particular made it clear that the tribunal's decision concerned a company which was doing work of a 'specialised' nature, work which 'was not only a *sine qua non* of the construction of the special machine tools required, but was an essential element in their manufacture'.[58] Not satisfied with this reasoning or with the decision, the Minister of Labour took the case to the House of Lords – the first to go there under the Selective Employment Payments Act – but was unsuccessful. The Lords refused to upset the tribunal's findings of fact.[59] Viscount Dilhorne was in no doubt that these findings were peculiar to the activities of the Reliant Tool Company:

While in the majority of cases it may be that the activity of designing is to be regarded as a distinct and separate activity from the making or building of what has been designed, *in particular cases* a finding that it forms part of the process of manufacture may be justified. *In each case it is,* in my view, *a question of fact.*[60]

As such, there was of course no inconsistency with the decision of the tribunal in the *Phillips case* above nor with various other decisions decided by tribunals on the question of designing. One of these was in fact given after the *Reliant Tool case* had been to the Court of Session and the conclusion reached that designing was not in the case before the tribunal a manufacturing activity. The case was *Engineering Designs (Ipswich) Ltd.* v. *Minister of Labour*[61] in which the company prepared diagrams and charts for electrical equipment and computers as well as diagrams and drawings for the manufacture and maintenance of installations. The tribunal, chaired by Sir John Clayden, held that these activities comprised professional and scientific consulting services and were thus not manufacturing. Sir John listed twenty-six decisions of tribunals, almost all of which were unreported, in which it had been held that a designing activity was not in each case part of a manufacturing process.[62] He noted that there was a contrary finding in the *Reliant Tool case* but said: 'In this case we are the tribunal', thus underlining the individuality of each case. To the extent of this individuality, any attempt to evaluate the finding in the *Reliant Tool case* that designing was a component part of manufacturing to a legal principle which could be applied directly to analogous activities in other industries must be regarded as misconceived.[63]

Although each case had been decided on its own facts, within any particular industry similar cases were normally treated alike, unless there were special features entitling a differentiation to be made. To do otherwise would be to offend the basic legal principle of consistency which will be discussed later (in Chapter 7). The need for consistency can of course also exist as between one industry and another but only where they are genuinely 'like' cases. The point can be illustrated by comparing two industries, each of which was concerned with work which might be thought to be of a preparatory nature. In one of these industries the work was held by tribunals to be a part of the manufacturing process which clearly followed it; in the other industry the tribunals consistently held that an activity which was in most respects analogous was not part of the manufacturing work that it preceded. The first of these industries was one where steel sheets were cut into various shapes and sizes; the companies concerned would buy the steel sheets, cut them to order, and then sell them to the manufacturers of various metal products. In a series of cases, it was held by the tribunals (and in one case affirmed on appeal by the Divisional Court[64]) that this was manufacturing and in no sense could the companies be said to be dealing in steel.[65] The second industry was the scrap industry in which various companies collected and sorted scrap materials and sold them to manufacturers who used the materials in the manufacture of their products. A typical example was *I. Goldman Ltd. v. Minister of Labour*[66] where the company bought off-cuts and clippings from clothing factories, sorted them and then sold them to manufacturers of shoddy and other products. The tribunal found that no shoddy manufacturer ever sorts his own rags and that there was accordingly a 'traditional demarcation between the person who sorts the rags or clippings and the person who makes them into shoddy'.[67] Notwithstanding that sorting was an essential part of the preparation of the raw material for the manufacture of shoddy, the tribunal was able to find therefore that the company was operating as a dealer in scrap materials. Other cases are of similar effect.[68] One can thus say that, broadly speaking, the scrap business is not a part of any manufacturing industry whereas those engaged in sorting and cutting steel plates are. Individual cases may still have special characteristics which distinguish them from the industrial norm, as in one scrap case where it was held that a company which purchased cotton wiping rags and then treated them before reselling them as cleaning cloths was engaged in the manufacture of such cloths.[69] Similarly, in another case,[70] a tribunal held that a company which was engaged in the excavation and delivery of minerals from old deposits of industrial waste was not operating as a dealer in industrial waste materials because the sale and delivery part of their activities was ancillary to the extractive part of the business.

The question as to when the manufacturing process ends has

been approached by the tribunals (and by the courts on appeal) in a similar way to the question of when it begins. In the Divisional Court Lord Parker put it this way: 'Just as the question when the manufacturing process begins is a question of fact ... so it seems to me that the question when it ends is likewise one of fact'.[71] The context of his remarks was a case where a company which purchased buttons packaged them as 'button bunches' and then resold them. The company claimed to be making button bunches but the tribunal had held that the company was merely adapting buttons for sale and, as such, was engaged in a distributive and not a manufacturing business. The Divisional Court refused to interfere with this clear finding of fact. Another illustrative case is that of *Hay's International Services London Ltd.* v. *Minister of Labour*[72] in which a company received tractors from the manufacturer and then tested them, replaced missing or defective parts, fitted wheels of a special kind to suit the particular requirements of customers and then packed the tractors in boxes for export. The tribunal held that these were not manufacturing activities because the only person who could be said to be engaged in manufacturing was the one who produced this final article. The Divisional Court, however, on appeal rejected this general proposition and said that 'the time when the manufacturing process ends must be a question of fact' in each case. It may well be, said the court, that the answer in this case was that the process had ended when the tractors left the manufacturer's works but, if so, the tribunal should have found so as a matter of fact. The case was therefore remitted to the tribunal to decide on the facts of the case as to just when manufacturing had ended.[73]

An activity which succeeds or follows manufacturing is not always of a distributive kind. In various cases the work of testing the finished product has been held to be a technical or scientific service.[74] Then in one case it was held that a company which cleaned new Jaguar motor cars for the manufacturer before they were delivered could not be said to be engaged in manufacturing motor cars[75] but was providing what was properly described as a miscellaneous service under the SIC.[76] There have also been several cases where it has been said that the installation of a product falls within heading 500 (Construction) and is not therefore part of the manufacture of the product. The line between manufacture and construction in such cases has been a particularly difficult one to draw. For example, in *Charles Wark & Sons v. Minister of Labour*[77] it was held that a company whose principal work was that of building joinery in schools and housing sites was properly classified as doing construction work while in *Minister of Labour v. Expamet Contracts Ltd.*[78] the fitting of office partitions was held to be a manufacturing activity. In the latter case the assembly of the various bits and pieces that went to make up the partitions was found to be a very skilled job, requiring the making of some adaptations to the original pieces, although it must nevertheless have been a borderline case.[79] A similar finding, however, was reached by the Court of Appeal in the *Prestcold case*[80] where it was held that a company which designed, assembled and installed cooling rooms at abattoirs, butchers' shops, supermarkets, hospitals, etc., was engaged in manufacturing and not construction, notwithstanding that the cooling unit was the only part actually made by the company. Similarly, in *Minister of Labour v. Pirelli General Cable Works Ltd.*[81] the Divisional Court affirmed a decision by a tribunal that a company engaged in installing electric cables was carrying on a manufacturing business. The Court found that the work was of a highly skilled nature and involved the fitting of the oil conductor as a continuous component. It was 'a different conception to a series of prefabricated pipes which merely have to be bolted together by comparatively unskilled labour'.[82] The same kind of point was also made by a tribunal in a case where the assembly of tanks and steel chimneys was held to be a part of the manufacturing process on the grounds that a certain amount of doctoring of the individual parts had to be done on the site and that the parts were then riveted and welded together to make the final product. The tribunal said, however, that its decision might have been different 'if the parts had been bolted together before being despatched, were then unbolted, then delivered to the site, and there merely had to be bolted together again'.[83] Although therefore the line is often difficult to draw in theory, it would seem that in fact it became tolerably plain on the examination of each case. Because the tribunals have always scrutinized these facts very carefully (making use of expert testimony where necessary) and, using their knowledge of industrial processes, have skilfully extracted the details of the activity, the results reached have, generally speaking, been consistently sound. This no doubt accounts for the exceptionally small number of tribunal decisions which have been reversed on the numerous appeals which have gone to the Divisional Court and to the higher courts, an aspect of SET cases which now falls to be considered.

5. APPEALS ON QUESTIONS OF LAW TO THE COURTS

The courts, in reviewing SET decisions, have shown great respect for the industrial tribunals, and for their knowledge and experience in particular.[84] This has led the courts to a practice of not interfering with the decisions of the tribunals except in the most exceptional of cases. This applies especially to the question of whether a particular activity is part of the manufacturing process because, as Lord Parker, LCJ said on more than one occasion and as his successor Lord Widgery has also said subsequently, 'the industrial tribunal, so far as the facts are concerned, is clearly the tribunal to answer that question'.[85] Of course the tribunals must group the industrial facts into the various categories of the SIC but even here, according to Lord Wilberforce,[86] 'Parliament must be taken to have intended to give to [the tribunals'] decisions on classification questions, including as they must consideration of the classificatory language, a strength only slightly less than that attracted by decisions of fact properly so called'. 'Certainly those decisions may be reviewed', he said, 'but the reviewing authority ... should start with the tribunal's findings, as those of a body which has the means and experience of knowing how industry works and is grouped, and see if the decision is one which reasonable men ought not to have come to, or if it is vitiated by some manifest misdirection'.[87] The principle that the reviewing court can only interfere where the decision is an unreasonable one or where there has been some manifest misdirection by the tribunal has been affirmed on many occasions.[88] In the absence of either of the latter vitiating factors, the court will bow to the superior expertise of the tribunal and will not upset the decision merely because it thinks that it might have come to a different conclusion itself.

The courts have also followed the lead given by a tribunal which said in one of the early SET cases that the SIC was never intended to provide statutory definitions.[89] Widgery, LJ, (as he then was) recounted in the Court of Appeal that, in the first SET appeals that went to the courts, there was a tendency to regard the SIC 'as if it were a schedule to the Act, and to be construed accordingly'.[90] However, he continued,

it is now accepted that this is the wrong approach because the Classification does not use the precise language of the Parliamentary draftsman and will not yield its true meaning to the application of rules of construction which assume that such precision was intended. In cases of doubt the primary concern is to give the words a meaning which is consistent with the general scheme of the Act and with the realities of the situation as understood to practical men with knowledge of industry.[91]

Lord Wilberforce (in the Reliant Tool case[92]) was probably the first judge to express this view of the SIC, namely that it was wrong 'to look too closely into its wording for solutions which it is not adapted to provide' and a similar doubt was shortly afterwards taken in both the Divisional Court[93] and the Court of Appeal. Lord Denning, MR, in the latter court, summarized the legal effect of the SIC in this way:

... the Standard Industrial Classification is not drawn up by lawyers for interpretation by lawyers. It is drawn up by economists and statisticians for use by Government departments ... the headings are illustrative, and not exhaustive.[94] They are not to be construed in legalistic fashion, according to the letter, but broadly according to the general intent. ... the task of classification is not a matter of law. It is a matter of fact and degree.[95]

The House of Lords[96] and other judges in the Court of Appeal[97] have subsequently taken the same approach to the interpretation of the SIC and this represents an encouraging jurisprudential advance in this field. Equally praiseworthy is the ready acknowledgement by the courts that the industrial tribunals are best equipped for analysing the organizational realities of industry against the background of the general scheme of the Act and for construing the SIC accordingly.[98] In this respect the Divisional Court has played a most significant role and has demonstrated what is, in my view, the correct appellate role which should be assumed by a court specializing in appeals from administrative tribunals. Doubtless, however, the skill and confidence of the tribunals themselves have been decisive in shaping the willingness of the courts to leave so much to the tribunals.

6. CONCLUSIONS

Despite the glowing picture of the work of the industrial tribunals in their SET jurisdiction which has been painted above, some serious reservations must still be expressed. So far as SET itself is concerned, nothing that the tribunals have been able to do has altered – nor of course could it alter – basic defects in the policy and in the objectives which SET sought to achieve. Certainly SET has been highly successful as a revenue-raising device – even its fiercest opponents acknowledged that much.[99] Professor Reddaway, in his report on the distributive trades also found that in the period 1966–9 there had been a substantial increase in productivity in the distributive sector over and above what would have been expected in the absence of SET. But, as he himself acknowledged and as others were also to point out, it was difficult, if not impossible, to assess quantitatively the effect which the abolition of resale price maintenance had had on this development.[100] In relation to the movement of labour Reddaway thought that the effects of SET 'had been un-sensational, but that they might nevertheless be of importance, particularly in the longer run'. The impact of SET, he said, 'seems to have been largely to *accelerate* the taking of action which would have been worthwhile anyhow – e.g. introduction of more self-service or more self-selection'.[101] On the other hand, in reviewing Reddaway's report, Marris took a more optimistic view and thought that there was at least a likelihood that, if SET had improved productivity, it would also move labour.[102]

Perhaps in response to the hostile criticisms that were made of the policies behind SET, the Government by the Finance Act of 1967 had modified SET by adding an additional premium – called the regional employment premium – which was to be paid to those qualifying for a rebate and premium as manufacturers where the establishment in or from which the employment was carried out was situated wholly within a development area.[103] This provided a partial answer to those who had claimed that selectivity should be based on a social yardstick.[104] But it did not answer the critics who could see no merit – social or economic – in preferring manufacturing to service.[105] Regional employment premiums, it should be noted, only applied to *manufacturing* establishments within development areas and to that extent, although 'the discriminatory purpose of the Selective Employment Payments Act, 1966, [was] not the same as that of s. 26 of the Finance Act 1967', the two enactments did 'operate in perfect harmony' as Lord Simon of Glaisdale was to say.[106] Nevertheless, premiums payable under the Selective Employment Payments Act were later abolished by section 7 of the Local Employment Act 1970, though regional employment premiums were retained.[107] The differentiation between manufacturing and services was thus reduced, though not eliminated. It was reduced even further when after the 1970 General Election the new Conservative Government halved the amount of SET payable. SET was finally phased out completely with the introduction of value added tax (itself equally controversial and also provided with an appellate tribunal system) on 1 April 1973.

In conclusion, when the full picture is re-examined from the point of the industrial tribunals, it must be said that one lingering, but serious, doubt cannot be dispelled. This concerns the claim made by the tribunals, and on their behalf by the High Court, that they knew the structure and workings of industry sufficiently well to be able to slot neatly into the categories provided by the Standard Industrial Classification the multifarious industrial activities which were examined by them. In other words, the edifice has been perched on a foundation of expertise which, if it were found not to be of substance, would bring the whole lot tumbling down. Certainly, by comparison with the High Court, these tribunals are expert bodies but, in conceding that, it must also be said that expertise is in all respects relative. On the other hand, it is true that the tribunals will hear expert testimony on the organization of a particular industry (for example, from a lecturer in technology) if it is available but evidence of this kind is not always given as of course. In jurisdictions of this kind, therefore, there may in fact be a case for commissioning a general fact-finding survey, or a number of such surveys, to which the tribunals would be entitled, and indeed compelled to have regard. There would obviously be difficulties with a proposal of this kind, notably in obtaining results quickly enough from the time the legislation is passed to enable the tribunals to begin work without too much delay. And yet the fact remains that, in relying on the expertise of tribunals to the extent that we do, we are taking an awful chance. Hunches and slight encounters are no substitute for hard specific facts scientifically and objectively determined.

7

Decision-making and tribunals 11: How different are tribunals from courts?

The process of decision making in tribunals, as in the courts, is shaped by the nature of the institutions, including their procedures by which evidence is heard, tested and examined and by which submissions on the relevant laws are made. It is commonly assumed that the composition and characteristics of tribunals differ from those of the ordinary courts and that this results in clear and ascertainable divergences in the form and substance of the decisions that are reached and also in the processes of reasoning by which those decisions are reached. This is a view which encompasses a picture of a court and another one of a tribunal which can readily be contrasted. It will be seen in the final chapter to this book that a glib juxtaposition of court and tribunal raises fundamental difficulties of definition. One problem, however, is that there has been little analysis or examination of tribunal decision-making to enable the necessary comparison between court and tribunal to be made.

1. INSTITUTIONAL AND PROCEDURAL ASPECTS OF TRIBUNAL DECISION-MAKING

Adam Kuper has recently said that there should be brought to the current interest in decision-making processes 'a greater respect for institutional constraints'.[1] Lawyers know a great deal about the processes of application and interpretation of legal material by judges; the second part of this chapter which examines the same subject in relation to tribunals will add little to our knowledge of those processes for we shall see that they scarcely differ in tribunals. But, taking Kuper's point, what lawyers have not studied are the effects which institutional and procedural matters have on the decision-making process, whether in courts or tribunals. There is after all, as one writer put it, an 'inherent unity of search, analysis, and evaluation'.[2] Lawyers have of course provided *descriptive* accounts of our legal institutions and their procedures but they have not undertaken the kind of case-by-case examination (whether on a systematic or on a more piecemeal basis) which would be necessary to tell us very much about the *real* institutional and procedural effects on judicial decision-making. As Bernard Brown has recently pointed out in relation to the operation of law in primitive New Guinea communities, this is surprising because emphasis on individual cases and procedures 'is the very stuff of the common law process and ought to have an attraction for the enquirer trained in law'. When it comes to studies of this kind, he says, lawyers seem to prefer the descriptive approach which 'backs away from the fact that ideal norms are mouthed but "oft-times honoured only in the breach" '.[3]

Abuses of 'ideal' procedural norms occur with monotonous regularity in the courts, particularly the lower courts. Legal literature is full of vivid accounts of judges who were subconsciously biased (by training or background) against particular parties, or who descended into the arena and allowed the dust of the conflict to cloud their eyes. Tribunals are scarcely different, as the following examples (put forward for illustration only) show:

(1) The parties (producers, retailers' organization and departmental officer) appear at a hearing to be held by a tribunal empowered to permit an increase in the maximum price at which the commodity concerned may be sold. At the beginning of what was expected to be a complex and protracted hearing, the tribunal chairman announces to counsel appearing for the parties that the hearing cannot run beyond two days because the room in which it is being held is not available beyond that period.[4] (Recorded in the transcript of a price tribunal hearing, New Zealand.)

(2) The members of a tribunal are paid by the half day. Part of a half day counts for this purpose as a complete half day. A hearing has entered its second day but looks as though it will end

at about 11.30 am. The chairman and one of the tribunal members agree to take it in turns to question the last witness until just beyond the luncheon adjournment so that they will qualify for two full days' payment. (Private address by a tribunal chairman to a legal advice clinic, England.)

(3) A medical appeal tribunal, consisting of a lawyer chairman and two specialist doctors, assesses the degree of permanent disability resulting from an industrial injury. The claimant is examined and medical reports and opinions are considered. The lawyer, after sitting on a number of cases and 'getting the feel' of them, determines that as chairman he should take full responsibility for the conduct of the investigation. Thereafter, he discourages questions from the medical members of the tribunal by leading the questioning on medical matters himself and otherwise exerting a dominant position. (Medical appeal tribunal, England.)

(4) The lawyer chairman of a tribunal concludes that he is able to elicit the necessary facts from the parties better than their representatives can do through the ordinary processes of examination-in-chief and cross-examination of the parties and their witnesses. Where the parties are legally represented he is unable to do much but wait while the lawyers perform the interminable ritual. Frequent signs of impatience are exhibited by him while this occurs. In cases where trade union officials and other non-legally qualified representatives appear (as they often do), he adopts a practice of telling the representative that before the latter takes his witness through his evidence, it is necessary for the tribunal to obtain 'a few formal particulars'. The chairman then proceeds to elicit 'all the necessary facts' from the witness, apologizing at the end of the case to the representative for having, unwittingly, usurped his function. (Industrial tribunal, England.)

(5) The appellant in a supplementary benefit appeal does not appear at the hearing and is not represented. The tribunal, which has read the Supplementary Benefit Commission's presenting officer's written statement of the reasons for rejection of the benefit, asks the officer if he has anything to add. The officer says no or comments shortly that it is not the Commission's policy to allow claims in the circumstances of the present case. The tribunal announces that the appeal is dismissed. (A common

supplementary benefit appeal; not uncommon also in some respects in national insurance local tribunals, England.)

(6) A tribunal chairman is unwilling to adjourn a case, on the grounds that it may be difficult to find another date convenient to all three members of the tribunal. (Industrial tribunal chairman's reason for a general practice of not allowing adjournments once a case is part-heard, England.)

(7) An unrepresented respondent is asked by a tribunal chairman if he wishes to cross-examine the applicant, who has just finished giving his evidence. The respondent, who has made notes throughout the applicant's testimony, begins a long, rambling question. The chairman interrupts and tells him that he will have his chance to give his evidence and to make submissions later. Bewildered, the respondent sits down. (Rent tribunal hearing, England.)[5]

(8) A personnel manager, representing his company in a redundancy case, is told by the tribunal chairman that he must appreciate the difference between making submissions and giving evidence. Bewildered, the manager allows the tribunal chairman to take over the complete conduct of the case. (Industrial tribunal, England.)

(9) As at March 1973 there are 1,229 chairmen who serve on supplementary benefit appeal tribunals.[6] From 1959 to 1973 a man files 132 supplementary benefit appeals. Twenty of these are heard by five different chairmen but the remaining 112 are heard by the same chairman, a clergyman. Feeling that he is not getting a fair deal from this chairman, the claimant writes in 1973: 'I complained to the council on tribunals about this four years ago and I had a brief respite; but now he is back on the job'.[7] (Supplementary benefit tribunal, England.)

(10) During the course of a hearing for unemployment benefit the local tribunal chairman comments that the tribunal is 'the guardian of the national insurance fund, which is in the red'. (National insurance tribunal, England.)[8]

These examples are not put forward as illustrations of procedural unfairness (though they may be that also) but rather to point out the fragile nature of the procedures by which tribunals obtain the material upon which their decisions as to the facts of cases must be based. It will be seen that the question of representation, or lack of it, figures prominently in a number of the instances given. It will be obvious that, when it comes to the determination of questions of law, the presence of a lawyer may be a vital element in the process. As to this, the point is often made, by industrial tribunal chairmen in particular, that many lawyers appearing before them do not know the jurisdiction and in some cases have not even read the statute that they are arguing about. Tales are told (no doubt true) of barristers who seek a ten minute delay to the start of the hearing so that they can read the brief. On the other hand the Chief National Insurance Commissioner, addressing a conference held by the Institute of Judicial Administration in Birmingham in 1971, said that he welcomed the assistance which counsel gave. It would seem, therefore, that the quality of representation is an important factor affecting the decision-making process. Whatever doubts may be felt generally about lack of representation in tribunal cases, from an observation of tribunal hearings one cannot but help conclude that the applicant or appellant without representation who is led through his evidence by an experienced and patient chairman will be better off than one with an incompetent or unprepared lawyer.

The examples above also provide instances of tribunal members whose character or personality will obviously have an effect on the decision-making process. Considerable attention has been given in the last few years to this question in relation to the judiciary.[9] Claire Palley has, for example, listed the background variables which determine judicial behaviour, under four main heads: personal background (class, family, education, professional traning, age, etc.) attitudes, small group relationships (between one judge and another, court officials, counsel, litigants) and the judge's conception of his role.[10] This is a good analysis which can usefully be applied to special tribunals. As we have seen, tribunals typically will have a lawyer chairman assisted by people who may have some special experience in the subject matter of the jurisdiction. (The very fact of a composite body is itself an important variable. A judge sitting alone may act differently from one sitting with assessors, or even from one sitting as a bench of three judges.) We do not know very much about the kind of people who are appointed to tribunals or their attitudes or their conception of their role.[11] But two articles published recently by Cavenagh and Newton point the way towards the research that needs to be done.[12] Not all tribunal chairmen are lawyers but it is probable that the majority act in a part-time

capacity and are barristers or solicitors. (In most tribunal jurisdictions the chairman *must* be a lawyer; in others lawyers are
preferred.[13]) National Insurance Commissioners are always full-
time appointments and are drawn from the ranks of senior
counsel. The same is true of the president of the Transport
Tribunal. There are a number of full-time industrial tribunal
chairmen; interestingly, most of those sitting in south-east
England have at some stage in their careers held office as colonial
judges in Africa.[14] The 'lay' members of tribunals vary
tremendously in background and experience.[15] The relationship
between them and the lawyer chairman is an interesting one.
Often at hearings they appear to be completely passive – as, for
instance, in one case where the chairman (a QC) did not bother
to consult with his brethren at the end of the hearing of the
evidence and submissions before dismissing the claim on a legal
ground. There are other instances, however, where lawyer chairmen have paid warm tribute to the part played by the laymen.
There is generally a power of dissent in tribunal cases but,
judging from the very small number of cases where dissents are
recorded, there would appear to be some pressures operating
towards the reaching of a common tribunal point of view. The
need for consensus would seem to be particularly strong in rent
tribunals and in rent assessment committees where a process of
taking the median appears to operate as a means of presenting a
unified decision as to the rent which should be payable.[16]

2. LEGAL REASONING AND TRIBUNAL DECISION-MAKING

There is a considerable body of literature on the subject of legal
reasoning as it exists in the ordinary courts. Legal reasoning
in tribunal jurisdictions has, by comparison, received little
systematic attention.[17] This is unfortunate both because it has led
to the perpetration of certain exaggerated asssumptions as to
'tribunal flexibility' and 'freedom from technicality' in decision-
making and because a knowledge of reasoning processes in
tribunal jurisdictions may reveal much about general principles
of legal reasoning as they apply in all jurisdictions, whether court
or tribunal. For this latter reason the examination of formal
tribunal decision-making which follows will be set in the wider
context of judicial decision-making generally.

There is some cause to believe that English judges are beginning to effect radical changes in their processes of reasoning and of interpretation and development of laws. A return to the golden age of the common law, when judges did not hesitate always to break new ground and to adapt laws to meet changing social and other conditions may not exactly be just around the corner but there are encouraging signs of improvement. It is possible, for example, to point to a radical loosening in recent years of the *formal*[18] rules of precedent, both in the House of Lords[19] and in the Court of Appeal.[20] Perhaps of greater significance, English judges are now showing a greater willingness to talk more openly of policy considerations underlying legal development. Lord Denning, in his influential position as Master of the Rolls, has led the way. Emboldened by earlier successes,[21] he has recently put the role of the English judge on a broader plane when, in *Dutton* v. *Bognor Regis UDC*,[22] he said:

In previous times, when faced with a new problem, the judges have not openly asked themselves the question: what is the best policy for the law to adopt? But the question has always been there in the background. It has been concealed behind such questions as : Was the defendant under any duty to the plaintiff? Was the relationship between them sufficiently proximate? Was the injury direct or indirect? Was it foreseeable, or not? Was it too remote? And so forth.

Nowadays we direct ourselves to considerations of policy.[23]

While one Lord Denning does not make a judicial summer, it is clear that many other judges are also increasingly making a more conscious attempt to relate their legal determinations to social problems and to the considerations relevant to those problems. The ascertainment and application of legislative objective figures more prominently in the interpretation of statutes[24] and precedents are more readily overthrown. Thus, the House of Lords recently disregarded one of its earlier decisions on the ground that it had been 'rendered obsolete by changes in physical and social conditions' and had become 'an incumbrance impeding the proper development of the law'.[25]

The idea that English judges may overtly consider policy alternatives in developing the law to meet new conditions, or may give a liberal interpretation to statutes in order to prevent a frustration of legislative objective, runs counter to what has consistently been said during the course of this century by the

judges themselves.[26] Certainly, since the last war, English judges
have constantly repeated the view that their law-making function
is considerably restricted and that, by undertaking too active a
role, they risk usurping parliamentary and governmental power.
Thus, Lord Evershed, Lord Denning's predecessor as Master of
the Rolls, writing in the *Columbia Law Review* in 1961, was
clearly happy to concede Professor K. C. Davis's comment in the
same journal that 'English judges strive to avoid consideration of
the policy aspects of the issues they decide and ... in strikingly
large degree they succeed'.[27] Any other course, Lord Evershed
said, would be tantamount to disregarding 'the essential meaning
of accepted parliamentary supremacy in twentieth-century demo-
cratic England'.[28] The correct position, as it was and ought to
be, had been stated by Lord Devlin, he thought, when the latter
had addressed the Bentham Society in 1956: 'In the old days the
judges had to stretch the law to meet a new situation which
otherwise would have been unregulated. Now that Parliament is
willing to exert itself judges are entitled, and indeed bound, to say
that it is for Parliament and not for them to make new law'.[29] In
this respect, there is the example of the *Suisse Atlantique* case
where Lord Reid said of standard-form contracts: 'This is a
complex problem which immediately affects millions of people
and it appears to me that its solution should be left to
Parliament'.[30] This is an attitude which is well known to English
lawyers and which scarcely needs elaboration here. It is based on
a recognition by the judges of the sovereignty of Parliament and
also assumes a high degree of efficiency in the legislative
machinery.[31] But parliamentary time has of course come increasingly under pressure; financial and economic measures inevitably
take precedence in a crowded legislative timetable and legal
reform tends to take a back seat. This in turn has added weight to
the kind of criticisms of English judges exemplified by the
remarks of Professor Davis quoted above. It may also help to
explain why the courts here are widely seen as being cautious and
inflexible in the extreme; and why legislators have been so ready
to turn to special tribunals as providing some hope of
improvement.

In this last respect one particular point that is often made in
favour of tribunals, as against the courts, is that they are not
bound by their own precedents. As we have seen, this is not
always true because, where there is a tribunal hierarchy, the

decisions of the higher tribunal will bind lower tribunals. Thus, local national insurance tribunals must apply the case law of the National Insurance Commissioners[82] and goods services licensing authorities are bound by precedents of the Transport Tribunal.[33] On the other hand tribunal hierarchies differ from those in the judicial system in that they are the exception rather than the rule; even the additional fact that tribunals will be bound to apply rulings given by the High Court on review or appeal does not of itself destroy the general point. In many jurisdictions there *is* a general body of tribunal precedents which effectively provides the legal materials by which cases are determined, though in theory none of these precedents is necessarily determinative of any case. The question that now requires examination is whether the theory matches the reality.

At least one writer, taking the point that tribunals are not bound to follow their own precedent decisions and relying principally on cases concerning the ad hoc adoption of policy rules by administrators,[34] draws the conclusion that tribunals are limited in the extent to which they can apply precedents and are not legally entitled to attain consistency 'by following precedents or general rules'.[35] Too much notice should not, however, be taken of declarations by tribunals that they are not bound by precedent. Such statements can be found in most, if not all, tribunal jurisdictions where selected decisions are published.[36] It is true that tribunals usually do start with every good intention; not only do they endeavour to avoid a *formal* doctrine of binding precedent but also they seek to preserve intact their freedom of future action by not building up too comprehensive a system of case-law. Flexibility is the ideal. Hence the early decisions of a tribunal in the first years of its operation tend to abound with such well-meaning phrases as 'we are not bound by precedent', 'each case must be decided upon its own facts' and 'we do not intend by this decision to lay down any general principle'. Inevitably, however, general principles do emerge, for the very good reason that an each-case-on-its-own-facts (or merits) approach leads before very long to an inconsistency problem. Demands too for predictability of decision, both from lawyers and from those engaged in the business or industry affected by the tribunal's decisions, contribute to the eventual establishment of an informal de facto system of precedent. The formal power to depart from earlier decisions remains and the 'general principles' laid down in the tribunal's case law will often have sufficient built-in exceptions and reservations to preserve a reasonable degree of flexibility. But the essential differences in practice from, say, the House of Lords or the Court of Appeal (where the hierarchical effects are less than in lower courts) are not as marked as one might think. In Chapter 3 it was seen how the industrial tribunals through their published case-law were inevitably drawn towards a practice of applying precedent decisions while at the same time pronouncing a formal theory that denied any binding characteristics to those precedents. By way of comparison it will be useful to undertake a brief examination of the development of case-law in the road transport licensing jurisdictions.

The Transport Tribunal is, by tribunal standards, of some antiquity. It was first set up as long ago as 1933. (Its name at that time was the Road and Rail Traffic Appeal Tribunal, its new title being given in 1951.) The principal function of the Tribunal was to hear appeals from decisions given by the various regional licensing authorities for goods service vehicles. In issuing public carriers' licences, the licensing authorities (and on appeal the Tribunal) had been given a wide discretion.[37] There were certain matters to which they had to have regard (such as 'the previous conduct of the applicant in the capacity of a carrier of goods', 'the need for providing for occasions when vehicles are withdrawn from service for overhaul or repair' and so on) but their principal instruction was simply to 'have regard primarily to the interests of the public generally'. No further statutory indication of what constituted the public interest was provided and the way was therefore open to the adoption of a flexible approach which would be able to embrace different temporal and locational circumstances. It was not surprising therefore that the familiar phrases 'each case depends on its own facts'[38] and 'no general question of principle is decided in this case'[39] should be common to the pages of the 'Traffic Cases' Reports in the first few years of the Tribunal's operation. The caution of the Tribunal in this respect is amusingly related by its first chairman, Mr Rowland Harker, KC, in the 1936 case of *G.W. & L.M.S. Rlys. v. Smart*:[40]

We were much interested to hear Mr Fox-Andrew's submission that it was no part of our function to lay down a principle in advance and that we should not decide any principle unless it was necessary for the decision of a particular case. This agrees with the views we ourselves have held since we started to function. In a number of cases we have been tempted by counsel to express an opinion upon some point which it was not necessary for us to decide for the purpose of our arriving at our decision in those cases. According to the headnotes of the *Traffic Cases* there is only one case in which we have fallen to such temptation, and in that case the learned counsel we were unable to resist was Mr Fox-Andrews.

'Each case must depend upon its own facts', the Tribunal concluded. 'When considering whether suitable transport facilities exist and whether they are or would be in excess of requirements, it is our view that this should be done in relation to current industrial and commercial conditions.'[41]

And yet there is little doubt that this was an overstatement of what the Tribunal was doing, even during this early period. General principles *were* being established, though as guidelines only. The perennial problem of uniformity had of course raised its head and the Tribunal felt constrained to give a lead to the regional licensing authorities. The best-known of these principles was that laid down in Enston's case, namely that an applicant for a public carrier's licence must show that the work which potential customers were willing to give him if he were granted a licence could not for any reason be done by other hauliers (road or rail) already established in business.[42] Another important principle was the 'Hawker formula', laid down in *H. W. Hawker Ltd.* v. *G. W. & L.N.E. Rlys.*[43] in 1935, viz, that in arriving at the amount of additional tonnage to which a licensee applicant was entitled, the tonnage of goods carried per ton of unladen weight of the vehicles already in use should be taken into consideration. Indeed, not only were such principles established by the Tribunal, but complaints were later to be made that their subsequent application had led to legalism and rigidity in the system. Two committees which were set up to investigate passenger and goods services licensing both made this criticism. The Geddes Committee, which reported on *Carriers' Licensing* in 1965, examined briefly the early principles laid down by the Tribunal and concluded that licensing authorities 'had to consult precedents before giving decisions'.[44] The Thesiger Committee, which had reported on *Passenger Services Licensing* in 1953, had made a similar criticism of the tribunal system operating in the goods services' jurisdiction. The decisions of the Tribunal, the Committee said, had 'become precedents which experience has shown ... it can break away from only with the greatest difficulty if at all'.[45] Enston's case was cited as the principal culprit.[46] Some writers have also noted Devlin, LJ's comments in the Court of Appeal in 1962 in the Merchandise Transport case:

> In my opinion a series of reasoned judgments such as the Tribunal gives is bound to disclose the general principles upon which it proceeds. I think that that is not only inevitable but also desirable. It makes for uniformity of treatment and it is helpful to the industry and to its advisers to know in a general way how particular classes of applications are likely to be treated. But the Tribunal may not in my opinion make rules which prevent or excuse either itself or the licensing authorities from examining each case on its merits. ...
> ... a tribunal must not pursue consistency at the expense of the merits of individual cases. If the discretion is to be narrowed, that must be done by statute; the tribunal has no power to give its decisions the force of statute.[47]

This does not mean, however, that the Transport Tribunal had in fact reached the point where it was hidebound by precedent and had lost all flexibility. On the contrary the correct conclusion is that the Transport Tribunal had laid down principles of general application but had hesitated to inhibit the statutory discretion conferred on it and on the licensing authorities by developing these into a series of specific legal rules, as the criticisms of Geddes, Thesiger and others suggest. Certainly, these principles had an important precedential effect but, whenever the Tribunal did express its findings in terms of principle, it always stressed the need for flexibility in any subsequent application and accordingly always left room for later development. Thus, in the year after the statement of the 'Hawker formula', the Tribunal warned that, although the formula was 'a useful guide to be applied in appropriate cases', regard should always be had to exceptional factors – for example, the carrying capacity of the vehicle[48] – which might affect its application.[49] The same caution was provided in the case of the Enston principle.[50] Exceptions to the principle were also readily formulated as the need arose: it was held not to apply to an applicant who intended to provide a new type of service, such as a regular daily service,[51] nor to railway company applicants (because of their statutory obligations in relation to collection and delivery[52]), nor to an applicant who could show that he could operate a more efficient service than established hauliers.[53] Finally, even the apparently stern comments of Devlin, LJ, lose much of their force when it is realized that neither he nor the other members of the Court of Appeal found that the allegations of allowing its precedents to preclude the Tribunal from investigating the merits of each case were true. On the contrary, as the Tribunal itself pointed out a year earlier,[54] the Court of Appeal expressly held that the Tribunal had not precluded itself by any of its rulings, from considering the merits of the case before it.[55]

3. LEGAL PRINCIPLES AND CONSISTENCY IN DECISION-MAKING

The conclusion reached above that the Transport Tribunal and, it is suggested, other tribunals[56] have laid down general principles for application in subsequent cases while stopping short of developing these into hard-and-fast legal rules needs some further explanation. The distinction between principles and rules has in recent years been given new emphasis by the writings of Professor Ronald Dworkin who saw rules (where they are applicable) as necessitating decisions in conformity with them; principles, on the other hand, had merely a 'dimension of weight or importance' which might lead a judge to a particular decision but which did not necessarily compel him to reach it.[57] The common law abounds with principles, which Dworkin saw as being based on requirements of 'justice or fairness or some other dimension of morality'. He discussed in particular the principle that no man should profit from his own wrong and showed how this explains and is reflected in the legal rule laid down in *Riggs* v. *Palmer*[58] that a murderer cannot inherit under the will of his victim. It can be added that there are many other legal rules in the common law which reflect this principle also.[59] But, more significantly from the point of view of this work, is the fact that that same principle was also applied by the Transport Tribunal, though not *eo nomine*, in its various formulations of the Enston principle. For example, in *L.M.S. Rly.* v *Motor Carriers (Liverpool) Ltd.*,[60] in restating the principle, the Tribunal said that the onus was on the applicant to prove that he had not 'wrongfully abstracted' traffic from the objectors (existing carriers). The point seems to be further borne out by the fact that each of the exceptions to the

Enston principle recognized by the Tribunal – the establishment of a new type of service (Smith), a more efficient service (Edwards) and railway companies with statutory obligations of collection and delivery (Anderson) – contains no element of the applicant's profiting (through the grant of a licence) from his wrongful taking of another's business. From this example in particular, the similarities of legal reasoning in the courts and in tribunals become more apparent. The same point seems to be valid also in relation to decision-making in other forums. In his recent work referred to on page 166 Adam Kuper says of African tribal councils: '. . . when a council deals with matters of law or ritual the members refer explicitly to general principles, recognized by everybody as binding, and, often, to precedents which may have the force of law'.[61]

If the conclusion seems inevitable that theoretical differences between the operation of precedent in courts and in tribunals have little practical significance, the explanation is to be found in what may be described as the first principle of justice – the basic premise upon which the whole of our law and of our legal system rests – namely the requirement of consistency, uniformity and equal treatment. This is in fact more than just a legal principle for it also constitutes an ideal in everyday life. We treat our children equally, social justice is thought to mean equal opportunities for all, democracy itself embodies it in the form of one man one vote. In this respect decision-making by courts and tribunals bears strong resemblances to other kinds of decision-making.[62] Consistency and equal treatment are just as necessary in the field of administration as they are in that of adjudication. Consistency in administration has its own special problems and justifications[63] but the result will be much the same. Hence the practice adopted in government departments of formulating administrative principles and rules to guide officials in the exercise of their discretionary powers – ministerial circulars to local authorities on planning matters, the Department of Health and Social Security's social security codes, etc. It is true that these rules have no legal status and can be changed at will but, while they remain operative, they are enforced in much the same way as legal rules are by courts and tribunals.[64]

It does not, however, follow from the conclusion that tribunals will tend to follow precedents just as readily as courts (and other bodies) that there are consequently no differences in the processes

G

of decision-making in courts and in tribunals. We have seen, for example, in an earlier chapter, that the High Court, the Court of Appeal and the House of Lords have accepted that the industrial tribunals have been able to give interpretations to the Standard Industrial Classification that the courts were not equipped to give. These were cases, it will be recalled, where classification decisions required an expert knowledge of the organization of industry which judges did not possess. Of course, once such a decision had been given by an industrial tribunal in a particular type of case, the forces of precedent would then tend to operate in the usual way. Nevertheless, the claim by a tribunal to special experience or knowledge may lead it into paths which a body of a more general jurisdiction would decline to enter. When making this point, however, one must return to a proposition made in the following chapter that courts exist (for example, the Commercial Court, Restrictive Practices Court and the National Industrial Relations Court) which will not hesitate to take a similar course.

8

Decision-making III:
The role of administrative
tribunals

No one still doubts the importance of administrative tribunals.
The number of tribunals, and their case load, listed in the Annual
Reports of the Council on Tribunals (including those referred to
in Chapter 1) grows almost year by year. And this is only a
part of the picture, for there are a great number of tribunals
which do not come under the supervision of the Council on
Tribunals. It is one of the unfortunate effects of the Tribunals
and Inquiries Act 1958,[1] which established the Council, that it
should have created a somewhat artificial division between
those tribunals which were specified as coming within the terms of
the Act and under the general supervision of the Council and
those tribunals which were not. Power was given in the Act for
new tribunals to be added to those initially listed but nowhere were
there any criteria laid down as to how a decision-making agency
was to qualify for inclusion. This means, among many other
things, that there is an obvious problem about trying to measure
the scale on which tribunals operate simply because no one has
provided a satisfactory definition of what a tribunal is. For
example, can the Monopolies Commission, the Restrictive
Practices Court, the Supplementary Benefits Commission, the
Alkali Inspectorate, various ad hoc commissions and committees
of inquiry and so-called domestic and house tribunals (none of
which is the concern of the Council of Tribunals) be said to be
tribunals? Could the Prices and Incomes Board? Or the
Consumer Council?[2] Will the new Price Commission and Pay
Board deserve the appellation? Perhaps it doesn't matter. But,
having regard to the particular mould into which Tribunals and
Inquiries Act tribunals have tended to be cast, perhaps it *is*

important to have some criteria by which different kinds of agencies can be classified and by which their functional and procedural purposes and characteristics can be assessed. Further, irrespective of the problems of definition, any really useful assessment and appraisal of the role which tribunals play in the modern State must surely take account of all forms of independent and semi-independent decision-making agencies, both as they operate in the judicial system as we normally understand it *and* in the administration of government.

The dichtomy just stated, between the judicial system and the administration of government, raises a fundamental functional matter. How is the function of tribunals best viewed? As another form of court, exercising powers and following procedures roughly categorized as 'judicial'?[3] Or as part of the machinery of administration? The Franks Committee, whose report in 1957 entitled *Administrative Tribunals and Enquiries*[4] has dominated thinking about tribunals in the last sixteen years, had no doubts at all on this point :

Tribunals are not ordinary courts, but neither are they appendages of Government Departments. Much of the official evidence, including that of the Joint Permanent Secretary to the Treasury, appeared to reflect the view that tribunals should properly be regarded as part of the machinery of administration, for which the Government must retain a close and continuing responsibility. Thus, for example, tribunals in the social service field would be regarded as adjuncts to the administration of the services themselves. We do not accept this view. We consider that tribunals should properly be regarded as machinery provided by Parliament for adjudication rather than as part of the machinery for administration. The essential point is that in all these cases Parliament has deliberately provided for a decision outside and independent of the Department concerned, either at first instance (for example in the case of Rent Tribunals and the Licensing Authorities for Public Service and Goods Vehicles) or on appeal from a decision of a Minister or of an official in a special statutory position (for example a valuation officer or an insurance officer). Although the relevant statutes do not in all cases expressly enact that tribunals are to consist entirely of persons outside the Government service, the use of the term 'tribunal' in legislation undoubtedly bears this connotation, and the intention of Parliament to provide for the independence of tribunals is clear and unmistakeable.[5]

It is argued, however, that this view is an unduly restrictive one which is potentially harmful to the future development of tribunals. There certainly are many tribunals which can properly be regarded as 'machinery provided by Parliament for adjudication'. Most of the tribunals which are listed by the Tribunals and Inquiries Act can reasonably be so described. But not all of them. It is difficult, for example, to describe the Transport Tribunal as an adjudicating body, at least in functional terms, even although it admittedly possesses many of the procedural trappings normally associated with courts. More than that, it is referred to in its enabling legislation as a 'court of record'; but in relation to the powers it possesses and to the sorts of considerations and criteria to which it has regard in making decisions it resembles many administrative bodies much more closely. The new Civil Aviation Authority is even less like the conventional judicial-type tribunal that Franks typified and in many ways represents an important development in the gradual evolution of independent or partly independent agencies exercising wide functions and powers along the lines of the American Federal regulatory agencies. And yet the Civil Aviation Authority has been brought into the list of tribunals now covered by the Tribunals and Inquiries Act.

Abel-Smith and Stevens, in their work *In Search of Justice*,[6] distinguish between what they call court-substitute tribunals and policy-oriented tribunals and this may be a useful distinction to use as a starting point for discussion on the ambit and scope of tribunals. Some of the features of each broad type of tribunal may be quite different; according to the respective role that is played, this may be entirely necessary and desirable. There is a tendency, for example, to provide the interested minister with the power to issue general directions, either as to procedure or as to substance, to the policy-oriented tribunals. This is true of the Transport Tribunal and transport licensing authorities, it is true of the Civil Aviation Authority and it is also true of the rent scrutiny boards which were established by the Housing Finance Act 1972. The Consumer Protection Advisory Committee and the reconstituted Monopolies and Mergers Commission, both established by the Fair Trading Act 1973, are also subject to ministerial direction on matters of procedure. These powers of intervention raise fundamental questions about the claim of such agencies to be regarded as independent decision-making bodies, a matter which will be discussed more fully below. The same might be said also of those agencies whose powers are recommendatory only and where the final decision is taken by the minister. Planning inspectors conduct public inquiries, listen to evidence, find facts and make policy recommendations, all without apparent interference from the minister, and yet at the end of the day it is the minister who decides whether the application for planning permission should be granted. The Monopolies Commission is scarcely in any better position from this point of view. Can it really be said, therefore, that policy-oriented tribunals are in essence in any different position from the civil servants who work in the minister's department? Are they true tribunals?

These questions raise again the problem of definition. But try as one might, no satisfactory definition can be given. There are too many exceptions to the model which is postulated. To the student of this subject it seems that there is an infinite variety of tribunals, whether looked at from a functional, operational or constitutional point of view. The search for the generic leads always to the fading of the concept into obscurity and ambiguity. Even the traditional distinction that is drawn between the ordinary courts and tribunals, and the differences in their characteristics, is fraught with the greatest difficulty. This is not to say, however, that no such distinction can be validly and usefully drawn, only that the task is not an easy one. The best approach may be to adopt Professor Putnam's 'cluster concepts'[7] and attempt to examine the characteristics or properties which tribunals commonly and collectively exhibit. If this approach is taken, and if the word 'tribunal' is transposed for the word 'man' in Putnam's original treatise, the tribunal picture looks something like this:

Suppose one makes a list of the attributes P_1, P_2 ... that go to make up a normal tribunal. One can raise successively the questions 'Could there be a tribunal without P_1?' 'Could there be a tribunal without P_2?' and so on. The answer in each case might be 'Yes', and yet it seems absurd that the word 'tribunal' has no meaning at all ... the meaning in such a case is given by a cluster of properties. To abandon a large number of these properties, or what is tantamount to the same thing, to radically change the extension of the term 'tribunal', would be felt as an arbitrary change in its meaning. On the other hand, if most of the properties in the cluster are present in any single case, then under suitable circumstances we should be inclined to say that what we had to deal with was a tribunal.

What are the properties of tribunals? The Franks Report thought that there were three 'basic characteristics: openness, fairness and impartiality',[8] The trouble with these qualities is that they are so vague as to be virtually meaningless, at least without being transposed into much more explicit features. Certainly, such features can be gleaned from the Franks Report itself. Thus, the Committee said that openness includes the promulgation of reasoned decisions and, more important, the holding of hearings in public.[9] It also thought that impartiality must mean a secured independence from departmental control or influence – for example, by vesting in the Lord Chancellor the power to appoint tribunal chairmen and in the proposed Council on Tribunals a similar power to appoint other members, thus replacing the practice of ministerial appointment.[10] The Council on Tribunals itself has subsequently made it plain, through its consultative powers in relation to the drafting of procedural rules for tribunals, just what it regards as essential features of a tribunal; and the Tribunals and Inquiries Act, which established the Council, has added further to the picture.

It is a major submission in this book that the tribunal picture provided by the Franks Committee and its creations – the Tribunals and Inquiries Act and the Council on Tribunals – is unduly restrictive and serves to exclude certain tribunals which have an indistinguishable constitutional and administrative purpose from *some* of those which are included. Before developing this point, however, it will be necessary to determine the Franks tribunal properties. It is suggested that they can be listed as follows:

(1) Subject only to any existing appeal or review powers existing in another tribunal or court, a tribunal has legal authority to make determinations or decisions which are final and which are thus legally enforceable;

(2) A tribunal is independent of any minister of the crown or department or other agency. Crucially, this independence pertains to the tribunal's decision-making processes, which it is thought must be free (and be seen to be free) from governmental direction or influence. Independence is also affected by such matters as appointment of tribunal personnel, their security of tenure, provision of staff (e.g. tribunal clerk) and location of hearing rooms;[11]

(3) A tribunal holds a public hearing which may be loosely characterized as judicial. That is to say, persons affected have the right to appear, either in person or through representatives (whether lawyers or not), and to submit evidence, cross-examine opposing witnesses and make submissions on the case. Typically, such hearings are relatively informal and in this sense compare better with county or magistrates' courts than they do with the High Court. They are not preceded by interlocutory proceedings of any complexity but at most by the filing of a simple application or appeal form followed sometimes by a short answer or response. Nor are the legal rules of evidence applicable; the tribunal will be free to receive whatever material or information it wishes, subject only to questions of relevance and requirements of disclosure;[12]

(4) Typically, a tribunal will be required to give reasons if requested to do so on or before notification of the decision;[13]

(5) A tribunal will possess expertise in the subject matter with which it is dealing or at least will be operating in a specialized or comparatively specialized jurisdiction. Some members of the tribunal may have been chosen for their expertise or experience in that subject matter; the chairman will normally, however, be a lawyer.

(6) An appeal on questions of law will lie to the High Court from the tribunal's decision.[14]

Taken collectively, it is obvious that very few, if any, tribunals possess all these features. This is true even of those tribunals which have been listed in the Tribunals and Inquiries Act, as the following examples will show. Transport licensing tribunals and the Civil Aviation Authority are subject to ministerial direction. Supplementary benefit appeal tribunals, mental health review tribunals and industrial tribunals hearing training levy appeals all sit in private; others have power to sit in private in special circumstances – for example, national insurance tribunals. Mental health review tribunals can even hear evidence in the applicant's absence where it is thought that the disclosure of medical evidence in his presence would be likely to affect adversely his health or other interests. Before the Immigration Act 1971 was passed, a specially constituted immigration appeal tribunal could also conduct unilateral proceedings of this kind where the Home Secretary had certified that matters of national security were at issue.[15] The legal rules of evidence are applicable in proceedings before the Lands Tribunal. Other tribunals, notably national insurance and to some extent industrial tribunals, have developed evidential rules and practices of their own which are referable to the ordinary legal rules of evidence; thus, the general principle very clearly established by the National Insurance Commissioners is that, while evidence can and will be heard which would not be admissible in a court of law, such evidence should be treated with caution and given less weight. In the national insurance jurisdictions also, use has been made of extra-hearing investigatory procedures, ranging from seeking information informally by letter from witnesses unable or unwilling to attend the hearing to employing local referees to conduct a formal examination of such witnesses. On-the-spot examinations and inspections are conducted regularly by rent tribunals, rent assessment committees and agricultural tribunals of different kinds, thus reducing considerably the importance of the hearing as the instrument of investigation. Appeals on law from the Transport Tribunal go directly to the Court of Appeal, and not as with other Tribunals and Inquiries Act tribunals to the Divisional Court. There is no direct appeal at all to any court from decisions of the National Insurance Commissioners and of the rent tribunals, though in each case judicial review by the Divisional Court through the appropriate prerogative order may have the same effect. Mental health review tribunals need not give reasons, if requested, if they consider that it would be undesirable to do so having regard to the interest of the patient or for other special reasons.

The essential point, however, is that such exceptions and irregularities do not necessarily destroy the claim of any of the tribunals mentioned to be properly described as a tribunal and to be classified for that purpose, for example, in any discussion relating to the allocation of decision-making powers of a certain kind. It may be that some irregularities will be sufficiently serious to warrant a denial of the tribunal classification. A lack of independence from governmental influence may be thought to be a disqualifying factor. Hence, it has been said of the transport licensing authorities that, because they are subject to ministerial direction, they are 'really only emanations of the Minister or ways of organising the department's work' and are 'not quite tribunals'.[16] Caution must be exercised here for ministerial directions have only been issued twice (in 1931) and the realities are that these licensing bodies are in fact independent. It is all really a question of degree and it is doubtful whether any of the agencies listed under the Tribunals and Inquiries Act, with the possible exception of the Civil Aviation Authority,[17] can be denied the epithet 'tribunal'. Even mental health review tribunals, which as seen above exhibit a number of irregularities, would seem on balance to have sufficient tribunal characteristics to qualify.

But the same is true also of many agencies which are not listed under the Act. The Criminal Injuries Compensation Board, for example, falls into this category and it also lacks a number of the Franks properties. It seldom holds a full hearing, normally delegating the power to determine a claim to an individual member of the Board; it possesses no special expertise and there is no appeal on questions of law to the High Court; most seriously of all, its decisions have no legal effect in that the payments which are made under the scheme are purely ex gratia. Further, the Board differs from other, more regular, tribunals because it was created by prerogative act of the Home Secretary and not by statute. These last matters are, however, not of great importance. No claimant in whose favour the Board has made an award has failed to receive a payment in compliance with that award and the Divisional Court has held that the Board is amenable to judicial review by certiorari, notwithstanding its lack of a statutory base and the ex gratia nature of the scheme.[18] Some other agencies give rather more trouble. The Monopolies Commission's decisions are recommendatory only and in a large number of instances the Government of the day has failed to implement them. And yet the Commission arrives at its findings by a process of independent investigation and, as reconstituted under the Fair Trading Act 1973, must generally provide a hearing to any persons having a substantial interest in the subject matter of a reference. The same considerations apply to planning inspectors, who hold public inquiries on planning applications, arrive at findings and make recommendations to the minister; in this case, the minister will more often than not adopt the inspector's recommendations. Similar considerations apply to matters of ministerial direction. The Supplementary Benefits Commission, the rents scrutiny boards, and the Consumer Protection Advisory Committee and the Monopolies Commission (as to procedure only) are all subject to such direction. Again, in other respects these bodies possess many of the tribunal characteristics listed above. Then there are the various bodies set up by the Industrial Relations Act 1971. The best-known of these is the National Industrial Relations Court, which in composition, procedure and function is scarcely all that different from the industrial tribunals which are listed in the Tribunals and Inquiries Act. Nor is the Industrial Arbitration Board so very different and even the Registrar of Trade Unions is as much a judicial tribunal for certain purposes as most of those listed under the Tribunals and Inquiries Act. The Commission on Industrial Relations is more complex but it too is an independent, investigative and decision-making body. Finally, mention of the National Industrial Relations Court brings to mind the Restrictive Practices Court, upon which it was largely modelled. These special courts highlight the difficulties of distinguishing tribunals from other bodies for they possess nearly all the characteristics (and claimed advantages) of tribunals over the ordinary courts.

One problem here is that no one has provided a satisfactory definition of what is an ordinary court. As Abel-Smith and Stevens have shown, the variations between one type of court and another can be quite considerable; yet there is a tendency to assimilate 'courts' to the High Court, although quantitatively 'this court is a very small part of the judicial system'.[19] Even the High Court itself is divided into separate divisions which are concerned with different subject matter and which operate differently. Thus, the Commercial Court bears little resemblance to a Crown Court; indeed it possesses all the Franks tribunal virtues of accessibility, freedom from technicality, expedition and expert knowledge, lacking only the final Franks quality of cheapness. It is tempting to conclude, therefore, that there are no basic or essential differences between courts and tribunals or, for that matter, between tribunals, as understood by Franks, and other agencies with a distinct existence. Abel-Smith and Stevens say that such differences as do exist between courts and tribunals 'are not in any sense fundamental but at most differences in degree'.[20] 'Properly understood', they say, 'tribunals are a more modern form of court'.[21] This view is irrefutable if one is talking of those tribunals which are essentially court-substitutes. But it is not true of the policy-oriented tribunals. In saying that, I do not intend to adopt the view that courts administer rules of law only while policy-oriented tribunals administer both law and policy. Abel-Smith and Stevens are rightly scathing in their condemnation of lawyers who regard such a distinction as fundamental:

We would maintain that no such clear line can or should be drawn. Indeed it was the evolution of this myth which helped establish the tribunal system by convincing the judges of the ordinary courts that they were concerned with legal but not with policy questions. But continued insistence on this unsatisfactory distinction makes it increasingly difficult to entrust new matters to the courts or to merge courts and tribunals.[22]

Their proposal, therefore, is that every effort should be taken to merge courts and tribunals : in this respect they do not distinguish court-substitute tribunals from their policy-oriented brethren.[23]

I would argue, however, that there *is* a key characteristic of policy-oriented tribunals which distinguishes them fundamentally from courts and court-substitute tribunals. This is to be found in the power which the minister retains to issue directions to such tribunals. In practice these directions may relate to procedure or, of vital significance here, to policy. In this latter case it is the minister and not the tribunal who determines policy. This does not mean that the tribunal does not also have some responsibility for policy determination in the same sense that courts and court-substitute tribunals have regard to policy considerations (or ought to do so). But it does mean that the minister retains ultimate control and responsibility for the formulation of the more important matters of policy; the tribunal's task is then limited to applying that policy to the individual cases that it determines. Many may be shocked that this should be so and it is certainly this reaction which has led to a denial of transport licensing bodies counting as tribunals.[24] Concern was expressed also about the Supplementary Benefits Commission in this respect;[25] in practice the Commission is indeed subject to a great deal of ministerial direction on policy. But its autonomy on day-to-day administration and in the determination of individual claims has never been seriously questioned. It is clear also that the newly created Civil Aviation Authority will be subject to regular direction on a number of crucial policy matters, following explicit legislation to this effect based upon the urgings of the Edwards Committee Report on Civil Air Transport.[26] The obvious parallel is that provided by the nationalized industries where the minister has the power (and the responsibility) to issue general policy directions but is not responsible for matters of day-to-day administration.[27] It is, therefore, in essence a matter of responsibility: responsibility, on the one hand, by the minister for general policy, and on the other hand by the tribunal (or public corporation or other agency) for administration and application of that policy.

If this perspective is adopted, then two things become clear:

(1) objections to the 'handing over of governmental power' to bodies 'remote from political control'[28] lose much of their sting;

(2) the advantages seen by, for example, the Fulton Committee on the Civil Service[29] in hiving-off the task of managing and operating policies to autonomous agencies can be realized without undue fear. There is enormous potential here for the growth and greater use of policy-oriented tribunals. But the concept of 'independence' must first be put in its correct place – with the courts and court-substitute tribunals. This is a matter which will be returned to later in this chapter.

Seen in this light there is a strong case for saying that the policy-oriented tribunals are so basically different – institutionally and constitutionally – that they should be regarded as being functionally distinct from courts and court-substitute tribunals. This would undoubtedly assist the debate over the allocation of decision-making powers (discussed in much of this book). It would, for example, pinpoint the unsatisfactory nature of the two extremes that were presented in the debate over the establishment of the Restrictive Practices Court. In short, the trouble with that argument was that it did not envisage the Court or other agency as a policy-oriented tribunal of the kind described here.

It is perhaps in this respect that, as a matter of definition and analysis, Wittgenstein's 'family relationships' prove to be just as useful as Putnam's 'cluster concepts'.[30] Certainly it is arguable that 'independence' is not a necessary characteristic of a tribunal but merely one of those qualities which, taken together with others, provides a picture of a paradigm or standard tribunal. And yet ministerial control over policy is surely *indicative* of a different functional task. The policy-oriented tribunal is an evolutionary body: its job is to assist the minister by constantly adapting its criteria and its investigative techniques, partly under his direction and partly in the light of its own experience, to ensure the best possible achievement of legislative objectives, having regard to changing conditions. In this sense there may be (and are) 'similarities, relationships, and a whole series of them at that'[31] between policy-oriented tribunals and court-substitute tribunals. But, from one to the other, certain 'common features drop out, and others appear'.[32] In particular the feature of independence in court-substitute tribunals is replaced by a new and different ministerial relationship in the policy-oriented tribunals. Certain important differences in investigatory techniques are also sometimes present. Paradoxically, in view of the weakness of its analysis in other respects, the Committee on *Ministers' Powers* provided an analogous distinction between those tribunals which were 'in fact free from ministerial influence, direct or indirect' (in the sense of ministerial powers of appointment and re-appointment rather than ministerial control through direction) and those tribunals which were not in fact free. The Committee referred to the former as 'specialised courts of law' and to the latter as 'ministerial tribunals'.[33] Specialized courts included professional disciplinary committees such as the General Medical Council, the Central Midwives Board and the Discipline Committee of the Law Society; arbitrators appointed to determine disputed compensation payable from the compulsory acquisition of land; the Railway and Canal Commission; the Chief Registrar of Friendly Societies; and the Special Commissioners of Income Tax.[34] Ministerial tribunals included the unemployment insurance officer, the Court of References and the Umpire; and the Pensions Appeal Tribunal established under the War Pensions Act 1921.[35]

It may be argued also that the functional and procedural differences between courts and court-substitute tribunals are such that they bear but a 'family relationship' to each other. Certainly Franks thought that these bodies were qualitatively different, at least in a procedural sense, so that the question of choice became of major importance. As we have seen, Abel-Smith and Stevens deny that such differences as exist are fundamental. Others have pointed to the fact that tribunals do not regard themselves as bound by their own precedents or by the rules of evidence and suggested that the processes of decision-making are thereby rendered distinct. Chapter 7 of this book has examined decision-making in court-substitute tribunals[36] with a view to testing this hypothesis. The conclusion drawn has been that differences in decision-making have been greatly exaggerated and to that extent

Abel-Smith and Stevens are right. This does not necessarily mean, however, that it would be desirable to merge courts and tribunals (of either kind), as they suggest. Chapters 2 to 5, which examined a number of tribunals in action, revealed some important procedural differences – for example, the practice and effect of site inspection by rent tribunals; informal extra-hearing investigations by national insurance tribunals; consultation of the parties by rent officers; conciliation by the Race Relations Board and its officers and in some of the industrial relations jurisdictions. It is not claimed that these are fundamental or unique to tribunals but the difficulties of obtaining a more general use of such procedures in the courts in England gives some support to the desirability of continuing the dichotomy, at least for the present. As one speaker said in the debates on the Immigration Appeals Bill of 1969, if the courts are defective, then let us reform the courts rather than establish yet another tribunal. But the opposition of two Lord Chancellors (past and present) to the minor reform of allowing solicitors to appear in the Crown Courts in limited circumstances would not seem to augur well for the kind of radical court reform that would be needed to halt the flow of new tribunals.

Similar considerations are true in relation to the policy-oriented tribunals. Britain, along with other western countries, is regarded as having a mixed economy, characterized by 'the co-existence of public and private economic power' and encompassing 'a variety of ways in which the power of the state is used to control or direct the economic system of the country, even insofar as it remains operated by private enterprise'.[37] The State's importance as an economic force and participant (for example, through the public or nationalized corporations) has received increasing attention;[38] the State's role as regulator of economic activity, both in the public and private sectors, remains more obscure. The key to this obscurity lies in the lack of analysis of the different institutions which individually wield regulatory powers and which collectively comprise the grand institution known as the State. Professor Friedmann has pointed out that the 'ubiquitous use of the word "state" . . . can easily disguise the fact that there are basically divergent philosophies of state': from the view taken by Hegel of the State as the embodiment of individual freedom to that of Marx for whom the State comprises the machinery by which the ruling class ensures its control over the means of production and the exploitation of the working class.[39]

The different philosophies of state objectives are important for they will determine co-incidentally our basic attitudes to the use of tribunals in the context of the administration of government. Do tribunals provide a necessary control over that part of the machinery of government which is all too susceptible to political pressures? Or are they a convenient method of enabling the heads of government to escape accountability, to get off the hook? Do tribunals enable government ministers to have it both ways – to exercise crucial and subtle influence over supposedly independent decision-making bodies while denying responsibility for the decisions that are taken?

An illustration of this last attitude arose in February 1971 when the Government announced that it did not intend to re-appoint Professor Hugh Clegg of Warwick University to a further term as chairman of the Civil Service Arbitration Tribunal.[40] There is no doubt that the Government was quite within its legal rights to take this action. Clegg's appointment was not being terminated; it was simply not renewed. On the other hand it was widely acknowledged that Clegg was in reality being given the sack. His predecessor had served a total of sixteen years in the post and the Prime Minister in fact publicly stated that, in the Government's view, Clegg was not suitable for reappointment. He had compromised his impartiality, Mr Heath said, by accepting a trade union nomination to membership of another industrial tribunal – the Scamp tribunal, an ad hoc committee of inquiry which had investigated and reported on the dustmen's pay dispute in 1970. In answer to a parliamentary question, the point was subsequently made by the Secretary of State for Employment, Mr Robert Carr, who said: 'There is no slight on Professor Clegg's integrity, but if one takes on a job which is judicial in nature one must, however reluctantly, refrain from doing things which otherwise one might have done quite properly'.[41] The legal validity of this assertion, as applicable in this case, was not beyond challenge for, as *The Times* pointed out, 'there is surely a distinction between a nominee to arbitrate and a representative'. Once he had accepted the job on the Scamp tribunal, *The Times* thought, 'it was Professor Clegg's duty to give impartial consideration to both sides of the case. There is no reason to suppose he failed in that duty'.[42] It is not surprising, therefore, that commentators were not slow to suggest that there were other, more important, reasons behind Clegg's 'dismissal'. Harold Jackson, writing in *The Guardian*, said: 'The whole question of a national policy for prices and incomes hung round the professor's receding figure'.[43] Certainly the Scamp Report had been criticized by the Government on the grounds that it had given too much to the dustmen; the suspicion arose as a result that Clegg was not being given further work to do because of his part on the Scamp tribunal and because his decisions on the Civil Service Arbitration Tribunal were regarded by the Government as being inflationary. At the time it was generally understood that, in the absence of a statutory incomes policy, the government's view was that wage increases should be kept down below an unofficial norm of eight per cent and that, in particular, increases in the public sector should not exceed this figure and so act as a leader to other sectors of the economy. The conclusion that was drawn, therefore, by Harold Jackson was the rather cynical one that 'Mr Heath is looking for arbitrators who are independently favourable towards his own economic policies'. He thus saw the Prime Minister 'not only to be moving towards the creation of a body of precedent by independent arbitrators but also to be trying to pre-empt their decisions in his selection of acceptable chairmen'. Similar doubts were later to be expressed about the whole operation generally of independent tribunal and arbitration wage-fixing bodies. The view was put forward in *The Financial Times*, for instance, that government pressure had been put on Wages Councils to keep increases down below the unofficial norm. In addition, the Department of Employment's Conciliation Service was apparently instructed not to assist in wage negotiations which looked as if they would result in a wage settlement in excess of the norm.[44] Not surprisingly, trade union confidence in the Conciliation Service soon fell and the TUC and the CBI later joined in demanding the establishment of a truly independent mediation service.

It would be a mistake, however, to see the use of tribunals in the field of administration just in terms of control or escape from accountability, as the case may be. Tribunals are often used because they provide a more effective form of management, where responsibility for decision-making is more clearly pinpointed and where structural organization is able to be less hierarchical and more efficient than in the regular civil service. The Fulton Committee, which reported on the workings of the civil service, was very much in favour of investigating the possibilities of a greater hiving-off of the task of managing and operating policies.[45] In principle, of course, reform of the civil service would meet criticisms about the inefficiencies of service hierarchy and indeed the Fulton Committee did recommend that 'bold experiments' should be undertaken by introducing ' "flatter" structures'.[46] But, as in the case of court reform, radical change of the established machinery such as the civil service always seems to be incapable of accomplishment.[47] For this reason, the radical attack is best directed to the creation and development of tribunals and other autonomous agencies, less established and hence more adaptable. It may be thought regrettable that this is the most realistic prospect for major improvement in administrative performance. But the dual system of administration comprising the civil service and autonomous agencies may in fact be the best approach in any event. The Fulton Committee was much impressed by the notion of a smaller civil service assuming greater and clearer responsibility for the formulation of policy and the administration of that policy being undertaken by independent agencies. It thought that the concept of ministerial responsibility meant that, under the present system, decisions were inevitably taken at a higher level than needed to be the case. This led to delays and a tendency to 'pass the buck':[48]

Often, from Executive Officer upwards, each level 'has a go' at a paper or a problem, adding comments or suggestions as it goes up the hierarchy until it reaches the point at which somebody takes a decision. This point is often higher than it would otherwise be because decisions may involve the Minister in having to answer for them in Parliament. In consequence, personal responsibility and authority are obscured; delay follows.[49]

Fulton was much impressed by the experience of Sweden where the role of central departments was largely restricted to policy-making, with the administration of policies being hived off to autonomous agencies. The system was used in Sweden not only for commercial activities but also for public services in social fields especially.[50] On the other hand it was acknowledged that the work of the independent regulatory commissions in the United States of America has attracted increasing criticism;[51] and that a complete separation of policy-making from execution would be harmful and would therefore need to be guarded against.[52]

The division of labour between policy formulation and administration is both efficient and institutionally necessary in order to prevent the daily pressures of administration swamping and swallowing the time and detachment needed for the working out of really good policies. Policy-oriented tribunals therefore have great potential as an aid to the processes of government. But a working link with the minister is obviously necessary so that the latter can hand down and adapt the policies from time to time which the tribunal must apply. This does not mean that the tribunal must always 'report back' to the minister before making some innovations. There will be great advantage – in some jurisdictions more than others – in delegating to the tribunals themselves the power to work out their own policies on certain matters, especially where the tribunals are better equipped to do so because of particular experience relevant to those matters. There is obviously enormous scope for flexibility of structural arrangement here; this would be accentuated even further if limited rule-making powers were given to tribunals so that case-law and precedent did not form the only means by which principles could be developed. Lest the lessons of the Supplementary Benefits Commission's 'A' Code be forgotten, however, the urgings of Professor K. C. Davis, that discretion should not only be structured but should also be controlled by the publishing of such rules and by openness in all matters of decision-making and administration, provide a timely warning.[53]

One final point requires brief examination. In Chapter 2 it was seen that the Fair Trading Act 1973 provides a new sophistication in the employment of tribunals in the implementation of government policies. The Act attempted in particular to meet the problem of dealing with continuing change in consumer and trade practices by juxtaposing formal tribunals (the Restrictive Practices Court and the Consumer Protection Advisory Committee) against a more informal, negotiating official (director general of fair trading). The formal tribunals, as investigating and decision or policy-making bodies, remained important in their own right but their principal value lay in the support which they gave to the more flexible, wider-ranging director who would seek to shape the pattern of trade and consumer practices through a system of 'conciliation and voluntary response'.

In a field where the nature of the problem which must be solved transcends the interests of two (or more) opposing parties or litigants and where the agency is wedded to a process of investigation by judicial hearing and problem-solving by adjudication or decision such a development is inevitable. Arguably, this development provides the next stage in the history of administrative law. Informal, expert tribunals, which have been willing to a certain extent to shrug off the constraints of rules of precedent and evidence, have evolved from and superseded to a large extent the ordinary courts because of deficiencies in the latter. But now it is seen that these very tribunals, differing ultimately only in degree and not in kind from the courts, find their procedures inappropriate and their final decisional solutions inadequate. As one American lawyer put it:

> Today ... social questions are multi-dimensional in that they deal with diverse matters such as land use, poverty, race, cities and baffling technical considerations. . . . Such questions defy clear and certain solutions. Solutions must be attempted, but they often cannot be anything but tentative working hypotheses, subject to continual reconsideration. An immutable rule, even one made under the best and most flexible of hearing procedures, is often inappropriate.[54]

The same writer continued to point out that the administrative process suffers from a misapplication of trial procedures. 'Due process is unnecessarily adhered to in situations where a consensus seeking mechanism would be far more appropriate', he said. Effectively the wheel has turned full circle for ' "the delays attendant upon formalism" which administrative law was created to remedy have now come back to plague administrative law as it deals with more complex and quasi-legislative questions'.[55]

It would seem highly likely that consensus-seeking mechanisms, informal and formal consultation, inquisitorial proceedings, the development of informal rule-making processes will provide the basis for administrative law in the latter quarter of the twentieth century. Such a pattern of regulation seems inevitable if the growing social and economic problems of society are to be contained. What remains unclear, however, is whether these new procedures and decision-making techniques will be exercised by tribunals constituted as we know them today or whether they will be undertaken by government or government-appointed officials as a preliminary step to determination by tribunals operating in the traditional, judicial way. If it is the latter, then there would seem little doubt but that the occasion for formal tribunal decision-making will diminish sharply and the role of tribunals will thus become an influential rather than determinative one.[56] The consequences of that development would clearly affect the present hierarchical structure of the civil service. It would also cast new light on the desirability of the hiving-off of administration to independent or semi-independent agencies where the function of such agencies had changed in the manner described.

Notes

Chapter One

1 *The Machinery of Justice in England*, 5th ed. (1967) p. 352.
2 H. W. R. Wade, *Towards Administrative Justice* (1963) p. 87.
3 F. J. Goodnow, *Politics and Administration* (1900); Simon, *Administrative Behaviour* (1945), p. 55.
4 See, for example, *R. v. Leman Street Police Station Inspector ex parte Venicoff* [1920] 3 K.B. 72.
5 House of Commons Debates, vol. 849, 22 January 1969, col. 502.
6 *Ibid.*, cols. 509–10.
7 See p. 29.
8 See p. 124.
9 'Appeals in Town and Country Planning Law' in *Administrative Tribunals at Work*, ed. Pollard, (1950) p. 114.
10 Report of the Committee on *Immigration Appeals* (1967) Cmnd. 3387.
11 [1942] A.C. 206.
12 *Ibid.*, 253; and see Viscount Maugham at p. 222.
13 In the United Kingdom there is also parliamentary control at the other end of the process because the Ombudsman is only able to investigate those complaints which are referred to him through Members of Parliament. This, and other restrictions which have served to limit his jurisdiction and the grounds on which he can criticize a departmental decision, have by comparison with his counterparts in Scandinavia and New Zealand reduced considerably the impact which he has had on public administration.
14 H.C. Deb. vol. 851, 23 February 1973, cols. 996–7.
15 *Ibid.*

16 *Justice in the Welfare State* (1968) (Hamlyn lectures), p. 57. Paradoxically, as Professor Street also points out (p. 58), complaints against a doctor's professional competence or integrity leading to a decision to strike him off the medical register are determined in public session by the Disciplinary Committee of the General Medical Council.

17 Immigration Appeals Act 1969, s. 9.

18 For a devastating analysis of the whole Dutschke Tribunal proceedings, see Hepple, 'Aliens and Administrative Justice: the Dutschke Case' (1971) 34 *Modern Law Review*, p. 501.

19 It is interesting to note that concern expressed in New Zealand over the operations of the security intelligence service in that country led to the enactment of a right of appeal for any person who claimed that 'his career or livelihood is or has been adversely affected by an act or omission of the New Zealand Security Intelligence Service': New Zealand Security Intelligence Service Act 1969, s. 17(1). The appeal was to lie to a special Commissioner of Security Appeals who was to be a barrister or solicitor of not less than seven years' standing and who was to use methods of inquiry along Ombudsman lines rather than adopt judicial hearing-type procedures.

20 H.C. Deb., vol. 738, 12 December 1966, col. 71.

21 *Ibid.*, col. 78, see also Mr Richard Sharples on this point : cols. 124–5.

22 *Ibid.*, col 107: and see other speakers at cols. 132, 176, 193–4.

23 H.C. Deb., vol. 745, 26 April 1967, cols. 1641–3.

24 *Ibid.*, col. 1650.

25 'Parole Procedure: An Alternative Approach' (1973) *British Journal of Criminology*, 6, p. 22.

26 [1968] A.C. 997.

27 *The Management of Government* (1972) p. 9.

Chapter Two

1 For a devastating analysis of the performance of Labour and Socialist parties in power, see R. Milliband, *The State in Capitalist Society* (1969).

2 Selective employment tax was abolished in 1973 and replaced by value-added tax (a virtually non-discriminatory measure).

3 The Industrial Training Act was itself a fiscal attempt to induce employers to provide more training for their employees and hence presumably in the long run to increase productivity.

4 See especially Industry Act 1972, s. 7.

5 *Ibid.*, s. 1; Local Employment Act 1972, s. 3.

6 Local Employment Act 1972, s. 4.

7 *Ibid.*, s. 6.

8 *Ibid.*, s. 7.

9 *Administrative Tribunals and Enquiries* (1957) Cmnd. 218. The spirit referred to is that of 'openness, fairness and impartiality': *ibid.*, p. 10, para. 41.

10 G. Ganz, 'The Control of Industry by Administrative Process' (1967), *Public Law*, 93, p. 100.

11 Compare the enforcement of much environmental legislation.

12 Ganz, in *PL*, 93, p. 101.

13 Ganz, in *PL*, 93, p. 101.

14 H. C. Deb., vol. 709, 30 March 1965, col. 665; Ganz, in *PL* 93, p. 103.

15 *Ibid.*, col. 667; 103.

16 Industrial Reorganization Corporation Act 1966, s. 2.

17 *Ibid.*, s. 2(5).

18 H.C. Deb., vol. 837, 22 May 1972, cols. 1014–5.

19 The device of advisory committees has been used before in other fields – for example, under the national insurance legislation – though some of them have tended to fall into disuse, or at least have not been used as much as they might have been. The National Economic Development Council, and the various industry 'neddies', which constitute joint consultative bodies on matters of general economic and industrial policy, have also not been used to their full potential.

20 Local Employment Act 1972, s. 3(1).

21 Cf. *Padfield* v. *Minister of Agriculture* [1968] A.C. 997.

22 Local Employment Act 1972, s. 4(1).

23 *Ibid.*, s. 4(5).

24 Industries Act 1972, s. 9.

25 S. 2; see now ss. 74–5, Town and Country Planning Act 1971.

26 Standing Committee, D, 30 March 1965, col. 665; Ganz, 'Allocation of Decision-making functions II' (1972), *PL* pp. 299, 300. On the subject of office location generally, see J. Rhodes and A. Kan, *Office Dispersal and Regional Policy* (1972), Univ. Cambridge, Dept. Applied Economics, Occasional Paper 30.

27 (1969) Cmnd. 3998, para. 485; Ganz, in PL, p. 300.

28 See Chapter 3.

29 *Modern Capitalism* (1965), p. 154; A. Fels, *The British Prices and Incomes Board* (1972), University of Cambridge Department of Applied Economics, Occasional Paper No. 29, p. 10.

30 *Modern Capitalism*, p. 154. And see Worswick, 'The British Economy 1950–59' in *The British Economy in the 1950s*, ed. Worswick and Ady (1962), p. 59; Fels, *The British Prices and Incomes Board*, pp. 9–11; H. Clegg, *How to Run an Incomes Policy and Why We made such a Mess of the Last One* (1971), p. 3.

31 Four references only were made.

32 Much of what follows, both in relation to the procedures used by the National Incomes Commission and those used by the National Board for Prices and Incomes, is based on Alan Fel's excellent work, *The British Prices and Incomes Board* (1972).

33 Fels, *The British Prices and Incomes Board*, pp. 19, 20.

34 *The British Prices and Incomes Board*, p. 22.

35 *Cf.*, Fels, p. 70, for a criticism of this reply.

36 I have written more fully on these sorts of procedures as they operate in New Zealand, both in tribunals and Government Departments there, in 'Tribunal Procedure Reform : A Process of Consultative Investigation' [1970], *New Zealand Law Journal*, p. 124.

37 Farmer in *NZLJ*, p. 38.

38 Farmer in *NZLJ*, p. 152.

39 Farmer in *NZLJ*, p. 43.

40 *Productivity, Prices and Incomes Policy after 1969*, para. 42.

41 See also the discussion of the Clegg case in Chapter 8.

42 See also Chapter 8.

43 See Chapter 3 on the operation of tribunals in the field of industrial relations.

44 See Chapter 3.

45 Under the Counter-Inflation (Temporary Provisions) Act 1972.

46 See also the views of Aubrey Jones, a former chairman of the Board, in his recent work on this subject.

47 S. 1(3).

48 The agencies are more obviously judicial than the Prices and Incomes Board in a procedural sense in so far as they are expressly required to give fourteen days' notice to affected parties before making a restriction order to allow them to make written representations: ss. 6(4)(5); 7(4)(5). It is too soon to say (at the time of writing) what basic form of investigation the agencies will adopt.

49 S. 2.

50 Ss. 6(2); 7(2).

51 See s. 21(1) for the various ministers to which this provision can refer.

52 S. 5(1).

53 See also Sched. 1, para. 18 for the Secretary of State's power to give general directions to the agencies as to their procedure and their power to publish information or advice.

54 H.C. Deb., vol. 346, 6 March 1956, cols. 2029–30. The debates on the establishment of the Restrictive Practices Court are now well known, following R. B. Stevens and B. S. Yamey's work

The Restrictive Practices Court (1965). See also V. Korah, *Monopolies and Restrictive Practices* (1968), p. 30; Ganz, 'Allocation of Decision-making Functions I', 215 (1972), *PL*, pp. 217–18.

55 H.C. Deb., vol. 350, 12 April 1956, col. 404.

56 *Ibid.*

57 Stevens and Yamey, p. 7.

58 Stevens and Yamey, pp. 7–8, for specific references.

59 Stevens and Yamey, p. 240.

60 Restrictive Practices Court Rules 1957, S.I. 1957 No. 603, r. 55.

61 Rule 49.

62 Rule 33, as amended by the Restrictive Practices Court (Amendment) Rules 1965, S.I. 1965 No. 22 r. 10.

63 Stevens and Yamey, pp. 3–4.

64 Letter dated 7 June 1971.

65 A similar procedure was proposed for monopolies and mergers through an official to have been called the Director of Research and Investigation.

66 The various provisions of the Fair Trading Act will be discussed below in so far as they are relevant to this work.

67 Similar provisions existed in respect of the export of goods and in relation to the application of a process of manufacture to goods.

68 See the Annual Report of the Board of Trade for 1956 in respect of the Monopolies Act for a summary of the jurisdictional division between the Commission and the Court.

69 Mr Douglas Jay (President of the Board of Trade) : H.C. Deb., vol. 709, 29 March 1965, col. 1218.

70 The Restrictive Trade Practices Act 1968 did bring information agreements within the Court's jurisdiction but, more significantly, it also allowed agreements which promoted industrial efficiency and which carried out a scheme of importance to the national economy to be exempted from registration and hence judicial scrutiny.

71 Annual Report by the Department of Trade and Industry on the Monopolies and Mergers Acts 1948 and 1965, p. 2, paras. 6–9.

72 S. 10 of the 1948 Act (as amended by s. 3 of the 1965 Act).

73 For a full discussion of the Commission's report, see A. Sutherland, *The Monopolies Commission in Action* (1970) Univ. Cambridge Dept. Applied Economics Occasional Paper No. 21, chapter 6.

74 H.C. Deb., vol. 745, 26 April 1967, col. 1610.

75 *Ibid.*, col. 1611 (Mr Ridley).

76 H.C. Deb., vol. 856, 23 May 1973, col. 465.
77 *Ibid.*, col. 465 (Mr C. Davis); see also col. 471 (Mr Wedgwood Benn).
78 *Ibid.*, col. 465 (Mr Davis); col. 469 (Mr Biffen).
79 *Ibid.*, cols. 469–70.
80 *Ibid.*, col. 471.
81 Cf. *Padfield* v. *Minister of Agriculture* [1968] A.C. 997 where the Minister gave as one of his reasons for refusing to refer a complaint to a statutory committee of investigation the fact that it would be politically embarrassing for him to reject the committee's findings if they supported the complainant.
82 *The Times*, 26 May 1973.
83 Fels, *The British Prices and Incomes Board*, p. 235.
84 'A New Look at Monopoly Policy', *Political Quarterly*, 41 (1970), p. 328; Fels, pp. 235–6. For a full account of Commission procedure, see Korah, *Monopolies and Restrictive Practices* (1968), pp. 44–8.
85 Sutherland, *The Monopolies Commission in Action*, pp. 76, 77.
86 Sutherland, p. 76.
87 Quoted by T. Hadden, *Company Law and Capitalism* (1972), p. 354.
88 Tribunals in the areas of social security and rent control and regulation will be examined in detail in later chapters.
89 A position now remedied, at least in part, by the Supply of Goods (Implied Terms) Act, 1973.
90 'Small Claims', 35 (1972), MLR, pp. 18, 27.
91 H.C. Deb., vol. 848, 13 December 1972, col. 456.
92 *Ibid.*, col. 457.
93 *Ibid.*
94 *Ibid.*, col. 460.
95 The 1971 Trade Practices Amendment Act has resurrected the Commission to some extent by allowing it to give approval to certain kinds of collective price agreement on direct application to the Commission.
96 See generally the outline given by Street, *Justice in the Welfare State* (1968), Hamlyn lectures, chapter 4.
97 Street, p. 72, contrasting the supply of essential services in coal, electricity and gas.
98 T. D. Corpe, *Road Haulage Licensing*, 2nd ed., pp. 1–2.
99 Corpe, pp. 1–2.
100 Report, p. 9.
101 Report, p. 11.
102 *Enston & Co. Ltd.* v. *L.M.S. Rly.* (1934) 22 Traf. Cas. 3.
103 See generally Transport Act 1968, ss. 60–74.

104 See, for example, Wade, *Towards Administrative Justice* (1963), p. 42.

Chapter Three

1 *The Worker and the Law* (1971), 2nd ed., p. 13
2 Renner, 'The Development of Capitalist Property and the Legal Institutions Complementary to the Property Norm' (1949), reproduced in *Sociology of Law*, ed. Aubert (1969), pp. 43–4.
3 For a discussion, see P. S. Atiyah, *Accidents, Compensation and the Law* (1970), chapter 14.
4 The development and operation of the national insurance and supplementary benefit systems will be discussed in detail in the next chapter.
5 Cmnd. 5034.
6 Possibly, however, the single-function judicial tribunal will remain as an appeal body: this is the case under the New Zealand Accident Compensation Act described on page 54.
7 See H.C. Deb., vol. 848, 19 December 1972, cols. 1119–20.
8 For a discussion of the Criminal Injuries Compensation Board, see Atiyah, *Accidents, Compensation and the Law*, chapter 13.
9 Similarly, other forms of misfortune, such as illness, require the same attention.
10 B. Hepple and P. O'Higgins, *Individual Employment Law* (1971), p. 4.
11 See, for example, the Water Officers Compensation Act 1960 and the London Authorities (Interim Action) Order 1964.
12 At the conference on administrative tribunals held at Birmingham in 1971 by the Institute of Judicial Administration.
13 K. W. Wedderburn and P. L. Davies, *Employment Grievances and Disputes Procedures in Britain* (1969), p. 251; McCormick, 'The Redundancy Payments Act in the Practice of the Industrial Tribunals', (1970), *British Journal of Industrial Relations* 8, pp. 334, 337; and see *Adams* v. *Macaire Mould & Co. Ltd.* (1966) 1 I.T.R. 441, 412. *Cf.* Rideout, 'The Industrial Tribunals', 21 (1968), Current Legal Problems, p. 178.
14 Of redundancy cases decided in 1966 and later reported, 41 per cent of workers appeared in person (50 per cent in 1969–70), 29 per cent were represented by a trade union official (18 per cent in 1969–70), 6 per cent (14 per cent) by counsel and 14 per cent (18 per cent) by a solicitor. Figures for employers were compar-

able, though with considerably higher figures in 1969–70 for presentation by counsel.

15 *On-Line Electronics* v. *Engineering Industry Training Board* (1967) 2 I.T.R. 242, 247. *Cf. Caskie* v. *Campbell and Isherwood Ltd.* (1967) 2 I.T.R. 276, 277 where representation by trade union and employers association officials was praised; but see also *Bruce* v. *NCB* (1967) 2 I.T.R. 159, 160 where an industrial relations officer's representation was termed 'complex sophistry'.

16 In *Current Legal Problems*, pp. 185, 189–92.

17 In *Employment Grievances*, pp. 274–5.

18 (1967) 2 I.T.R. 84.

19 (1967) 2 I.T.R. 229.

20 In *Employment Grievances*, p. 269.

21 As Wedderburn and Davies implicitly suggest was the effect of the *Morton Sundour Fabrics case*: *Employment Grievances*, p. 267.

22 (1967) 2 I.T.R. 59, 61.

23 (1967) 2 I.T.R. 59.

24 *Ibid.*, 61. Underemployment has been described by Allan Flanders as 'an economic calamity and social evil' that ranks with unemployment: see *The Fawley Productivity Agreements* (1964).

25 Construction Industry Training Board Guide, p. 3.

26 *Scaffolding (G.B.) Ltd.* v. *Construction Industry Training Board* (1966) 1 I.T.R. 219, 220.

27 (1966) 1 I.T.R. 225

28 *Ibid.*, 226.

29 *Sterling Products Ltd.* v. *Minister of Labour* (1967) 2 I.T.R. 539, 541; *Szerelmey Ltd.* v. *Construction Industry Training Board* (1966) 1 I.T.R. 193, 195; *Altmiths Ltd.* v. *Construction Industry Training Board* (1966) 1 I.T.R. 196, 197; *Jossaume* v. *Construction Industry Training Board* (1966) 1 I.T.R. 130, 132.

30 See for example, Rideout, in *Current Legal Problems*, pp. 189–91.

31 (1967) 2 I.T.R. 138.

32 *Ibid.*, 139.

33 Redundancy Payments Act 1965, s. 2(4). The wording of the section may be at least partly at fault; some tribunal members say that the section was intended for another statute but found its way into the Redundancy Payments Act by mistake!

34 *Gotch and Partners* v. *Guest* (1966) 1 I.T.R. 65, 66; *Tyler* v. *Cleveland Bridge and Engineering Co. Ltd.* (1966) 1 I.T.R. 89, 90; *Rawe* v. *Power Gas Corporation Ltd.* (1966) 1 I.T.R. 154, 157; *Silver* v. *The J.E.L. Group of Companies* (1966) 1 I.T.R.

238, 240; *Morrison and Poole* v. *Cramic Engineering Co. Ltd.* (1966) 1 I.T.R. 404, 406; *Gregg* v. *NCB* (1967) 1 I.T.R. 30, 31; *Bruce* v. *NCB* (1967) 2 I.T.R. 159, 160; *Watson* v. *Bowaters United Kingdom Pulp and Paper Mills Ltd* (1967) 2 I.T.R. 278, 279.

35 *Bainbridge* v. *Westinghouse Brake Co. Ltd.* (1966) 1 I.T.R. 55; *Tyler* v. *Cleveland Bridge & Engineering Co. Ltd.* (1966) 1 I.T.R. 89; *Rose* v. *Shelley and Partners Ltd.* (1966) 1 I.T.R. 169; *Silver* v. *The J.E.L. Group of Companies* (1966) 1 I.T.R. 283; *Strachan* v. *W. J. Clifton & Co. Ltd.* (1966) 1 I.T.R. 552; and see also *Belle* v. *Fielding and Johnson Ltd.* (1966) 1 I.T.R. 16; *Cahuac, Johnson and Crouch* v. *Allen Amery Ltd.* (1966) 1 I.T.R. 313; *Gay* v. *The Commander, US Naval Activities, United Kingdom* (1966) 1 I.T.R. 347.

36 (1967) 2 I.T.R. 484.

37 *Ibid.*, 488

38 (1966) 1 I.T.R. 169.

39 (1966) 1 I.T.R. 170.

40 (1966) 1 I.T.R. 546.

41 (1967) 2 I.T.R. 7.

42 (1966) 1 I.T.R. 347.

43 (1966) 1 I.T.R. 367.

44 (1966) 1 I.T.R. 347, 349.

45 (1966) 1 I.T.R. 367, 369.

46 For a less optimistic view of the part played by industrial tribunals in the administration of the Docks and Harbours Act, see Wedderburn, *The Worker and the Law* (1971), 2nd ed., p. 151.

47 (1968) 3 I.T.R. 92.

48 *Ibid.*, 100.

49 A similar point may be applicable in the case of the new unfair dismissal jurisdiction established by the Industrial Relations Act 1971; see page 65.

50 116 (1966), *NLJ*, p. 1214; and see Wedderburn, 'Labour Courts?', *New Society*, 6 December 1965, p. 9.

51 H.C. Deb.,26 April 1965, col. 46.

52 (1968) Cmnd. 3623.

53 Report, pp. 156–7, paras. 573–7.

54 Both the Labour and Conservative parties accepted the Donovan proposals in preference to those of the NJAC: see *In Place of Strife* (1969) Cmnd. 3888 and *Fair Deal at Work.*

55 Both matters will be discussed on pages 70–4.

56 *Brindle* v. *H. W. Smith (Cabinets) Ltd.* (1973) 8 I.T.R. 69, 70–1.

57 Notably in *Nagle* v. *Feilden* [1966] 2 Q.B. 633 and *Edwards* v. *SOGAT* [1970] 3 W.L.R. 713.
58 In fact there were House of Lords decisions which effectively denied a legal right to work: *Allen* v. *Flood* [1898] A.C. 1; *Weinberger* v. *Inglis* [1919] A.C. 606; *Faramus* v. *Film Artistes Association* [1964] A.C. 925.
59 *Hewitson* v. *Anderton Springs Ltd.* (1972) 7 I.T.R. 391, 396.
60 *Marriot* v. *Oxford and District Co-op Society Ltd.* (1969) 4 I.T.R. 377 per Lord Denning, MR.
61 Section 24.
62 See Chapter 8 below.
63 *Simmons* v. *Tom Garner Motors Limited* (1972) 7 I.T.R. 246.
64 See, *Ridgway* v. *Hungerford Market Company* (1835) A. & E. 171, 172.
65 See, for example, *Pepper* v. *Webb* [1969] 1 W.L.R. 514.
66 [1964] A.C. 40.
67 *Ibid.*, 65.
68 See, for example, *Malloch* v. *Aberdeen Corporation* [1971] 2 All E.R. 1278; cf. *Vidyodaya University Council* v. *Silva* [1965] 1 W.L.R. 77.
69 [1965] 1 W.L.R. 77.
70 (1972) 7 I.T.R. 312.
71 As to the Code, see page 77.
72 (1972) 7 I.T.R. 324, 329.
73 *Wood* v. *Louis C. Edwards & Sons (Manchester) Ltd.* (1972) 7 I.T.R. 335, 337; *Hewitson* v. *Anderton Springs Ltd.* (1972) 7 I.T.R. 391, 394.
74 (1973) 8 I.T.R. 33.
75 *Ibid.*, 35.
76 *Ibid.*, 39.
77 The refusal of Parliament to provide the remedy of reinstatement to a worker who has been unfairly dismissed underlines this point. The Act does authorize the tribunals to recommend re-engagement but the employer need not comply with such a recommendation. His failure to do so will, however, be reflected in the quantum of compensation which is awarded against him: see ss. 106 (4)(5), 116 (4).
78 In *Employment Grievances*, p. 275; and see Wedderburn, *New Society* (note 50) where the view is expressed that the desire to bring all types of labour dispute under the umbrella of one system of labour courts is 'little more than the unhelpful approach of an unduly tidy mind'.
79 And as to collective contracting-out of the Act, see C. Grunfield, *The Law of Redundancy* (1971), pp. 30–1.
80 This right has been held to extend to the case where the worker

has evidenced an intention to join a union but has not yet determined which union so that the possibility of his joining an unregistered union remains open : *Cotter* v. *Lynch Bros.* (1972) 7 I.T.R. 354 (NIRC).

81 See ss. 6–18.
82 This does not include a right to the use of the employer's premises: *Post Office* v. *Ravyts and Smith* (1972) 7 I.T.R. 285 (NIRC).
83 S. 5(1).
84 For example, a refusal of overtime: *Jones* v. *Vauxhall Motors Ltd.* (1972) 7 I.T.R. 250.
85 S. 5(2).
86 S. 5(3). If the action complained of constitutes a dismissal or refusal to employ, the tribunal may also make a recommendation for re-engagement or engagement: if the recommendation is not accepted by the employer an award for compensation will be made (subsections (4) and (5)).
87 As in *Nagle* v. *Fielden* [1966] 2 W.L.R. 1027 and *Edwards* v. *Society of Graphic and Allied Trades* [1970] 3 W.L.R. 713.
88 A number of such cases had found their way into the law reports: see *Taylor* v. *National Union of Seamen* [1967] 1 W.L.R. 532; *Birch* v. *National Union of Railwaymen* [1950] Ch. 602; *Lee* v. *Showmen's Guild* [1952] 2 Q.B. 329; *Lawlor* v. *Union of Post Office Workers* [1965] Ch. 712; *Leary* v. *National Union of Vehicle Builders* [1970] 3 W.L.R. 434.
89 S. 65. Similar provisions exist in the case of employers' organizations so that individual employers against whom improper action is taken by such an organization are also protected; see sections 69, 70.
90 S. 66.
91 S. 107 (3)(b). In addition, a trade union which applies for registration under the Act must submit its rules for approval to the Registrar of Trade Unions and Employers' Association (s. 75); the rules must comply with the guiding principles and also with certain express requirements contained in Schedule 4 to the Act before approval will be given.
92 *Golding* v. *Baldwin* (1973) 8 I.T.R. 104.
93 *Spring* v. *National Amalgamated Stevedores and Dockers Society* [1956] 2 All E.R. 221; *Andrew* v. *National Union of Public Employees, The Times,* 9 July 1955.
94 (1973) 8 I.T.R. 87.
95 *Ibid.,* 95.
96 *Ibid.,* 97.
97 Wages Councils Act 1959; and compare Agricultural Wages Act 1948.

H

98 *Labour Law: Old Traditions and New Developments* (1968), p. 8.

99 S. 99.

100 Indeed the Court of Appeal on one occasion commented on the fact that the NIRC had sat long hours to dispose of an emergency application and said that it was 'very difficult for the judicial process to be properly conducted in such haste': *Secretary of State* v. *ASLEF (No. 2)* [1972] 2 All E.R. 949, 963, 969.

101 *Challinor* v. *Taylor* (1972) 7 I.T.R. 104, 105–6; *Gibb* v. *Lanarkshire Bolt Ltd.* (1973) 8 I.T.R. 53, 55; *Street* v. *Wrights Insulations Ltd* (1973) 8 I.T.R. 5; *Norton Tool Co. Ltd.* v. *Tewson* (1973) 8 I.T.R. 23, 26; *Earl* v. *Slater & Wheeler (Airlyne) Ltd.* (1973) 8 I.T.R. 33, 38.

102 Recounted in *Heatons' Transport Ltd.* v. *TGWU* [1972] 2 All E.R. 1214, 1248 by Buckley, LJ.

103 *Ibid.* And see also *Churchman* v. *Joint Shop Stewards' Committee* [1972] 1 W.L.R. 1094, 1100.

104 See ss. 2, 3.

105 H.L. Deb., 29 June 1971, cols. 248–50.

106 (1972) 7 I.T.R. 188.

107 *Ibid.*, 190; and compare *Simpson* v. *Dickinson* (1973) 8 I.T.R. 40, 42 and *Langston* v. *AUEW* [1973] 2 All E.R. 430, 436–7.

108 See Chapter 2, pp. 21–8, for a fuller account of incomes policies.

109 Ss. 138–40.

110 *Secretary of State* v. *ASLEF* [1972] 2 All E.R. 853.

111 *Ibid.*, 860–1.

112 S. 141.

113 *Secretary of State* v. *ASLEF (No. 2)* [1972] 2 All E.R. 949.

114 See Chapter 1 for a consideration of further misuses of tribunal jurisdictions in this context.

115 [1972] 2 All E.R. 853, 858.

116 *Heatons' Transport* v. *TGWU* [1972] 2 All E.R. 1214, 1222.

117 See generally Industrial Relations Act 1971, ss. 44–53. Another important agency established by the Act is the Industrial Arbitration Board, formerly known as the Industrial Court exercising a voluntary jurisdiction but now given limited compulsory decision-making powers: ss. 125–6.

118 See Industrial Relations Act, ss. 121–3.

119 S. 120.

120 Sched. 3, para. 31 (2).

121 *Ibid.*, para. 36.

122 S. 121 (1).

123 The principle of conciliation, though in the context of and as a

preliminary to formal decision-making, has been recognized in the Act: see ss. 1 (1)(b); 146.

124 *Labour Law: Old Traditions and New Developments,* p. 3.

125 There is scope for their further expansion in section 113 of the Act which empowers the Lord Chancellor by statutory order to bring all contract of employment actions (other than personal injuries) under the tribunals.

Chapter Four

1 Beveridge Report on Social Insurance and Allied Services (1942) Cmnd. 6404, p. 11, para. 20 et seq.; p. 141, para. 369.

2 See the Report of the Royal Commission on Social Security in New Zealand (1972), p. 316, para. 24.

3 The fact that national insurance was based on the notion of contract has been said to be the reason for its original popularity: Rodgers, *The Battle Against Poverty I* (Routledge and Kegan Paul 1969), p. 77.

4 Report, p. 42, para. 182; and see also p. 41, para. 179.

5 *Introduction to Social Welfare* (1968, 3rd ed.), pp. 292–3.

6 Report, p. 12, para. 24.

7 *Poverty in Britain and the Reform of Social Security,* University of Cambridge Department of Applied Economics Occasional Paper No. 18 (1970), p. 24.

8 *Poverty in Britain,* p. 24 and fig. 1.2, p. 25.

9 Second Reading of Ministry of Social Security Bill, 24 May 1966, H.C. Deb., vol. 729, col. 336 per the Minister of Pensions and National Insurance (Miss Margaret Herbison). But cf. V. George, *Social Security: Beveridge and After* (1968), p. 75.

10 H.C. Deb., vol. 729, 24 May 1966, col. 336; and see cols. 340, 348.

11 *Ibid.,* col. 411.

12 *Ibid.,* col. 417.

13 *Ibid.,* col. 340.

14 H.C. Deb., vol. 729, 24 May 1966, col. 339.

15 'Civic Rights and Social Services', 40 (1969), *Political Quarterly,* pp. 90, 91–2.

16 'Civic Rights'.

17 See an interesting and extensive article in *The Sunday Times,* 8 August 1971 : 'The Secret Machinery of the Poverty Code'. See also Hill, 'The Exercise of Discretion in the National Assistance Board' (1969), *Public Administration* pp. 75, 77.

18 *The Sunday Times,* 8 August 1971.

19 There have been two revisions subsequently : in April 1971 and December 1972.

20 Handbook (April 1971), p. 2.
21 See Tony Lynes, *The Penguin Guide to Supplementary Benefits* (1972), p. 20.
22 Handbook. p. 26.
23 Handbook, p. 3.
24 Handbook, p. 1.
25 And see Lynes, *The Penguin Guide*, p. 200.
26 'Welfare "Rights", Law and Discretion', 42 (1971), *PolQ*, p. 113.
27 *Discretionary Justice* (1969), p. 65.
28 And see *Blackpool Corporation* v. *Locker* [1948] 1 K.B. 349 per Scott, LJ.
29 Titmuss, in *PolQ*, p. 127.
30 Titmuss, p. 117–18.
31 Titmuss, p. 126.
32 Titmuss, p. 118.
33 *Discretionary Justice.*
34 See Reich, 'Individual Rights and Social Welfare : The Emerging Legal Issues', 74 (1965), *Yale Law Journal*, pp. 1245, 1252 : 'Because welfare clients seldom have legal assistance, statutory interpretations by administrators have generally gone unchallenged. But when a real challenge is made, a significant change in prevailing practice may result. Absent challenge, welfare administrators are permitted broad areas of discretion in which they make the law by administrative interpretations under the pressures of current public opinion – interpretations that may be neither consistent from one jurisdiction to another nor in accord with the original purposes of the legislature.'
35 See generally Murphy, 'The National Environmental Policy Act and the Licensing Process: Environmentalist Magna Carta or Agency Coup de Grace', 72 (1972), *Columbia Law Review*, p. 963.
36 Melvin Herman, *Administrative Justice and Supplementary Benefit Appeal Tribunals* (1971), citing unpublished departmental figures.
37 S. 39(4) and 7th Sched.
38 7th Sched., paras. 1, 3.
39 Ministry of Social Security Act 1966, Sched. 3, para. 6(1)(b) and Tribunals and Inquiries Act 1971, s. 10.
40 S.I. 1971 No. 680.
41 R.11(10).
42 R.11(2).
43 R.11(3).
44 R.11(9).
45 R.11(6).

46 R.12(1).
47 Annual Report for 1971, Table 132, p. 361. The comparable figures for 1970 were 4,596 sittings and 23,593 appeals.
48 Under s. 6 of the Selective Employment Payments Act 1966 and under the Family Income Supplements Act 1970.
49 By way of comparison, the number of appeals and proportion of those that were successful in the national insurance and industrial injuries jurisdictions was as follows :

	Local appeal tribunals		NI Commissioners	
	1971	1970	1971	1970
National insurance				
Appeals	24,031	28,965	1,546	1,681
Allowed	4,256	5,337	408	359
	(18 per cent)	(18.4 per cent)	(26 per cent)	(21 per cent)
Industrial injuries				
Appeals	4,661	5,903	624	789
Allowed	1,850	2,230	187	202
	(40 per cent)	(37.8 per cent)	(30 per cent)	(26 per cent)

50 See note 49 above.
51 See page 95.
52 Herman, *Administrative Justice*, p. 42.
53 Hill, 'The Exercise of Discretion in the National Assistance Board' (1969), *Public Administration* p. 75.
54 Hill, in *Public Administration*, p. 84.
55 Report, pp. 11–12, para. 21.
56 As to these, see the Report of the Committee on *Ministers' Powers* (1932) Cmnd. 4060, pp. 87, 131–3.
57 See the Franks Report, pp. 39–40, paras. 171–4. See also pp. 40–1 paras. 175–7 for other differences.
58 Report, p. 33, para. 138.
59 Following a recommendation to that effect by the Franks Committee: Report, p. 42, para. 184.
60 As the National Insurance Act 1965 and the National Insurance (Industrial Injuries) Act 1965. 1965 also saw the consolidation of the family allowances legislation.
61 Source: Annual Reports of the Department of Health and Social Security. The figures have been reasonably consistent: in 1960 insurance officers decided over twelve and a half million national insurance claims and one million industrial injuries cases and in 1965 fourteen million and one million respectively.
62 1970 figures were 28,965 and 5,903 respectively; 1960: 32,317 and 6,978; 1965: 29,200 and 7,020.
63 1970: 1,681 and 789; 1965: 1,627 and 989; 1960: 1,849 and 861.

64 For example, *R.* v. *Industrial Injuries Commissioner, ex parte Ward* [1965] 2 Q.B. 112; *R.* v. *Deputy Industrial Injuries Commissioner, ex parte Jones* [1962] 2 All E.R. 430.

65 National Insurance Act 1965, s. 71(1). As to the 'awkward division of function' between the statutory authorities and the minister, see Decision R(S) 3/68.

66 National Insurance (Industrial Injuries) Act 1965, s. 38(1).

67 *Ibid.*, s. 39(2).

68 National Insurance (Industrial Injuries) Act 1965, s. 39(2).

69 National Insurance (Industrial Injuries) Act 1965, s. 42(1); and see Part IV of the National Insurance (Industrial Injuries) (Determination of Claims and Questions) Regulations 1967, S.I. 1967 No. 1169. There is no right of appeal against an exercise of the discretion given to it by s. 40(4) of the Act: see Decision R(I) 15/68. The decision of a medical appeal tribunal may be reviewed in the High Court by prerogative order: see *R.* v. *Medical Appeal Tribunal, ex parte Gilmore* [1957] 1 Q.B. 574; *R.* v. *Medical Appeal Tribunal, ex parte Hubble* [1959] 2 Q.B. 408.

70 National Insurance Act 1965, s. 68(1), as amended by the Ministry of Social Security Act 1966, s. 39 and Sched. 8.

71 H.C. Deb., vol. 729, 24 May 1966, col. 339.

72 *Ibid.*

73 See Chapter 8.

74 See Decision R(G) 3/62.

75 The Parliamentary Commissioner for Administration has recommended ex gratia payments in these situations. There is also the possibility of a legal liability under the principles of *Hedley Byrne* v. *Heller* [1964] A.C. 465.

76 S.I. 1967 No. 1168.

77 Reg. 5(3). The time limit for the appeal is measured from the date of that notification: *ibid.*

78 Reg. 5(4).

79 As related by departmental officers.

80 Clause 79(2).

81 Source: internal departmental memorandum.

82 *Social Security: Beveridge and After* (1968), p. 85.

83 An American writer, however, claims that negro welfare claimants prefer to deal or bargain with a 'power patron' in the form of a government official than to obtain benefit through an independent legal institution: Zeitz, 'Survey of Negro Attitudes towards Law', 19 (1965) *Rutgers LR.* pp. 288, 304; Gellhorn, *When Americans Complain* (1966), p. 214.

84 National Insurance Act 1965, s. 77(1).

85 McCorquodale, 'The Composition of Administrative Tribunals' (1962), *PL* pp. 298, 299.

86 National Insurance (Determination of Claims and Questions) Regulations 1967, S.I. 1967 No. 1168, reg. 9(1).

87 Atiyah, *Accidents, Compensation and the Law* (1970), p. 383.

88 *Ibid.* The case referred to is presumably *Minister of Social Security* v. *A.E.U.* (*No. 2*) [1967] 1 A.C. 725, 728 *et seq.*

89 Both insurance officers and local appeal tribunals (but not, surprisingly, the Commissioners) have statutory power to use local referees to investigate and report on questions of fact: S.I. 1967 No. 1168, reg. 17. In practice, insurance officers do not use local referees and, as stated above, local tribunals only use them where the claimant cannot be present at the hearing. One writer has complained of local referees in general that 'supplementary questions cannot easily be posed when local referees report': Kathleen Bell, *How to Get your Industrial Injuries Benefit* (1966), p, 244.

90 See 116 (1966), *NLJ*, p. 1098.

91 As note 90.

92 Harry Street, *Justice in the Welfare State* (1968), p. 17. For an important general statement of the duties of local appeal tribunals to help unrepresented defendants, see Decision R(I) 6/69: see also Decisions R(I) 29/61 and R(U) 2/71; but cf. Decision R(I) 3/70.

93 Report, p. 25, para. 104.

94 The number and proportion of successful appeals, both at the local appeal and Commissioner stages have been given on page 215 as a comparison with supplementary benefit appeal tribunals: see p. 97.

95 Tribunals and Inquiries Act 1971, s. 13.

96 Report, p. 26, para. 108; the Committee also thought that no appeal should lie to the High Court from decisions of national assistance appeal tribunals: p. 26, para. 108.

97 National Insurance Act 1966, s. 9.

98 Annual Report of Department of Health and Social Security.

99 Source: internal departmental memorandum.

100 S.I. 1967 No. 1168, reg. 11(1).

101 See Decision R(1) 4/70 where a Commissioner refused the appellant's request for an oral hearing on the ground that the appeal could properly be determined without one. The appellant was in fact successful.

102 Interview with Commissioners. The claimant must, it seems, request a hearing: see Decision R(I) 2/71.

103 S.I. 1967 No. 1168, reg. 11(3).

104 See, for example, Decision R(I) 7/68 where a tribunal of three

Commissioners considered and refused to follow an earlier Commissioner's decision (R(I) 10/66).

105 In 1960 37 national insurance, 46 industrial injuries and 8 family allowances appeals (out of 2,758 cases) were selected for publication. The 1965 figures were 13, 14, 1 out of 2,665. The 1971 figures were 24 in all out of 2,212. The question of reporting is in fact complicated by the availability to the Commissioners of 'numbered' decisions and also the use of unreported, unnumbered decisions.

106 See Decisions C.S.G. 9/49; C.S. 414/50; R(I) 34/57.

107 The most recent study – and one which is critical of the system – is the Society of Labour Lawyers Report by Julian Fulbrook, Rosalind Brooke and Peter Archer, *Tribunals: A Social Court?* (Fabian Tract 427 – December 1973).

Chapter Five

1 E. J. Mishan, *Twenty-one Popular Economic Fallacies* (1971), p. 34.

2 M. J. Barnett, *The Politics of Legislation* (1969).

3 Under the Rent of Furnished Houses Control (Scotland) Act 1943.

4 Under the Furnished Houses (Rent Control) Act 1946.

5 (1930–1), Cmnd. 3911.

6 (1945), Cmnd. 6621.

7 The Government of the day was apparently strongly opposed to the suggestion that the new system of rent control should be administered through the ordinary courts: see H.C. Deb., 13 November 1945, vol. 415, col. 1941.

8 First Annual Report (year ending 31 December 1959), p. 17, para. 84.

9 The Francis Committee summarized the tenancies which are normally regulated as being those where:
   (1) the amount of the rent which is fairly due to attendance or to the use of the furniture (having regard to its value to the tenant) is not a substantial part of the whole rent;
   (2) the rent does not contain anything for board;
   (3) the tenancy is a legal tenancy and not simply a licence (e.g. a tied licence);
   (4) the tenancy is not rent controlled: Report on *The Rent Acts* 1971), Cmnd. 4609, p. 121.

10 See Rent Act 1968, Part VI.

11 For a full description of the security of tenure provisions and their exceptions (now brought forward into Part VI of the Rent

Act 1968), see the Francis Report, pp. 124–5.

12 See the Annual Reports for 1964 and 1966 of the Council on Tribunals, App. C; cited by Yardley, 'Rent Tribunals and Rent Assessment Committees' (1968), *PL* 135, 139.

13 A landlord may also apply to the tribunal at any time during an extension of a notice to quit under the Act for an order reducing that extension on the grounds that the tenant is not complying with the terms of his contract or is causing a nuisance or annoyance to his neighbours or is causing deterioration to the condition of the premises: Rent Act 1968, s. 80(2).

14 *Justice in the Welfare State* (1968). See also Adjutor, 'Furnished Houses Rent Tribunals' in *Administrative Tribunals at Work,* ed. Pollard (1950), pp. 67, 70.

15 Street, *Justice in the Welfare State,* pp. 36, 41.

16 Rent Act 1968, s. 73(1).

17 *R.* v. *Tottenham Districts Rent Tribunal, ex parte Fryer* [1971] 3 W.L.R. 355.

18 *Ibid.,* 358–9.

19 *Ibid.,* 359.

20 *Ibid.*

21 For a history of rent control, see Barnett, *The Politics of Legislation* (1969), chs. 3 and 4.

22 See now the Rent Act 1968, s. 2; and see the summary given by the Francis Report, pp. 3–7.

23 See now Rent Act 1968, s. 44(3).

24 Rent Act 1965, s. 22(2); now Rent Act 1968, s. 40(1). And see the letter from Mr M. Calman to *The Times,* 30 April 1973, referred to on page 126.

25 See also Adjutor, in *Administrative Tribunals,* pp. 73–4.

26 S. 7.

27 [1948] 2 All E.R. 528.

28 [1948] 98 L.J. 724.

29 H.C. Deb., 5 April 1965, vol. 710, col. 48.

30 Annual Report for 1965, p. 6, para. 20.

31 Report, p. 6, para. 21.

32 H.C. Deb., 30 June 1965, vol. 710, col. 678.

33 H.C. Deb., 16 June 1965, vol. 710, col. 958; Annual Report of the Council on Tribunals for 1965, p. 7, para. 23.

34 1965 Report, pp. 7–8, paras. 24–6.

35 S. 41 of the Act.

36 Annual Report for 1966, p. 15, para. 67.

37 Annual Report for 1968, p. 5, para. 18.

38 Report for 1968, p. 5, paras. 17, 18.

39 112 (1968), *SoJ,* p. 429.

40 112 (1968), *SoJ,* p. 526; but see 112 *SoJ,* p. 507.

41 Street, *Justice in the Welfare State*, p. 54; Yardley, *Rent Tribunals*, pp. 147–8.
42 Report, ch. 32 at p. 203.
43 Report, p. 206.
44 Report.
45 Report, p. 207.
46 Report, p. 209.
47 See p. 139 for a discussion of these provisions.
48 S. 52(3).
49 Part V of the Act.
50 S. 53(5).
51 S. 54(1).
52 S. 55(1) and see s. 56(3)(4) for the procedure which must be followed where there is any disagreement with assessments made by the local authority.
53 S. 55(2)(3).
54 S. 55(4).
55 S. 55(5).
56 See Chapter 8 in this book.
57 See s. 55(6).
58 Mr T. Rowlands, H.C. Deb., 8 May 1972, vol. 836, col. 954.
59 H.C. Deb., 15 November 1971, vol. 826, col. 50.
60 *Ibid.*, cols. 51–2; and see col. 53.
61 Mr R. C. Mitchell, col. 139 and H.C. Deb., 8 May 1972, vol. 836, col. 987 (3rd reading); Mr T. Rowlands, 3rd reading, cols. 953–4; Mr N. McBride, 3rd reading, cols. 999–1001; but cf Mr J. Amery, 2nd reading, col. 153; Mr G. Finsberg, 3rd reading, col. 959.
62 3rd reading, cols. 999–1001.
63 S. 51(1).
64 S. 51(4).
65 *The Times*, 21 April 1973 (Mr H. Cutler).
66 *The Times*, 26 April 1973 (Mr J. V. Lach).
67 30 April 1973 (Mr M. Calman): and see Rent Act 1968, s. 40(1).
68 Rent Act 1968, Sched. 6, para. 4.
69 *Ibid.*
70 *Ibid.*, para. 5.
71 *Ibid.*, para. 4(3).
72 (1971) Cmnd. 4609, p. 108.
73 *Ibid.*, p. 109.
74 H.C. Deb., 5 April 1965, vol. 710, col. 35.
75 *Ibid.*, col. 52; see also col. 40 where the minister referred to ending 'the cold war between landlord and tenant'.
76 *Ibid.*, col 49.

77 H.C. Deb., 30 June 1965, vol. 715, col. 684 (Mr Boyd-Carpenter).
78 H.C. Deb, 5 April 1965, vol. 710, col. 125 (Mrs Butler); col. 132 (Mr Lubbock); cols. 152, 153 (Mr Hogg); cols. 668–9 (Mrs Thatcher).
79 H.C. Deb., 5 April 1965, vol. 710, col. 47.
80 *Ibid.*, col. 48.
81 *Ibid.*, col. 153.
82 *Ibid.*, col. 159.
83 H.C. Deb., 30 June 1965, vol. 715, col. 668 *et seq.*
84 1965 Act, Sched. 4; now 1968 Act, Sched. 7.
85 H.C. Deb., 30 June 1965, vol. 715, col. 670.
86 Mrs Thatcher moved an amendment to the bill, which was defeated, requiring a mandatory qualification of not less than five years' practical experience in valuing dwelling houses in the ten-year period immediately preceding the appointment as rent officer: see H.C. Deb., 30 June 1965, vol. 715, col. 668 *et seq.*
87 H.C. Deb., 5 April 1965, vol. 710, col. 49.
88 *Ibid.*, col. 50.
89 H.C. Deb., 30 June 1965, vol. 715, col. 671.
90 *Ibid.*, col. 679.
91 *Ibid.*, cols. 678–9.
92 Report, p. 9.
93 Report. Rent tribunal clerks were also specifically mentioned.
94 Report, p. 37.
95 Report.
96 Report, pp. 37–8.
97 Table 24, p. 42.
98 1 January 1970 to 23 October only.
99 Report, p. 41.
100 As stated to the Francis Committee by the President of the London Rent Assessment Panel: Report, p. 41.
101 Table 25: 1969 figures only supplied. (Percentage rent decreases: 14.4 per cent; increases: 43.3 per cent; no change: 42.3 per cent).
102 Tables 25 and p. 44 (England only).
103 See page 128.
104 Francis Report, pp. 55–6.
105 Report, pp. 14 *et seq.*
106 Report, Ch. 9, p. 67.
107 Report, p. 67.
108 Report, p. 68.
109 Report, p. 67.
110 Report, p. 11.
111 Report, pp. 14–15.

112 Report, pp. 15–16.
113 Report, p. 6.
114 Report.
115 Report.
116 Report, p. 19; App. I.
117 Report, pp. 19, 20 (especially in the stress areas).
118 Report, p. 20.
119 Rent of Furnished Houses Control (Scotland) Act 1943, Sched., para. 1; Furnished Houses (Rent Control) Act 1946, Sched., para. 1. As to the position of clerks and other staff, note the concern expressed by the council on tribunals in its Annual Reports for 1959 (p. 18, paras. 89–90; p. 19, para. 96), 1962 (p. 11, para. 49) and 1965 (pp. 7–8, paras. 27–8).
120 [1948] 2 All E.R. 528, 533.
121 Annual Report for 1959, p. 17, para. 85; see also Annual Report for 1960, p. 12, para. 59.
122 Yardley, *Rent Tribunals*, pp. 139–40; Street, *Justice in the Welfare State*, p. 34.
123 Cavenagh and Newton, 'The Membership of Two Administrative Tribunals' (1970), *Public Administration* pp. 449, 451.
124 Rent Act 1968, Sched. 5, paras. 1–3.
125 As to this as a factor in the decision not to require rent officers to have a qualification as valuer, see the debate on Amendment No. 27, Report Stage, H.C. Deb., 30 June 1965, vol. 715, cols. 668–86, especially col. 679. And see the Annual Reports of the Council on Tribunals for 1961 (p. 11, para. 46) and 192 (p. 11, para. 47).
126 Rent Act 1968, Sched. 5, para. 6.
127 Francis Report, p. 45.
128 *Ibid.*, p. 48.
129 Furnished Houses (Rent Control) Regulations 1946, S.I. 1946, No. 781.
130 *Ibid.*, rule 8(1).
131 *Francis Jackson Developments Ltd.* v. *Hall* [1951] 2 K.B. 488, 494.
132 See Annual Report for 1959, p. 18, para. 87; 1960 Report, p. 12 para. 59; 1961 Report, pp. 10–11, paras. 41–5; 1962 Report, pp. 10–12, paras. 42–4; 1964 Report. p. 22, paras. 56–9. See also Adjutor, in *Administrative Tribunals*, p. 70.
133 Rent Assessment Committees (England and Wales) Regulation 1971, S.I. 1971 No. 1065; and see Rent Assessment Committees (Scotland) Regulations 1971, S.I. 1971 No. 1101 (S. 138).
134 Annual Report for 1967, p. 8, para. 72, App. B; 1970 Report, p. 27, para. 98. The Francis Committee was initially against

having formal rules but eventually accepted the Council's views on the matter : see Report, p. 50.

135 Reproduced as App. VI to the Francis Report. See p. 50 for the position in Wales.

136 Littlewood, 'The Practice of the London Rent Assessment Panel', 111 (1967), *SoJ*, p. 3.

137 Street, *Justice in the Welfare State,* pp. 53–54. And see Scott, 111 (1967), *SoJ*, p. 58.

138 90 (1946) *SoJ*, p. 461.

139 Adjutor, in *Administrative Tribunals, p. 70.*

140 As to this, see *R. v. City of Westminster Assessment Committee* [1941] 1 K.B. 53.

141 Furnished Houses (Rent Control) Act 1946, s. 2(1).

142 1946 Regs., First Sched. As to the need to disclose all information received by the tribunal to all the parties, see the Annual Report of the council on tribunals for 1964, p. 22, paras. 56–9 and R. E. Megarry, *The Rents Acts*, 10th ed., p. 513.

143 1946 Regs., r. 6(1).

144 *Perseus Ppty. Co. Ltd.* v. *Hampstead and St Pancras Rent Tribunal* [1954] E.G.D. 357.

145 Sir Sydney Littlewood, in 111 (1967), *SoJ*.

146 Report, p. 48.

147 S.I. 1971 No. 1065, r. 7(2). The parties must be notified and allowed to attend.

148 111 (1967) *SoJ*. Compare Adjutor, in *Administrative Tribunals,* p. 73: 'An inspection more desirably takes place after the hearing, because the tenant has had his say, has seen the tribunal and has sufficient trust as a rule, not to feel he must take further time off work to be present at the inspection'. For a strong criticism of this view, see Yardley, *Rent Tribunals,* pp. 149–50.

149 111 (1967), *SoJ*, p. 144 : and see para. 15 of his Notes of Guidance (Francis Report, App. VI).

150 111 (1967), *SoJ*, p. 3. For a lengthy defence of the after-hearing inspection, see the evidence to the Francis Committee of the president and vice-presidents of the London Panel: Report, pp. 46–8.

151 S.I. 1971 No. 1065, r. 7(4).

152 Francis Report, pp. 46, 144; Street, *Justice in the Welfare State,* p. 35; Alec Samuels, 'Assessing the So-called Fair Rent', 110 (1966), *SoJ*, pp. 878, 880.

153 Francis Report, p. 45.

154 Report, p. 46.

155 1946 Regs., r. 8(1); 1971 Regs., r. 3.

156 Para. 4.

157 1946 Regs., r. 7; 1971 Regs., r. 4.
158 Para. 4.
159 Lord Chancellor's Report, p. 72, para. 8; comparable figures are given in the Francis Report, p. 51, and by Sir Sydney Littlewood, in 111 (1967), *SoJ*.
160 Report, p. 72, paras. 10, 11.
161 Report, p. 72, para. 9.
162 Francis Report, p. 51. And see the Lord Chancellor's Report for the income limits: p. 72, para. 9.
163 Francis Report, pp. 50–3.
164 See, for example, the letter from Mr J. S. Richardson, chairman of the East Midland Rent Tribunal to *The Times*, 23 April 1973: '. . . This Rent Tribunal is dealing with up to 1,000 cases per annum but only very rarely is the tenant represented. Justice can rarely be seen to be done when the tenant who cannot afford a solicitor tries to represent himself, and the landlord is represented by a solicitor or even counsel. . . .'
165 Francis Report, p. 45.
166 H.C. Deb., 5 April 1965, vol. 710, col. 48.
167 See H.C. Deb., 5 April 1965, vol. 710, col. 91 (Mr Temple); cols. 132–3 (Mr Lubbock); cols. 152–3 (Mr Hogg) and H.C. Deb., 30 June 1965, vol. 715, cols. 681–2 (Mr Boyd-Carpenter). See also similar criticisms of the rent tribunals' jurisdiction in H.C. Deb., 24 January 1949, col. 589 (Lt-Col Elliot).
168 Clause 22 of the bill; s. 27 of the Rent Act 1965; s. 46 of the Rent Act 1968; and compare s. 50 of the Housing Finance Act 1972.
169 *Loc. cit.*, 4; criticized by Scott, 111 (1967), *SoJ*, p. 878.
170 Samuels, *Assessing the So-called Fair Rent* (1966) 110 *SoJ*, p. 878.
171 S. 2(2).
172 Annual Report for 1961, pp. 11–12, paras. 49–52; see also the Council's Report for 1962, pp. 10–11, paras. 45–6; Street, *Justice in the Welfare State*, pp. 41–2; 'Landlord and Tenant Notebook', 90 (1946), *SoJ*, p. 461.
173 [1952] 2 Q.B. 258; quoted in the Francis Report, pp. 146–7.
174 As to the giving of ministry directives to tribunals, see Street, *Justice in the Welfare State*, pp. 51–3; Annual Report of the Council on Tribunals for 1964, p. 22, para. 58. In the absence of express authority to give directives, they should be confined to providing references to recent court decisions.
175 See the evidence of Yardley given to the Francis Committee: Report, pp. 147–50.
176 Francis Report, p. 53; Annual Report of the Council on Tribunals for 1961, pp. 10–11, paras. 43–5; and see Street, *Justice*

in the Welfare State, p. 43; Megarry, *The Rent Acts* (10th ed.)
p. 515.
177 S.I. 1971 No. 1065, r. 10.
178 [1968] 1 W.L.R. 815.
179 Under the Tribunals and Inquiries Acts of 1958 and 1971.
180 [1968] 1 W.L.R. 815, 831–2.
181 The controversy continues: see the editoral in *The Times*, 17
April 1973 and the correspondence provoked by it: 21, 23, 26
and 30 April 1973.

Chapter Six

1 *Selective Employment Tax* (1966) Cmnd. 2986.
2 7 May 1966, p. 559.
3 H.C. Deb., vol. 727, 3 May 1966, cols. 1452, 1453.
4 *Ibid.*, col. 1452.
5 Cmnd. 2986, para. 2.
6 *Ibid.*, para. 4.
7 *Effects of the Selective Employment Tax* (1970).
8 *Effects of the Selective Employment Tax*, p. 5; and see pp.
19–21.
9 H.C. Deb., vol. 727, 3 May 1966, col. 1454.
10 *Ibid.*
11 *Ibid.*, col. 1457 and see col. 1458 where the Chancellor
described SET as 'first, as a means of raising revenue, and also
as an incentive for labour economies and manpower
redeployment'.
12 *Loc. cit.;* and see also 7 May 1966, p. 606.
13 See Byatt, 'The Selective Employment Tax' (1966), *British Tax
Review*, p. 171; and see Judith Reid, 'The Selective Employment Tax II' (1967), *British Tax Review*, p. 245.
14 Mr Fletcher-Cooke, H.C. Deb., vol. 732, 20 July 1966, cols.
697–8.
15 Sir Douglas Glover, *ibid.*, col. 703.
16 H.L. Deb., 8 August 1966, vol. 276, col. 1623.
17 Foley and Harvey, 'A Replacement for SET', 210 (1970),
Bankers' Magazine, p. 13.
18 'SET and the Shop Assistant', 7 March 1970, p. 57.
19 Cmnd. 2986, paras. 19–20, 22.
20 *The Economist*, 7 May 1966, p. 559.
21 Cmnd. 2986, para. 21.
22 Minister of Labour (Mr Gunter), H.C. Deb., 23 June 1966, vol.
731, col. 941; Minister of Defence for the RAF (Lord
Shackleton), H.L. Deb., 8 August 1966, vol. 276, col. 1613.

23 H.C. Deb., vol. 731, col. 951; and see Viscount Masereene and Ferrard, H.L. Deb., vol. 276, col. 1647.

24 Now Selective Employment Payments Act 1966, s. 7(5).

25 Sir Douglas Glover, H.C. Deb., vol. 732, col. 704.

26 H.C. Deb., *ibid.*, col. 713. As to the example postulated, see *Alan S. Deniff Ltd.* v. *Minister of Labour* (1967) 2 I.T.R. 368, where a tribunal held that the making and distribution of ready-mixed concrete was a manufacturing activity.

27 The numbers of the minimum list headings are in order but are not always consecutive.

28 Order III food, drink and tobacco; IV chemicals and allied industries; V metal manufacture; VI engineering and electrical goods; VII shipbuilding and marine engineering; VIII vehicles; IX metal goods not elsewhere specified; X textiles; XI leather, leather goods and fur; XII clothing and footwear; XIII bricks, pottery, glass, cement, etc.; XIV timber, furniture, etc.; XV paper, printing and publishing; XVI other manufacturing industries.

29 See s. 10(5) of the Act : '. . . in determining the activities falling under any particular minimum list heading in the Standard Industrial Classification, regard shall be had to any express provision of any other such heading'.

30 See Lord Shackleton, H.L. Deb., vol. 276, col. 1600.

31 Para. 4.

32 N. S. Ross, *Constructive Conflict* (1969), p. 78. But cf. the report of the Industrial Advisory Group, *The Case Against Selective Employment Tax* (1970); Foley and Harvey, 'A replacement for S.E.T.', 210 (1970), *Bankers' Magazine* p. 13.

33 H.C. Deb., vol. 732, col. 696; see also his speech in vol. 731, col. 1019 and see too Mr Alfred Morris, vol. 732, col. 706; Mr Peter Blaker, vol. 731, col. 1022 and Mr R. Chichester-Clark, vol. 732, col. 747.

34 H.C. Deb., vol. 732, col. 724.

35 H.L. Deb., vol. 276, col. 1624; and see Lord Archibald at col. 1650. That contribution to exports was not a relevant criterion was later recognized in *Ocean Pictures (Southampton) Ltd.* v. *Minister of Labour* (1967) 2 I.T.R. 445 and *Sterling Products Ltd.* v. *Minister of Labour* (1967) 2 I.T.R. 539, 541.

36 H.C. Deb., vol. 731, col. 1014 (italics supplied).

37 7 May 1966, p. 559; and see p. 606.

38 Reprinted in part in his 1970 Report, at pp 212–14.

39 See Judith Reid, 'The Selective Employment Tax II' (1967), *British Tax Review*, p. 245; and for an analysis of other S.E.T. decision, see Mrs Reid's article 'Cases on Selective Employment Tax' (1969) *British Tax Review*, p. 343.

40 (1967) 2 I.T.R. 80.

41 *Ibid.*, 82.

42 (1967) 2 I.T.R. 89.

43 *Ibid.*, 92.

44 *Skyfotos Ltd.* v. *Minister of Labour* (1967) 2 I.T.R. 573, 574.

45 *Minister of Labour* v. *Genner Iron & Steel Co. (Wollescote) Ltd.* (1967) 2 I.T.R. 640. Dictionary meanings of the word 'manufacture' have in fact been discussed on occasion by industrial tribunals and by the courts on appeal: see *I. Goldman Ltd.* v. *Minister of Labour* (1967) 2 I.T.R. 514, 516; *E. Austin & Sons (London) Ltd.* v. *Minister of Labour* (1967) 2 I.T.R. 546, 550; *Samuel Johnson & Sons (London) Ltd.* v. *Minister of Labour* (1967) 2 I.T.R. 602, 605 (tribunal) and (1968) 3 I.T.R. 246, 250 (Div. Court).

46 *R. Gordon (Kingston) Ltd.* v. *Minister of Labour* (1967) 2 I.T.R. 644, 646; *Turnill* v. *Minister of Labour* (1967) 2 I.T.R. 456.

47 *Book Centre Ltd.* v. *Minister of Labour* (1967) 2 I.T.R. 615, 618; *Drumry Testing Co. Ltd.* v. *Minister of Labour* (1967) 2 I.T.R. 312, 313.

48 (1967) 2 I.T.R. 615.

49 (1967) 2 I.T.R. 594.

50 *Ibid.*, 596.

51 *I. Goldman Ltd.* v. *Minister of Labour* (1967) 2 I.T.R. 514, 518. The chairman of the tribunal in that case, Mr G. M. Smailes, told me that where the tribunal did not itself have expert knowledge of the organization of a particular industry, it would hear expert testimony on the point e.g. from a lecturer in technology.

52 *Drumry Testing Co. Ltd.* v. *Minister of Labour* (1967) 2 I.T.R. 312, 313; *Book Centre Ltd.* v. *Minister of Labour* (1967) 2 I.T.R. 615, 618.

53 *Rank Xerox Ltd.* v. *Minister of Labour* (1967) 2 I.T.R. 399.

54 *Fisher-Bendix Ltd.* v. *Secretary of State for Employment and Productivity* (1970) 5 I.T.R. 157.

55 (1967) 2 I.T.R. 172. There were in fact two earlier decisions but these were not reported and were cases where it had been conceded that designing was not part of the manufacturing process: see (1967) 2 I.T.R. 176, 177, 178 (the *Reliant Tool case*).

56 (1967) 2 I.T.R. 176.

57 *Ibid.*, 177 (italics supplied).

58 (1967) 2 I.T.R. 498, 499.

59 Reported as *Lord Advocate* v. *Reliant Tool Company* (1968) 3 I.T.R. 70.

I

60 *Ibid.*, 74 (italics supplied).

61 (1968) 3 I.T.R. 62.

62 See also *The Woodside Drawing Company* v. *Minister of Labour* (1967) 2 I.T.R. 429.

63 For example, the comment by Salmon, LJ, in *The Central Press Photos Ltd.* v. *Department of Employment and Productivity* (1970) 5 I.T.R. 270, 278–9 that, having regard to the subsequent decision of *Reliant Tool Company*, the judgement in the earlier case of *Minister of Labour* v. *Southam News Services of Canada* (1968) 3 I.T.R. 8, in which he had concurred, must no longer be regarded as correct. In the *Central Press Photos case* itself, Salmon LJ, argued that 'by a parity of reasoning' with the *Reliant Tool case*, just as designing is a definite part of the manufacture of machine tools, so the work done by press photographic agencies is a definite and integral part of the whole process of producing a newspaper: (1970) 5 I.T.R. 270, 275. This conclusion may well be correct but, in my view, will only be so if it coincides with the facts of the newspaper publishing business. It cannot be established as such a fact by analogous reasoning with the machine tool manufacturing industry which is an entirely unrelated industry.

64 *Minister of Labour* v. *Genner Iron & Steel Co. (Wollescote) Ltd.* (1967) 2 I.T.R. 640.

65 *Lye Trading Co. Ltd.* v. *Minister of Labour* (1967) 2 I.T.R. 522; *Glen Metals Ltd.* v. *Minister of Labour* (1967) 2 I.T.R. 430; *H. A. Bore Ltd.* v. *Minister of Labour* (1967) 2 I.T.R. 455; cf. *A. Schulman Inc. Ltd.* v. *Minister of Labour* (1967) 2 I.T.R. 236 (polythene pellets to order).

66 (1967) 2 I.T.R. 514 (aff'd. on appeal to the Div. Court: (1968) 3 I.T.R. 206)

67 *Ibid.*, 518.

68 *A. & T. Jenkins (London) Ltd.* v. *Minister of Labour* (1967) 2 I.T.R. 600; *Minister of Labour* v. *Wandex Plastics Ltd.* (1968) 3 I.T.R. 156 (Div. Court); *Carfax Waste Paper Co. Ltd.* v. *Minister of Labour* (1968) 3 I.T.R. 150 (Div. Court and tribunal); *W. C. Jones & Co. Ltd.* v. *Minister of Labour* (1968) 3 I.T.R. 280 (Div. Court and tribunal).

69 *E. Austin & Sons Ltd.* v. *Minister of Labour* (1967) 2 I.T.R. 546.

70 *Holytown Building Materials Ltd.* v. *Minister of Labour* (1968) 3 I.T.R. 175.

71 *Samuel Johnson & Sons (London) Ltd.* v. *Minister of Labour* (1968) 3 I.T.R. 246, 249.

72 (1968) 3 I.T.R. 210.

73 *Ibid.*, 214–15.

74 *Drumry Testing Co. Ltd. Minister of Labour* (1967) 2 I.T.R.
312; *Vu-ray Industrial Radiography Service Ltd.* v. *Minister of
Labour* (1967) 2 I.T.R. 427; *Metallurgical Radiologists Ltd.* v.
Minister of Labour (1967) 2 I.T.R. 551.
75 *Roystan Factory Services Ltd.* v. *Minister of Labour* (1967) 2
I.T.R. 448.
76 Under minimum list heading 899(9): 'Other services: other'.
77 (1967) 2 I.T.R. 311.
78 (1969) 4 I.T.R. 152 (Div. Court).
79 An earlier unreported decision in which a tribunal reached an
opposite conclusion on apparently similar facts – *Universal
Erectors Ltd.* v. *Minister of Labour* – was distinguished by the
Divisional Court as being one where the full facts were not
available.
80 *Prestcold (Central) Ltd.* v. *Minister of Labour* (1969) 4 I.T.R.
1; see also *R. Gordon (Kingston) Ltd.* v. *Minister of Labour*
(1967) 2 I.T.R. 644.
81 (1968) 3 I.T.R. 394 (Div. Court).
82 *Ibid.*, 396–8. Cf. *MacKnight* v. *Minister of Labour* (1967) 2
I.T.R. 648.
83 *Turnill* v. *Minister of Labour* (1967) 2 I.T.R. 456.
84 See *Esso Petroleum Co. Ltd.* v. *Minister of Labour* (1968) 3
I.T.R. 306; *Earlham Colour Studios Ltd.* v. *Minister of Labour*
(1969) 4 I.T.R. 149; *Minister of Labour* v. *Expamet Contracts
Ltd.* (1969) 4 I.T.R. 152, 154; *Prestcold (Central) Ltd.* v.
Minister of Labour (1969) 4 I.T.R. 1, 5; *Watts of Calcot Ltd.* v.
Minister of Agriculture, Fisheries and Food (1970) 5 I.T.R. 40,
41; *The Central Press Photos Ltd.* v. *Department of Employment and Productivity* (1970) 5 I.T.R. 75, 80 (Div. Court);
(1970) 5 I.T.R. 270, 272 (citing Lord Wilberforce in *Maurice's
case* – note 86) (Court of Appeal); *Lord Advocate* v. *Reliant
Tool Company* (1968) 3 I.T.R. 70, 73.
85 *Earlham Colour Studios Ltd.* v. *Minister of Labour* (1969) 4
I.T.R. 149, 151; and see the decisions of the Divisional Court
cited in note 88 below.
86 *C. Maurice & Co. Ltd.* v. *Minister of Labour* (1969) 4 I.T.R.
186, 190 (cited by Salmon, LJ, in *The Central Press Photos case*
(note 84) at pp. 272–3).
87 *Ibid.*
88 *Carfax Waste Paper Co. Ltd.* v. *Minister of Labour* (1968) 3
I.T.R. 150; *Esso Petroleum* v. *Minister of Labour* (1968) 3
I.T.R. 306; *Earlham Colour Studios Ltd.* v. *Minister of Labour*
(1969) 4 I.T.R. 149; *Minister of Labour* v. *Expamet Contracts
Ltd.* (1969) 4 I.T.R. 152; *Como Confectionery Products Ltd.* v.
Secretary of State for Employment (1969) 4 I.T.R. 199;

Prestcold (Central) Ltd. v. *Minister of Labour* (1968) 3 I.T.R. 216, 220; (1969) I.T.R. 1, 5 (C.A.); *Fisher-Bendix Ltd.* v. *Secretary of State for Employment and Productivity* (1970) 5 I.T.R. 157, 160; *Secretary of State for Employment and Productivity* v. *Vic Hallam Ltd.* (1970) 5 I.T.R. 108, 110, 112; *The Central Press Photos Ltd.* v. *Department of Employment and Productivity* (1970) 5 I.T.R. 75, 80; *Secretary of State for Employment* v. *Building & Construction Ltd.* (1972) 7 I.T.R. 414, 417. (All the above Divisional Court unless otherwise indicated.)

89 *Halkett* v. *Secretary of State for Employment and Productivity* (1967) 2 I.T.R. 453, 454.

90 *Fisher-Bendix Ltd.* v. *Secretary of State for Employment and Productivity* (1970) 5. In fact, it is difficult to see that this is true of any of the decisions of either the Divisional Court or the Court of Session or, for the most part, the Court of Appeal, all of which have consistently taken what Lord Parker described as a 'common sense' approach (*Minister of Labour* v. *Genner Iron & Steel Co. (Wollescote) Ltd.* (1967) 2 I.T.R. 640, 643). There has been some legalistic reasoning in the House of Lords decision of *C. Maurice & Co. Ltd.* v. *Minister of Labour* (1969) 4 I.T.R. 186 (note 94) and Widgery, LJ's comments were probably true of Lord Guest's judgement in the *Reliant Tool case* ((1968) 3 I.T.R. 70, 80–1) but certainly not of Lord Wilberforce's judgement in that case.

91 (1970) 5 I.T.R. 157, 162; and see *Secretary of State for Employment* v. *Building & Construction Co. Ltd.* (1972) 7 I.T.R. 414, 417.

92 (1968) 3 I.T.R. 70, 82.

93 *Prestcold (Central) Ltd.* v. *Minister of Labour* (1968) 3 I.T.R. 216, 220.

94 On this point, see also *Minister of Agriculture, Fisheries & Food* v. *Ratsouris Ltd.* (1969) 4 I.T.R. 244; *Rank Xerox Ltd.* v. *Minister of Labour* (1968) 3 I.T.R. 399; *Minister of Labour* v. *C. Maurice & Co. Ltd.* (1968) 3 I.T.R. 32, 35, 38 (D.C.); *Lord Advocate* v. *Reliant Tool Company* (1968) 3 I.T.R. 70, 82 (H.L.) and (1967) 2 I.T.R. 498, 504 (Court of Session); *I. Goldman Ltd.* v. *Minister of Labour* (1967) 2 I.T.R. 514, 516; *Esso Petroleum Co. Ltd.* v. *Minister of Labour* (1968) 3 I.T.R. 306, 307.

95 *Esso Petroleum Co. Ltd.* v. *Minister of Labour* (1968) 3 I.T.R. 306, 307. But cf. Sachs, LJ at 312.

96 *C. Maurice & Co. Ltd.* v. *Minister of Labour* (1969) 4 I.T.R. 186; [1969] 2 All E.R. 37. It should be noted that the result in *Maurice's case* is open to serious doubt in so far as it is based on

the view that it was unfair, and therefore legally incorrect, if work done in the public sector were to qualify for a refund of tax while the same work done in the private sector were not: see Lord Wilberforce's judgement and more especially that of Lord Denning, MR, in the Court of Appeal ([1968] 2 All E.R. 1030, 1031). On this point the reasoning of Lord Parker in the Divisional Court is in my view to be preferred. The point should also be made that, despite the holding that the SIC was not to be construed as a lawyer's document, much of the reasoning of the Lords remained of a 'legalistic fashion, according to the letter': see particularly the judgements of Lords Guest and Pearson.

97 *Secretary of State for Employment* v. *The Mitchell Construction Co. Ltd.* (1972) 7 I.T.R. 24, 28.

98 Where a tribunal does not pretend to make use of its industrial expertise or does not hear expert evidence when deciding a question of industrial organization, the Court will be more ready to intervene, especially if it hears such evidence or receives it on affidavit: *Central Press Photos Ltd. case* (above) at p. 275.

99 'S.E.T. and the Shop Assistant', (7 March 1970), *The Economist*, p. 57; and 'Counter Reddaway' (11 April 1970), *The Economist*, p. 67. See also 'S.E.T.: It is the Miracle Tax' (5 March 1970), *The Times.*

100 See Foley and Harvey, 'A Replacement for S.E.T.', 210 (1970) *Bankers' Magazine*, p. 13; Marris (1971), *Economic Journal*, p. 393 (review of Reddaway Report).

101 Report, pp. 210–11.

102 (1971), *Economic Journal*, pp. 393, 394.

103 Finance Act 1967, s. 26(1).

104 See the comments of Mr Geoffrey Rhodes and *The Economist* above.

105 See Mr T. L. Higgins, H.C. Deb., 14 June 1967, vol. 748, col. 595.

106 *Lord Advocate* v. *Babcock & Wilcox (Operations) Ltd.* (1072) 7 I.T.R. 168, 174.

107 See H.C. Deb., 5 November 1969, vol. 790, col. 1033 per Mr E. Varley, Minister of State, Ministry of Technology.

Chapter Seven

1 'Council Structure on Decision-making' in *Councils in Action*, ed. Richards and Adam Kuper (1971), p. 28.

2 A. Downs, *Inside Bureaucracy* (1967); *Decisions, Organizations and Society*, ed. F. G. Castle, D. J. Murray and D. C. Potter,

(1971), p. 79: see also Braybrooke and C. Lindblom, *A Strategy of Decision* (1970), p. 57: '... evaluation and empirical analysis are closely intertwined'.

3 B. J. Brown, 'Legal Research in New Guinea', 1 (1971), *Melanesian LJ*, pp. 59, 67, citing on this last point Frank, 'Lawlessness', in *Encyclopaedia of the Social Sciences* vol. IX (1933), pp. 277–8.

4 As to this example, see Downs, *Inside Bureaucracy*: 'Search is greatly affected by the time pressure associated with a given decision. . . . There is an inverse relationship between the extension of search and the time pressure on the decision.'

5 The sequence in which evidence is presented may be an important factor in decision-making and in determining biases: see R. J. Audley, *Decision Making* (1967); *Decisions, Organizations and Society*, p. 62.

6 Rosalind Brooke, (22 March 1973) *New Society*, p. 648.

7 Letter to *New Society*, 5 April 1973, from Mr H. J. P. Priest.

8 Compare the not infrequent public announcements by the Department of Employment that the Redundancy Payments Fund is in the red.

9 See the surveys given by Brian Abel-Smith and Robert Stevens, *Lawyers and the Courts* (1967), pp. 299–301; *In Search of Justice* (1968), pp. 174–8.

10 *Decision making in the area of public order by English courts*, Open University materials on decision-making, Public Order, 45, pp. 55–9.

11 The most common view expressed by tribunal chairmen to whom I have spoken as to the role of the tribunals over which they preside is that they exist to provide a cheap, simple, informal brand of justice. 'We act as a poor man's court', as one industrial tribunal chairman put it. In this respect, compare the statement by Sir John Donaldson that the National Industrial Relations Court is a 'small claims court'.

12 'The Membership of Two Administrative Tribunals', 48 (1970), *Public Administration*, p. 449; 'Administrative Tribunals: How People become Members', 49 (1971), *Public Administration*, p. 197.

13 See Susan McCorquodale, 'The Composition of Administrative Tribunals' (1962), *Public Law* p. 298.

14 The comment was made – in jest – by one tribunal chairman who had not held a colonial judgeship to one who had that the latter had 'progressed from grinding the faces of the black to grinding the faces of the poor'.

15 *New Society* reported recently (5 April 1973, p. 24) that in Liverpool a trade unionist member of the panel for local sup-

plementary benefit appeal tribunals complained that over the course of the previous twelve months he had been invited to serve on a tribunal on only nine occasions; by contrast, inquiries revealed that a retired schoolmaster had served twenty-five times during the same period.

16 On the need for consensus generally, see Downs, *Inside Bureaucracy*.

17 Some of the better studies are Benjafield, 'Statutory Discretions', 2 (1956), *Sydney Law Review* 1, p. 23 *et seq.;* Sheridan, 'Late National Insurance Claims: Cause for Delay', 19 (1956), *MLR*, p. 341; Safford, 'The Creation of Case Law under the National Insurance and National Insurance (Industrial Injuries) Acts', 17 (1954), *MLR*, p. 197; Julius Stone, *Social Dimensions of Law and Justice* (1966), ch. 14; N. D. Vandyke, 'National Insurance Adjudication', 7 (1953), *Industrial Law Review*, p. 176; R. J. W. Pollard, *Administrative Tribunals at Work* (1950); K. C. Davis, *Discretionary Justice* (1969). There is published literature on the United States regulatory agencies and their decision-making processes.

18 But cf. Stone, 'Loosing the Chains of Precedent: 1966 and all That', 69 (1969), *Col LR* at p. 1201, who makes the point that changes in the formal doctrine of precedent make no effective change to the freedom of judges to distinguish cases at will. With respect, this would seem an overly simplistic view.

19 *Practice Statement (Judicial Precedent)* [1966] 1 W.L.R. 1234.

20 *Gallie* v. *Lee* [1969] 2 Ch. 17, 36–7; *Barrington* v. *Lee* [1971] 3 W.L.R. 962, 970; but cf. *Broome* v. *Cassall & Co. Ltd.* [1972] 2 W.L.R. 645.

21 Notably as a result of *Hedley Byrne* v. *Heller* [1964] A.C. 465 where the approach taken by him in his earlier, dissenting, judgement in *Chandler* v. *Crane Christmas & Co. Ltd.* [1951] 2 K.B. 164 was vindicated.

22 [1972] 2 W.L.R. 299.

23 *Ibid.*, 313.

24 See, for example, the judgements of Lords Diplock and Wilberforce in *Malloch* v. *Aberdeen Corporation* [1971] W.L.R. 1578 and that of Lord Diplock in *Kammins Ballrooms Ltd.* v. *Zenith Investments Ltd.* [1971] A.C. 850.

25 *Herrington* v. *British Railways Board* [1972] 2 W.L.R. 537, 575; and see also 'The Atlantic Star' (11 April 1973) *The Times*, where Lord Reid showed some change in emphasis from his remarks in *Suisse Atlantique* (note 30). In relation to the question of jurisdiction to try a maritime collision claim, he said that it was 'a function of the House to try, so far as possible, to keep the development of the common law in line with the

policy of Parliament and the movement of public opinion. The time was ripe for a reexamination of a rather insular doctrine.'

26 Though one can find various instances where judges have in fact applied policy considerations. Two outstanding examples are *Roberts* v. *Hopwood* [1925] A.C. 578 and *Prescott* v. *Birmingham Corporation* [1955] Ch. 210.

27 'Judge-Made Law in England', 61 (1961), *Col LR*, p. 202. On this subject generally, see Abel-Smith and Stevens, *In Search of Justice* (1968), pp. 172-3.

28 61 (1961), *Col LR*, p. 762.

29 'The Common Law, Public Policy and the Executive', 9 (1956), *Current Legal Problems*, pp. 7, 12.

30 *Suisse Atlantique Société d'Armement Maritime S.A.* v. *N.V. Rotterdamsche Kolen Centrale* [1967] 1 A.C. 361, 406; and for a more recent instance, see *Knuller* v. *D.P.P.* [1972] 3 W.L.R. 143.

31 Professor Louis Jaffe makes the point that the English judge's performance must be viewed as a part only of the total legal performance in England (including that of Parliament). This, he says, is often overlooked by American lawyers who draw unfavourable comparisons between English judges and their (more adventurous) American counterparts: *English and American Judges as Lawmakers* (1969), p. 5.

32 N.I. Decisions C.P. 93/49; R(G) 3/62.

33 *Railway Executive* v. *Archbolds (Transport) Ltd.* (1950) 29 Traf. Cas. 270.

34 *R.* v. *London C.C. ex parte Corrie* [1918] 1 K.B. 68; *R.* v. *Port of London Authority, ex parte Kynoch Ltd.* [1919] 1 K.B. 176.

35 H. J. Elcock, *Administrative Justice* (1969), pp. 7-10.

36 See N.I. Decisions C.P. 93/49; R(G) 3/62; R(I) 23/63; and see *Richards* v. *Fielding Ltd.* (1966) 1 I.T.R. 376, 379; *Sergeant's Appeal* (1948) 29 Traf. Cas. 84.

37 The Transport Act 1968 has removed much of this discretion by changing the whole basis upon which the licences are to be issued: see especially s. 74.

38 *G.W. & L.M.S. Rlys.* v. *Smart* (1936) 24 Traf. Cas. 273, 282; *Watts* v. *'L.N.E. & L.M.S. Rlys* (1937) 25 Traf. Cas. 187, 201; *J. M. Burgess Ltd.* v. *L.N.E. Rly.* (1939) 27 Traf. Cas. 142, 143.

39 *Charman* v. *Garlick, Burrell and Edwards Ltd.* (1938) 26 Traf. Cas. 177, 183; *J. M. Burgess Ltd.* v. *L.N.E. Rly.* (1939) 27 Traf. Cas. 142, 143-4; and see *B.T.C.* v *Chas. Alexander Partners (Transport) Ltd.* (1957) 31 Traf. Cas. 113, 115.

40 (1936) 24 Traf. Cas. 273, 280.

41 *Ibid.*, 281-2.

42 *Enston & Co. Ltd.* v. *L.M.S. Rly.* (1933) 22 Traf. Cas. 3. The
Enston principle was limited to newcomers to the transport
industry (*L.M.S. Rly.* v. *Palmer* (1925) 23 Traf. Cas. 76) but a
similar principle (requiring a proof of a general expansion of
the industry in the district) applied to established hauliers in
Ridgewell & Co. Ltd. v. *Sthn. Rly.* (1933) 22 Traf. Cas. 6.

43 (1935) 23 Traf. Cas. 23.

44 Report, p. 22, para. 248; see pp. 14–15, para. 2.22 for an
account of the leading cases decided in the period 1933–7.

45 Report, p. 64, para. 198.

46 Both Committees explained a 1953 amendment to the legislation as being necessary to free the licensing authorities from the
unduly inhibiting effect of Enston's case. The amendment,
which was designed to increase competition among hauliers,
expanded the statutory directive to have regard to 'the interests
of the public generally' to provide: 'to the interests of the
public generally including primarily those of persons requiring
facilities for transport and secondarily those of persons providing facilities for transport'.

47 *Merchandise Transport Ltd.* v. *B.T.C.* [1962] 2 Q.B. 173, 193;
32 Traf. Cas. 19, 44; commented on by H. W. R. Wade, 'Anglo-
American Administrative Law: Some Reflections', 81 (1965),
Law Quarterly Review pp. 357, 378; Elcock, *Administrative
Justice*, pp. 9–10; Corpe, *Road Haulage Licensing* (1964, 2nd
ed.) pp. 7, 27.

48 Other factors were later mentioned in Beazley's case (1936) 24
Traf. Cas. 112.

49 *H. W. Hawker Ltd.* v. *G.W. & L.M.S. Rlys.* (*No. 2*) (1936) 25
Traf. Cas. 99, 112–13.

50 See, for example, *Thornley & Son* v *L.M.S. Rly.* (1935) 22
Traf. Cas. 249.

51 *Smith* v. *L.M.S. Rly.* (1935) 22 Traf. Cas. 262.

52 *L.N.E. Rly.* v. *Anderson* (1935) 22 Traf. Cas. 171.

53 *Edwards* v. *L.M.S. Rly.* (1935) 23 Traf. Cas. 67.

54 *Clark* v. *B.T.C.* (1962) 32 Traf. Cas. 107, 111.

55 Devlin, LJ's finding to this effect (32 Traf. Cas. at p. 55) comes
some eleven pages in the Traffic Cases Report after his comments above and, most significantly, does not appear at all in
the law report of the case. This seems to me to have led some
commentators to assume that the charge against the Tribunal
had been accepted as proven: see, for example, 81 (1965),
LQR, p. 378.

56 Consider, for example, the case law of the National Insurance
Commissioners on the provisions in the national insurance legis-

lation relating to 'good cause for delay' in making claims. See especially Decisions R(S) 2/63; R(P) 10/59.

57 'The Model of Rules', 35 (1967), *Univ. Chicago LR*, p. 14; reprinted in *Essays in Legal Philosophy* (1968) ed. Summers. See also his more recent article, 'Social Rules and Legal Theory', 81 (1972), *Yale LJ*, p. 855. For a slightly different analysis, in which the distinction between rules and principles is nevertheless recognized, see Davis, *Discretionary Justice* (1969), ch. 4.

58 115 N.Y. 506, 22 N.E. 188 (1889). For an analogous finding in English law, see *In re Estate of Crippen* [1911] p. 108.

59 For example, the rule relating to self-induced frustration in the law of contract; the decision in *Cohen* v. *Sellar* [1926] 1 K.B. 536, esp. 548; and see also *Gray* v. *Barr* [1971] 2 W.L.R. 1334, 1354.

60 (1935) 23 Traf. Cas. 164.

61 In *Councils in Action*, p. 18.

62 The wider point has been made that 'the basic processes by which decisions are made have common features' in *Decisions, Organizations and Society*, p. 15.

63 See Davis, *Discretionary Justice* (1969), 108. Professor Davis points out that the inefficiency involved in rethinking a question that has been resolved to an administrator's or agency's satisfaction supports the practice of following precedents.

64 *Quaere*, the Franks Committee's analysis of administrative decisions as those which are 'arbitrary', 'made without principle, without any rules' and which are 'unpredictable' and constitute merely 'a wise expediency' (Report, p. 6, paras. 2, 29, 31).

Chapter Eight

1 Now superseded by the Tribunals and Inquiries Act 1971.

2 Both the Prices and Incomes Board and the Consumer Council are now defunct but were eventually replaced by somewhat analogous bodies, discussed in Chapter 1.

3 The categorization of 'judicial', 'administrative' and 'quasi-judicial' powers is a notoriously difficult one. The committee on *Ministers' Powers* attempted to provide dividing lines ((1932) Cmnd. 4060, pp 73–4) but its views are scarcely regarded as even respectable today. For a critique, see W. A. Robson, *Justice and Administrative Law* (3rd ed., 1951).

4 Cmnd. 218.

5 Report, p. 9, para. 40.

6 (1968), 220-1.

7 *The Analytic and the Synthetic,* ed. Feigl and Maxwell (1962), 3 Minnesota Studies in the Philosophy of Science, pp. 378; cited by Sartorius, 'Hart's Concept of Law' in *More Essays in Legal Philosophy,* ed. Summers (1971), pp. 142–4.

8 Report, p. 10, para. 41.

9 Report, p. 19, para. 76.

10 Report, pp. 11–12, paras. 45–54. The suggestion that the Council on Tribunals should appoint non-lawyer members of tribunals was not adopted.

11 As to these last matters, see the Franks Report, pp. 13–14, paras. 59–61; pp. 15–16, paras. 65–6.

12 By comparison with the courts, Franks thought that the chief attributes of tribunals were 'cheapness, accessibility, freedom from technicality, expedition and expert knowledge of their particular subject': p. 9, para. 38.

13 Tribunals and Inquiries Act 1958, s. 12; 1971, s. 12.

14 *Ibid.,* s. 9; 1971, s. 13.

15 As in the famous Dutschke case : see above, p. 10–11.

16 G. Marshall and G. C. Moodie, *Some Problems of the Constitution,* 4th (revised) ed., p. 109.

17 See page 183.

18 *R. v. Criminal Injuries Compensation Board, ex parte Lain* [1967] 2 Q.B. 864.

19 *In Search of Justice* (1968), p. 64.

20 *In Search of Justice,* p. 224.

21 *In Search of Justice,* p. 228.

22 *In Search of Justice,* pp. 227–8.

23 *In Search of Justice.*

24 See p. 186.

25 See p. 93.

26 *British Air Transport in the Seventies* (1969) Cmnd. 4018, pp. 157–8, paras. 639–40.

27 For the difficulties involved in drawing the line, see the Reports of the Select Committee on Nationalised Industries.

28 See p. 6.

29 (1966–8) Cmnd. 3638, p. 50, para. 147; pp. 61–62, paras. 188–91.

30 As pointed out by Sartorius, the two are separate concepts: in *More Essays in Legal Philosophy,* p. 143.

31 Wittgenstein, *Philosophical Investigations,* trans. Anscombe (1968), p. 31, para. 66.

32 *Philosophical Investigations,* pp. 31–2, para. 66.

33 Report, p. 82.

34 Report, pp. 83–6.

35 Report, pp. 87–8.

36 And in those tribunals which, for this purpose, can be compared with court-substitute tribunals – because in fact ministerial directions are not issued. The best known examples are the transport licensing authorities and the Transport Tribunal.

37 W. Friedman, *The State and the Rule of Law in a Mixed Economy* (1911), pp. 2-3.

38 For example, *Government Enterprise* (1970) eds. Friedmann and Garner.

39 W. Friedmann, *The State and the Rule of Law in a Mixed Economy*, pp. 6-7.

40 The matter was briefly debated in the Lords: see H.L. Deb., 18 February 1971, vol. 315, cols. 719-724.

41 H.C. Deb., 25 March 1971, vol. 814, col. 852; see also Lord Drumalbyn, Minister without Portfolio: 'this is a case of Caesar's wife – 'independent arbitrators must be absolutely above reproach' H.L. Deb., 18 February 1971, vol. 315, col. 723.

42 19 February 1971.

43 'Too many men, not enough middle', 19 February 1971.

44 22 November 1971.

45 *The Civil Service* (1966-8), Cmnd. 3638, pp. 61-2, paras. 188-90.

46 *The Civil Service*, p. 53, para. 159.

47 Although the Heath Government made substantial changes in the organization of administration as between one department and another, and new departments created and others merged, the 'bold experiments' urged by Fulton in relation to departmental structure were not undertaken or even contemplated seriously in the Government White Paper *The Reorganisation of Central Government* (1970), Cmnd. 4506.

48 Report, p. 53, para. 158.

49 Report, p. 53, para. 159.

50 See A. H. Rosenthal, *The Social Programs of Sweden* (1967).

51 Report, p. 61, para. 189.

52 Report, para. 190.

53 Davis, *Discretionary Justice* (1969).

54 Carson, 'Consultative Law: An Emerging Legal Development', 68 (1968), *Col LR*, pp.1496, 1497-8.

55 Carson, in *Col LR*, p. 1500. The phrase 'the delays attendant upon formalism' is taken from an address of J. Landis in 1937, quoted in W. Getlhorn, *Administrative Law, Cases and Comments II* (1940), pp. 7-18.

56 Cf. the experience of the New Zealand Trade Practices Commission outline above at p. 43. And cf. also P. Woll, *Administrative Law – The Informal Process* (1961).

Cases referred to

Index